TURF
and Other Corporate Power Plays

Pamela Cuming

Prentice-Hall, Inc. Englewood Cliffs, New Jersey

Prentice-Hall International, Inc., *London*
Prentice-Hall of Australia, Pty. Ltd., *Sydney*
Prentice-Hall Canada, Inc., *Toronto*
Prentice-Hall of India Private Ltd., *New Delhi*
Prentice-Hall of Japan, Inc., *Tokyo*
Prentice-Hall of Southeast Asia Pte. Ltd., *Singapore*
Whitehall Books, Ltd., *Wellington, New Zealand*
Editora Prentice-Hall do Brasil Ltda., *Rio de Janeiro*
Prentice-Hall Hispanoamericana, S.A., *Mexico*

© 1985 *by*

Pamela Cuming

Library of Congress Cataloging-in-Publication Data

Cuming, Pamela
 Turf and other corporate plays.

 Includes index.
 1. Office politics.   2. Executives.   I. Title.
HD38.C83   1985   658.4′095   85-12362

ISBN 0-13-933102-6

Dedication

It is with admiration and gratitude that I dedicate this book to all of my clients who have willingly shared their problems, visions, and hopes with me. I thank them both for their confidence in me, and for the opportunity to learn even while I taught.

Acknowledgments

A special thank you is due each of the following individuals. Without their assistance, TURF could not have been written.

To NEAL GILLIATT, for making me aware of the importance of the marketing role within corporations, and for providing me with the model of a fine mentor.

To TERESA HANKS, for her patience and perseverance in typing the many drafts of the manuscript, and for cheering me on each time the effort seemed impossible.

To MOLLIE LEDWITH, for her insightful critique of the first draft.

To RON LEDWITH, for his confidence in me, and for his assistance in designing the format of the book.

To EILEEN MARKOWITZ, for her comments which added both zest and realism to the story.

To CAROLE CONGRAM, for her ongoing support and her demonstrated belief in me and the concepts represented in this book.

To my children, MONICA and MELISSA, for their patience during the many hours I devoted to the writing of this book.

To ROBERT L. SMITH, for the many hours we spent discussing organization power dynamics.

Introduction

"Nothing gets done around here. Everybody is too busy protecting his turf."

"Step on someone else's turf, and they stab you in the back."

"People spend more time building up their empires and guarding their turf than they do attending to the business."

I hear these complaints more and more often in the course of my work with organizations. Fiefdoms proliferate, each headed by a lord whose worth is a function of the number of serfs he controls and the size of the territory he dominates. If a serf dares request a transfer in the interest of personal growth, the lord responds as though a traitorous act has occurred. If a product line or function is moved to another area in the interest of organizational efficiency, the lord experiences the decision as an attack, an invasion.

Would-be lords ally themselves with those who appear to have the largest domains, or those who make the turf allocation decisions. Lords in power fear the clever princes who aspire to the throne, and urge the promotion of those who are less threatening and less competent.

Persons in one area of the organization fail to share needed information with other areas. Information gives them an edge, an extra measure of control, in a game which they perceive as competitive. By refusing to share information, they attempt to make their borders impenetrable. In the game of turf protection, the strength of the unit is of more concern than the health of the organization as a whole.

Executives who have grown accustomed to running functions, such as marketing or manufacturing, resist structural changes designed to replace the functional organization with an organization form that emphasizes accountability for a specific account, product, or region. The function, or the discipline, has become their territory, their turf, and they defend it vigorously.

The concern with turf, and its protection or enhancement, is so widespread as to constitute an organizational theme. Turf is *the* organizational power play, and the stimulant for a number of other games designed to solidify the player's power base.

The games are all based on the assumption that the amount of power is finite; that a power pie exists, and that for you to get a bigger piece requires that I accept a smaller piece. The assumption is that all organizational decisions involve a win for some and a loss for others. Those who make such an assumption spend an inordinate amount of energy attempting to prove that they are more competent, more valuable, more important than others. The measure of success is not the accomplishment per se, but the size or scope of the accomplishment relative to that of others.

It is no wonder that power is widely regarded as a "dirty word." When people think of power, they generally remember times when they or the people they care about were caught up in dysfunctional power plays designed to enhance one person's position at the expense of another.

But power is more than a game designed to protect or enhance turf. It is the *ability to make happen that which we want to happen,* or, conversely, the *ability to block the occurrence of events that are undesirable to us.* More simply, power is the ability to choose.

Power is not inherently dirty. While apparently powerful people may harm others, it is not their power that is harmful, but their need or desire to win at others' expense. To feel empowered is fundamental to leading a healthy, active, fulfilled life. It is not power that is the antagonist, but powerlessness.

- The worker who feels unempowered turns to sabotage in order to exert some form of control over a hostile organizational environment.
- The labor union that experiences a lack of power makes unreasonable demands in an attempt to show management that it is a force to be taken seriously.

- The professional who feels precluded from demonstrating the power of his expertise leaves the firm, taking clients with him.

- The manager who feels incapable of reaching objectives begins to invest her energies in protecting her territory, and covering up mistakes rather than attempting to influence outcomes.

- The unempowered employee does just enough to get by, retiring on the job.

- Workers devote energies to complaining that they don't have the authority to accomplish their objectives. Gripe sessions consume the energies that should be devoted to acquiring power, to getting in a position to influence outcomes.

During my thirteen years as a consultant on organizational effectiveness to business and industry, I have tried everything imaginable to alleviate the symptoms of powerlessness and the abuses of games designed to protect turf.

Redrawing the organization chart hasn't helped. It realigned people, and even put persons on top who had been on the bottom. Yesterday's losers became today's winners, and vice versa. The balance of power shifted. The players changed, but the game remained the same.

New policies and procedures were introduced in an attempt to mandate behavioral changes. Additional controls further reduced commitment and motivation. New programs were resisted.

Training programs were introduced to stimulate greater productivity. They helped for a while. Eventually, however, the old behaviors reemerged, reinforced by the system of rewards and punishments that had remained unchanged.

Hired by client organizations to help them remove the barriers to productivity and employee satisfaction, I began to get extremely discouraged about my ability to introduce lasting changes. While a few interventions worked, most had only a short-term impact.

I began to devote my energies to attempting to understand the success stories, the change programs that worked over the long haul. I began to study successful individuals; persons within my client organizations who had found a way to realize their objectives while maintaining sound interpersonal relationships. Some common themes began to emerge.

The organizations that were successful paid close attention to the impact of policies, procedures, relationships, and culture on power dynamics. They understood, for example, that introducing a steep functional hierarchy encourages reliance on the formal chain of command, and discourages leadership based on expertise. They understood that a punitive culture or climate discourages innovation and the willingness to take risks. They understood that centralizing support services would make managers in the field feel less empowered.

A closer look revealed that it was not the organization per se that had such a good grasp of power dynamics, but rather it was the decision makers in the system who understood the uses and abuses of power. *It became obvious that the reason these people had succeeded in climbing the corporate ladder was due to one part luck, one part talent, and eight parts the feeling of personal empowerment—coupled with the ability to acquire and use a variety of types of power in the interest of* both *personal and corporate goals.*

Excited by this insight, I redefined my purpose as assisting individuals in their efforts to understand corporate power dynamics, and to enhance their own personal power base in ways which were straightforward, nonmanipulative, and in the interest of the organization as a whole.

Writing this book represents one of the ways in which I hope to accomplish this purpose. Three years ago, I attempted to do something similar. I wrote a textbook on power entitled *The Power Handbook*. While the reviews were positive, and while clients told me that they found the text helpful, I was not content with its impact.

Power is a basic concept, a reality that affects everything we do. Every interaction we have with another person either enhances or diminishes our power base, our ability to influence that person. The majority of our actions are designed to make an impact, to affect outcomes in ways that meet our needs. Power and influence are as central to our existence as are eating and sleeping. As concepts, they need to be understood by everyone who has a goal, a desire, a hope, an ambition.

Textbooks are the product of academics, and, all too often, are of interest only to students. To study power is to develop an abstract understanding. My goal is to help others feel powerful, and be powerful. I believe this can happen better through a close look at one individual's climb up the corporate ladder than through a lengthy theoretical narrative.

In using a fictitious framework through which to present organizational realities, I know that I am inviting critics to claim that TURF represents an attempt to replicate the success experienced by the authors of such books as *The One Minute Manager*. These kinds of books are both appealing and misleading in their simplicity. The power plays that fill the pages of TURF are realistic and, therefore, complex. TURF does *not* offer a handful of rules that guarantee success. It mirrors organizational life in its full complexity. Strategies and tactics that work in one situation may fail in another, given changes in the task and the people involved.

Through the trials, tribulations, successes, and failures of the book's heroes and anti-heroes, it becomes obvious that the successful trek through the corporate maze depends on the ability to acquire a variety of types of power or leverage *and* on the ability to select the most appropriate influence strategy.

In the pages that follow, you will get to know Larry Michaelson, and to participate in his struggle to become sufficiently empowered to realize his dream. Larry believes that marketing is the heart and soul of the corporation, any corporation. It is his dream to become the chief marketing officer, residing in the executive suite, and reporting directly to the chief executive officer. Larry's dream is ambitious. He aspires not only to a high ranking office, but also to a position that requires that he function almost as a prophet or a seer, predicting social and cultural trends far enough in advance to allow the organization to respond with new products in a timely way. It is Larry's dream to become a high-powered organizational maverick, a person who functions simultaneously as a creative visionary and a pragmatic businessman.

We first meet Larry at his graduation from business school. We find him to be an individual with aspirations, energy, stamina, who suffers from impatience and a tendency to appear to be arrogant. Larry's apparent arrogance stems not from a belief that he is better than others, but rather from a lack of self-confidence. Like most of us, Larry has some insecurities which he tries valiantly to hide from both himself and others.

It is because of these insecurities, in fact, that Larry periodically forgets the lessons of his mentor, William Werth, and engages in power plays designed to capture a piece of organizational turf. Disaster is often averted only as a result of Bill's wisdom and timely intervention. Bill's sixty-eight years taught him a great deal about power and organization dynamics. Now retired, Bill has the time and energy to serve as a guide and a mentor. You will have an opportunity to meet Bill as the story unfolds, and to learn about his perception of the key to the effective management of corporate politics and power plays.

You will also meet other people who serve as Larry's allies and supporters. And, of course, you will meet the enemy; the adversaries who attempt to undermine Larry's efforts. Reginald Sterling and his lackey, Joel, personify the destructive and devious tactics that too often characterize corporate power plays.

While the organization and the characters are fictitious, as are the events themselves, all are modeled after actual occurrences. In telling Larry's story, I hope to both entertain and educate. It is my hope that you will both enjoy and profit from the experience.

Contents

"This is my executive suite and this is my executive vice-president, Ralph Anderson, and my executive secretary, Adele Eades, and my executive desk and my executive carpet and my executive wastebasket and my executive ashtray and my executive pen set and my..."

Drawing by H. Martin; © 1974
The New Yorker Magazine, Inc.

1

Introducing the Players and Their Arena

IT WAS GRADUATION DAY at the business school. Watching proudly as Larry received his degree were Larry's parents and Bill Werth, Larry's retired friend and mentor.

While they watched the procession, Larry's father reminded Bill of the important role he had played in stimulating Larry's interest in business. "I think that Larry's interest in climbing the corporate ladder is a direct result of the many conversations you and he have had over the years, Bill. From the beginning, he has been fascinated by your tales of corporate intrigue."

Larry's father was right. Larry had indeed been fascinated by the corporate world described over the years by his father's friend, Bill. Bill had been influential in Larry's life since the Michaelsons and the Werths became neighbors fifteen years prior, when Larry had been a child of eleven.

Even at that age, Larry attracted Bill's interest. Bill was intrigued by Larry's curiosity, and by his tendency to ask questions that did not seem typical of a child. "Why does our government send so much money to poor people in other countries when so many of the people in this country don't have enough to eat?" "Why do people like to gossip?" "Why do people get so upset about nuclear power?"

Bill was often the person to whom Larry turned for answers. A philosopher by nature, Bill enjoyed lengthy discussions about political strategy.

When Larry ran for president of the high school Student Council, it was Bill who helped him plan his campaign strategy. And, it was Bill who had empathized with Larry's intolerance of "the system" that prevailed at college. Intellectually curious, Larry would spend hours probing areas of interest. Intolerant of the educational system itself, he spent almost no energy on subjects or issues he regarded as irrelevant or unimportant. Refusing to adhere to the policies and procedures of the institution, he persisted in being a maverick. His poor grades belied his intellectual abilities.

During Larry's two years in graduate school, Bill often helped him analyze the case studies that formed the basis of the course of study. And it was Bill who encouraged Larry in his choice of marketing as an area of concentration. Like Larry, Bill believed marketing to be the most critical of corporate functions. And, like Larry, Bill had been highly ambitious and impatient as a young man. But let me allow Bill to introduce himself to you.

"I saw a lot of action during my forty years with the company. Restless and ambitious as a young man, I was not content unless I was associated with the unit or the department that was on the cutting edge. No matter how efficient the status quo, it never satisfied me. I was always thinking of better ways to accomplish objectives. For that matter, I was always contemplating objectives that the organization should pursue and was not. Yes, as a young man, I was a malcontent and a maverick.

"There were times when I'm sure the organization would have preferred to get rid of me. In hindsight, I'm convinced that the promotion to director of Australian and Far East operations was not, in fact, a vote of confidence, but rather an attempt to get me out of the way, and out of the mainstream. What the organization did not appreciate was that Australia and the Far East represented the key to the organization's future.

"I managed that opportunity well, if I do say so myself. And I learned a lot in the process. Having to manage others taught me a lot about how to accomplish things. I learned to be a little more savvy politically, and to communicate with others in a less abrasive fashion. I grew less arrogant and more effective during my tour in the Far East.

"I also learned about the importance of really understanding the customer. Selling power tools to Australians who must work with one of the densest woods in the world is very different from selling the same product in the Orient. While overseas, I learned to listen, actively listen, to what the customer was saying.

"Marketing became my first love. And I do mean first love. For several years after returning to the States, I did almost nothing but work. That was a mistake. I missed a lot of living in those years. And I learned a valuable lesson about the importance of maintaining a balance in life. But that is another story; one that will undoubtedly come up again before our conversation is finished.

"By the time I was thirty-four, I was functioning as corporate director of marketing for professional products. That was a big job and a difficult job. You see, it was my responsibility to see that sales of professional products were strong, and yet I did not have the authority to direct the activities of the regional directors. Members of the sales force reported both to me and to their regional managers. At least, that was true in theory. In actuality, the regional directors were the ones who decided about raises and promotions. The sales person-nel knew that. I had to persuade them to do things on the basis of their belief in me and my approach. I could not issue directives and make them stick.

"At the time, I was terribly frustrated by what I perceived to be responsibility without authority. Looking back, that position taught me a great deal about power and organization dynamics. It is possible to make things happen in organizations without having the benefit of formal clout. In fact, formal clout can get in your way. My instincts were good, and I managed to succeed in the position of director of marketing.

"Fortunately for me, the chief executive at that time had a strong marketing background, and appreciated what I was doing. When the position of vice-president of U.S. operations opened up, he offered me the job. A couple of people were really upset by that. I guess they had expected to get the job themselves. Traditionally, that job represented the next step on the ladder for the individual who managed the European operation.

"By forty, I was extraordinarily successful in business. I was happily married to a woman who enjoyed my successes, but who had enough interests of her own to remain an independent person. Our three children were seemingly well-adjusted. Life had never been better, or so it seemed to me, when my eldest son taught me a lesson I will never forget.

"Shortly after his sixteenth birthday, his behavior changed

dramatically. He started hanging around with a new group of kids, kids who spent more time roving around town than studying. His grades dropped dramatically. As I was to learn much later, he also became heavily dependent on drugs.

"But that was not the worst of it. Peter then met a young woman who was a firm believer in one of those cults that demand a sacrifice of family and worldly possessions in exchange for membership in a 'community of true believers.' Well, Peter bought it all.

"His disappearance was devastating to us. Even more devastating was his refusal to return home once we found him. Oh, he had been brainwashed, all right, but that was not the full explanation for his refusal to return to his family. During one particularly painful phone call, Peter told me that he had no reason to return to a family that treated him as though he was an insignificant, even invisible, entity. 'I have found a new family,' he said, 'a family that values me for who I am, and for what I can do, and not as an extension of their own dreams and ambitions.'

"Peter eventually learned that his 'new family,' as he called it, was more interested in its own growth and wealth than in him as a person. Eventually, he returned home, and after two years of therapy, he was again functioning as a happy and integrated young adult. In the process, I learned as much about myself as Peter learned about himself.

"In effect, my definition of success changed. Success was no longer a function of dollars in the bank, or of position on the organization chart. No, those things, those trappings of success, became means and not ends. Peace of mind, love, contentment... those became my objectives. I became a more thoughtful person as a result of my son's experience. I learned to be patient, and less evaluative of others. I matured and became a person who spent as much time reflecting as acting.

"My management approach changed dramatically. Visibility became far less important to me than the opportunity to give others a chance to develop, and to realize their potential. Instead of seeking credit for my own brilliance, I began to focus on creating opportunities for others to shine.

"In giving away power, I became more empowered. Four years after my son's return, I was named chief operating officer of the corporation. In appointing me second in command, the chief executive officer told me that the reason for my promotion was that I had finally demonstrated the ability to inspire trust in me as a person as well as respect for my business acumen. His exact words remain with me to this day... *'The true measure of leadership ability is the willingness of others to follow due to their belief in the leader as a worthwhile person. That is the only power that sustains.'*

"At the age of fifty, I was named chief executive officer of the corporation I had served all of my adult life. In fifteen years, the firm grew from an annual sales volume of two-hundred million to one billion. It is now one of the major multinational firms in the world. And I am sought after by firms and individuals who want to learn the secrets of success. Perhaps I do know those secrets; perhaps it is not necessary to learn the hard way.

"It pleases me that young people want to listen to me. In this society, age does not confer power. On the contrary, people over sixty are often assumed to be mentally slower and less wise than those who are at mid-life or in their youth. As George Chapman once said, 'Young men think old men are fools; but old men know young men are fools.'

"Seriously, there is an important perspective that comes with time. I have always looked to history to inform present decisions. Perhaps that's why I'm so fond of quoting persons who lived a long time ago. Somehow, I find wisdom in these quotes. I suppose I'm viewed as somewhat of an eccentric in this regard. No matter.

"Anyway, Larry Michaelson is different. He feigns a fascination with my quotations and continues to seek my opinions. He reminds me of myself at age twenty-four. Oh, he is arrogant with me at times. Eager, ambitious, arrogant and impatient, he offends as often as he impresses. Yet I persist in offering as much advice as he will accept. Why? Perhaps I remember how it feels to have a dream, and because I know how difficult it is to maneuver through organizations in order to realize that dream."

Larry's dream and the organization he had chosen in which to realize his dream became the focus of discussion during dinner the night of the graduation. With great enthusiasm, Larry described Software Systems, Inc., the organization that had made him an offer only weeks before graduation.

"Software Systems, Inc. is in the business of developing and producing software and video discs for the government, private industry, and educational institutions. It's a relatively small business, doing only about twenty-five million dollars a year in volume, but it is growing fast. In spite of the fact that it is eight years old, it still retains many of the qualities that characterized its start-up days. I guess that's what appeals to me. Everybody is encouraged to be innovative and to think like an entrepreneur.

"At least that's what they're saying to new recruits. And I have good reason to believe it's true. I've done a lot of checking with people who know people who work there. And I've requested and had meetings with a couple of the key people.

"I think I can make a mark in that place, and in a short period of time. I mean, they have a lot to learn about marketing. Why, they still regard technology as the driving force of the organization. More of the organization's energies are devoted to staying at the cutting edge of technology than to developing marketing strategies. I think I can convince them that they need to be market-driven, not technology-driven."

Bill and Larry's parents toasted Larry's confidence, choosing not to dampen his enthusiasm with mention of the fact that shifting an organization's culture was a difficult task at best, and certainly one that could not be spearheaded by a trainee. Bill made a mental note to talk with Larry about the realities of corporate life, and the dangers of pushing too hard too fast. Encouraged by the toasts, and spurred on by the interest all displayed, Larry continued, drawing a picture of the organization on a napkin to help describe his new organizational home.

"The emphasis on technology, and the entrepreneurial spirit are both a direct reflection of the bias and preference of Peter Topper, chief executive officer.

CHIEF EXECUTIVE OFFICER
TOPPER

"A systems engineer by training, he is also the son of the founder of the company. The father, the founder that is, died only a year or so ago. The son is every bit as entrepreneurial as was his father.

"The misfit, as far as I can determine, is the chief operating officer, Harold Softner. People don't seem to regard him as very influential.

"Apparently, he is a holdover from the video company, which Software acquired two years ago. He was the president of Video Inc. I guess you don't simply get rid of presidents. Anyway, no one is quite sure why he continues to work. I mean, he made a fortune when

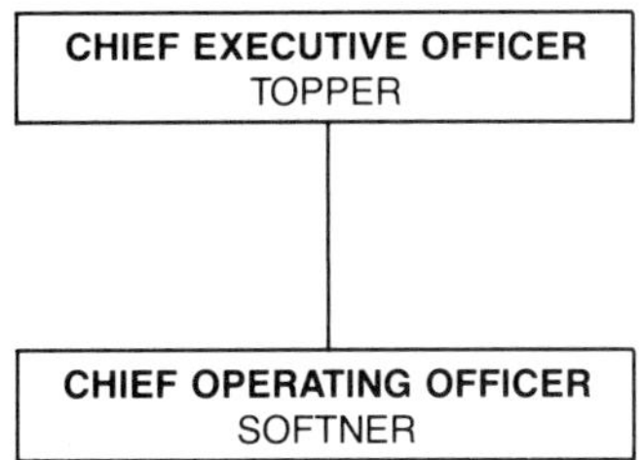

Software bought the company. The best thing I heard about him is that he stays out of people's way, pretty much letting them do their own thing.

"Another key player is the senior vice-president of software, Ralph Willit. He, by the way, is a second cousin of the chief executive officer. They really keep it in the family.

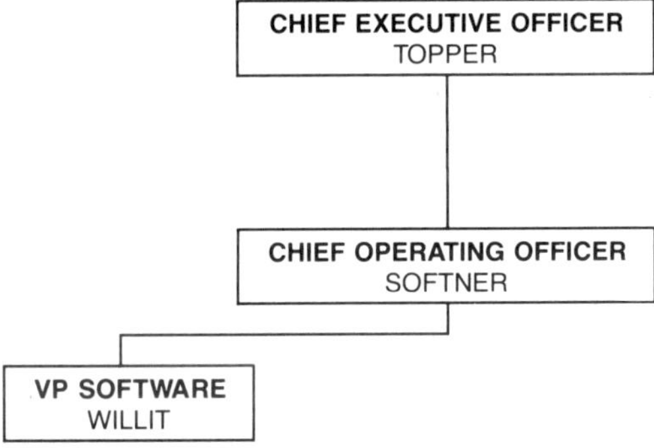

"Anyway, Willit is not your typical systems person. He is outgoing, and more of an inventor than anything else. And he encourages people to try new things.

"I think I'm going to like Tyler Watch, the vice-president of the video division. He is a colorful individual.

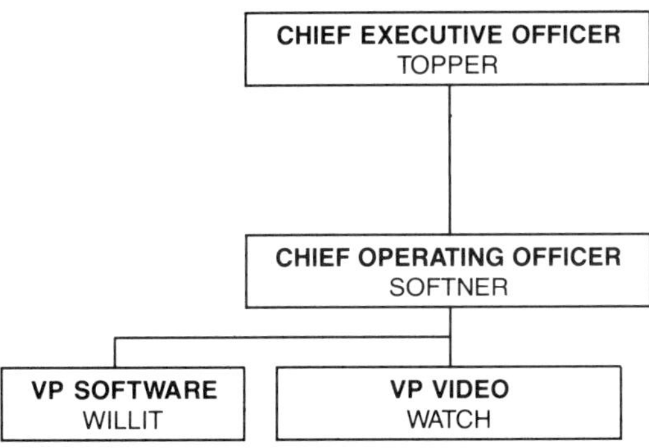

"Before getting into this business, Watch was a director in a Hollywood studio. He has a Hollywood manner about him, if you know what I mean. In addition to being extremely good looking, he is a real charmer. He could sell you the Brooklyn Bridge.

"I also look forward to getting to know the director of strategic planning, George Foresight. He is the only bachelor in the place, and is a real avid golfer. He is not even that much older than I am. In the three years since he joined the company, he has really made a name for himself.

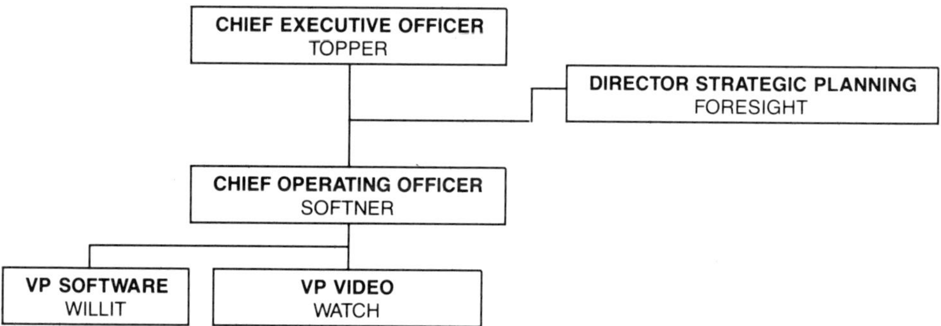

"Unlike many strategic planners, Foresight is a visionary who puts as much faith in intuition as in analysis. He is an incredibly well-rounded guy, comfortable with both numbers and with abstract notions."

Bill commented that the company sounded more like an adult playground than an orderly business. Misunderstanding his intent, Larry took offense.

"It's not child's play, Bill. The company plans to double its volume every year for the next five years! And they've got what it takes to do it. A company doesn't have to be stodgy to be successful."

Bill tried to clarify that he had intended only to compliment Larry on his choice of a company which had the energy and the willingness to take risks, to experiment. But Larry was not finished with his defense.

"In addition to entrepreneurs, inventors, Hollywood directors, and visionaries, the company also has a few extremely conservative people in high places. The most conservative is the chief financial officer, Peter Buck.

"Buck, I am told, does not have an ounce of imagination in him. A stickler for detail, he insists on a very tight budgeting process.

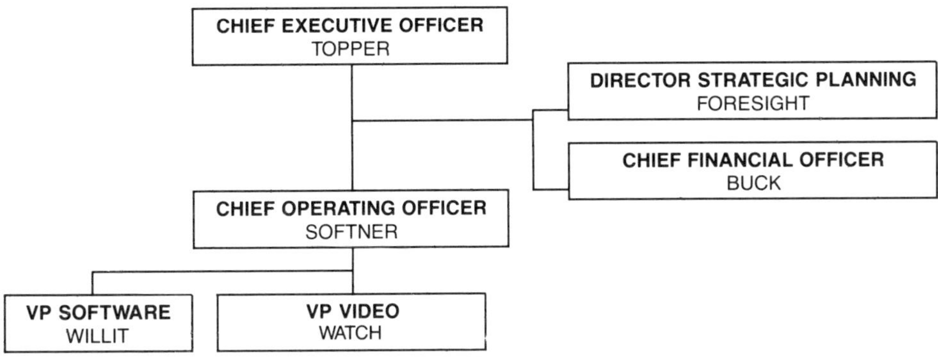

And he is completely analytical in his approach. The answer to everything, according to Buck, lies in numbers. While he wouldn't win any popularity contests, he does introduce that element of caution that you seem to feel distinguishes a business from an adult playground, as you call it.

"Last and probably least is the vice-president of administration, Wendell Gladhand. Wendell is in charge of recruiting, so I have had the pleasure of his company for several hours already.

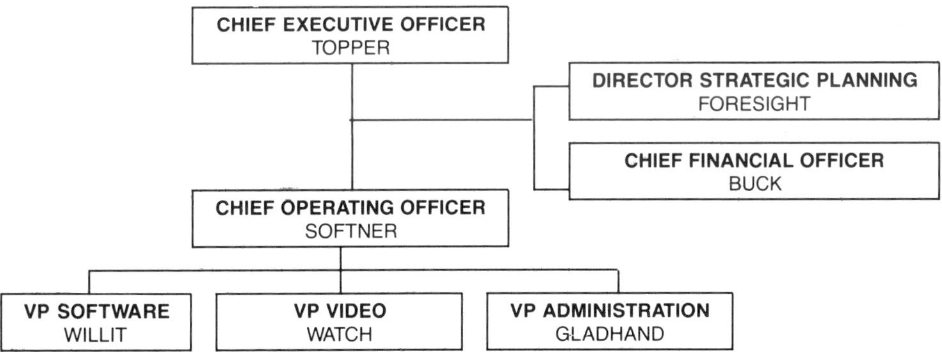

"Wendell could be the most boring individual I have ever met. He, too, is a carryover from the video company. I guess they didn't think they could fire a man in his late fifties. Instead, they put him on the shelf, so to speak, and put him in charge of administration. I guess they figured he could do little damage in a staff position. Well, that wasn't true. A couple of people told me he antagonized the chief executive when he introduced compensation systems that discouraged people from innovating and taking risks. You know, he advocated pay grades with ceilings and the like. Well, that stuff may work in a giant bureaucracy, but it has no place in a company like Software Systems. It took an outside consultant to straighten out the damage Gladhand created."

Completing the graphic that now consumed the entire napkin, Larry indicated that below the level of vice-president, there was a director level, a manager level, and a supervisory level.

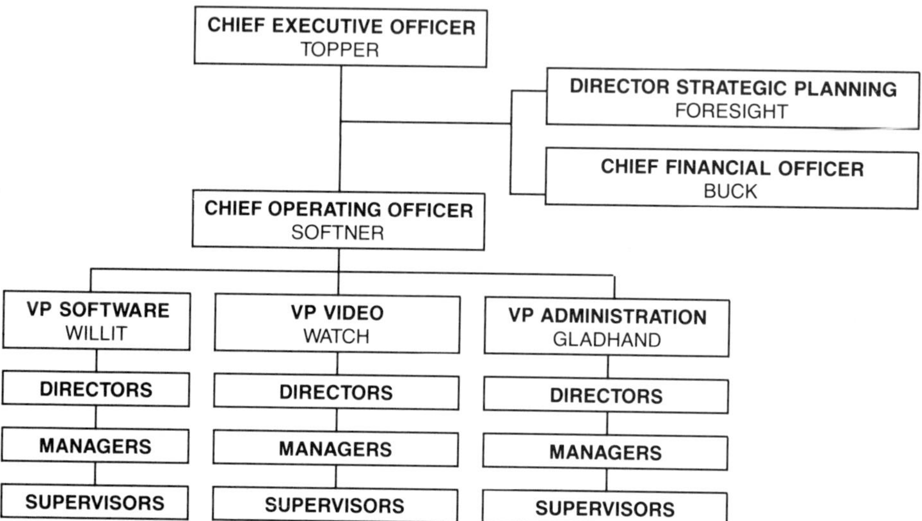

With pride, Larry announced that the company employed approximately 400 people, most of them professionals in their fields. "And *I*, Larry Michaelson, have the honor of being one of a highly select group of twelve carefully picked trainees!"

Bill could not resist taking advantage of an opportunity to use one of his favorite quotations. Raising his glass, he proposed a toast to Larry, and to his dream.

"As Theodore Roosevelt once said, 'Far better it is to dare mighty things, to win glorious triumphs, even though checkered by failure, than to take rank with those poor spirits who neither enjoy much nor suffer much, because they live in the gray twilight that knows not victory or defeat.'

"You, my friend, are determined to dare mighty things. More power to you. Let us talk a little before you begin your job. Perhaps there is a way to maximize the likelihood of victory, and minimize the possibility of defeat."

Larry eagerly agreed to several golf dates with Bill. By the time August first arrived, Bill managed to convince Larry that realization of his dream would require more than the strength of conviction. They agreed to get together periodically to review Larry's strategies, and to analyze the power plays that were occurring in the organization. Their objective was to equip Larry to

- distinguish between and to build each of seven kinds of power;
- select the most appropriate influence strategy;
- avoid manipulation and participation in other corporate power plays;
- create and maintain sound interpersonal relationships;
- create a network of supporters throughout the organization;
- determine who really makes things happen in the organization, regardless of the official chart;
- affiliate with the right people at the right time;
- make others feel like winners, avoiding win-lose situations, and refusing to win at another's expense if possible;
- master the art of timing, or selecting the appropriate moment for action.

The evening before Larry was to begin his new job, Bill and he had dinner. During dinner, they agreed that Larry was just commencing his education as a student of corporate power dynamics, and that the stakes were a lot higher than simply grades on a report card.

SOFTWARE SYSTEMS, INC.

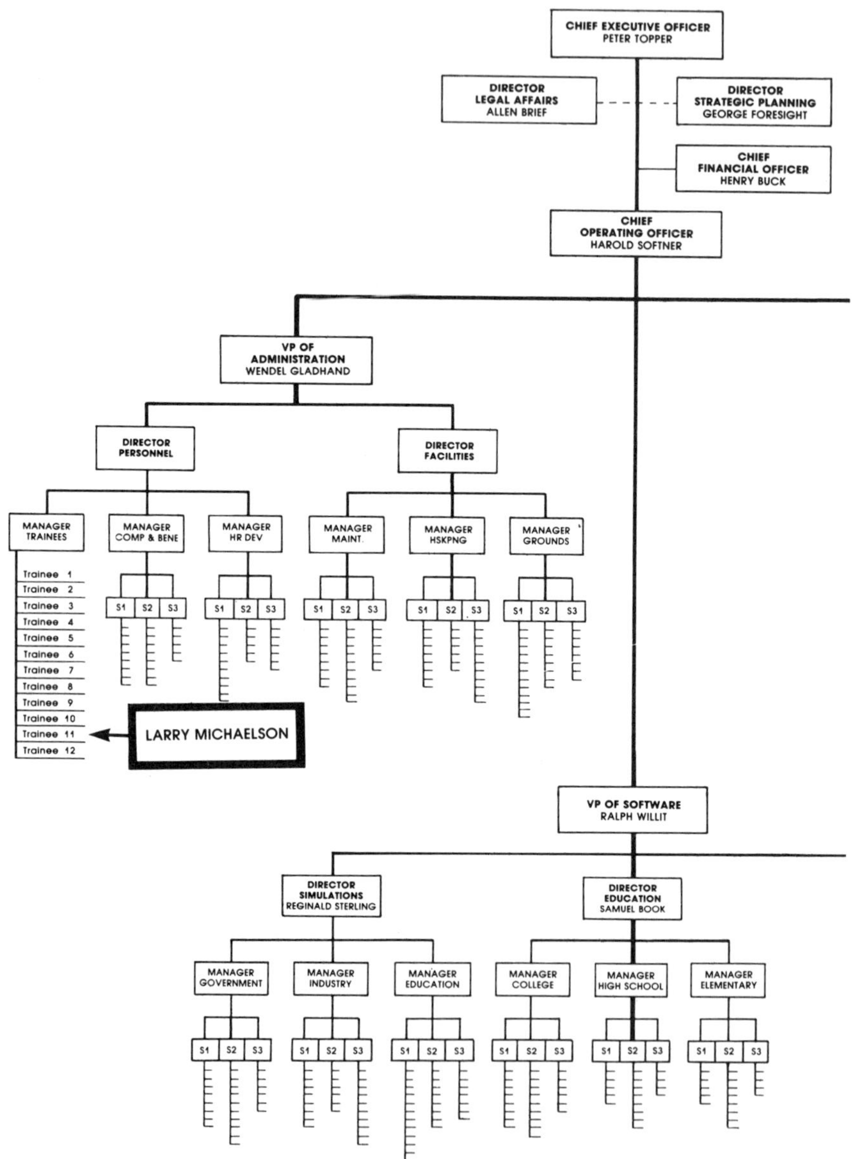

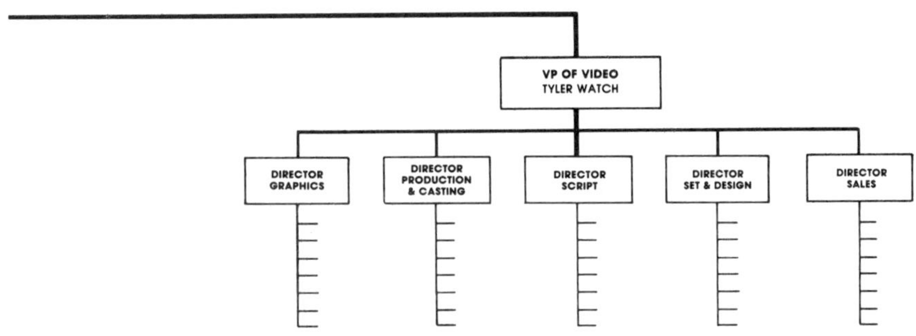
VP OF VIDEO
TYLER WATCH
DIRECTOR
GRAPHICS
DIRECTOR
PRODUCTION
& CASTING
DIRECTOR
SCRIPT
DIRECTOR
SET & DESIGN
DIRECTOR
SALES

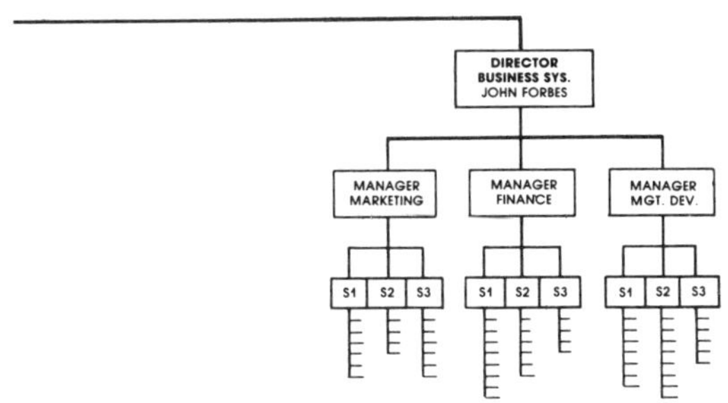
DIRECTOR
BUSINESS SYS.
JOHN FORBES
MANAGER
MARKETING
MANAGER
FINANCE
MANAGER
MGT. DEV.
S1 S2 S3
S1 S2 S3
S1 S2 S3

2

Turbulent Times for the Trainee

FIRED WITH AMBITION, and intent on realizing his dream as soon as possible, Larry embarked on his career as a management trainee with Software Systems, Inc. It was with a great deal of impatience and frustration at being unable to get on with the business at hand that Larry tolerated the first eight weeks of classroom training in programming and video technology.

Larry's incessant questions earned him the reputation of being an inquisitive, though somewhat obnoxious, trainee. Valuing energy, stamina, and drive as the organization did, however, it looked upon Larry with favor, ignoring for the moment his inability to determine when inquisitiveness ended and pestering began.

Larry and his peers then began a nine-month program which required that they rotate through all of the departments in the company, learning the functions and responsibilities of each. Each tour of duty lasted anywhere from two to four weeks.

Being a quick study, Larry was generally able to master the basics after only a week in each area. He then occupied himself with looking for opportunities to improve the effectiveness or efficiency of the operation. Wanting to stand out as the brightest of his group of trainees, Larry did not hesitate to recommend that changes be made. He did so in what he believed were the best interests of the company. After all, when he was hired, he had been told that the organization valued innovation and change.

It troubled Larry that his suggestions failed to generate action. In many instances, he got no response at all to his memos. Giving his new employer the benefit of the doubt, he assured himself that change would come in time, and that silence indicated acceptance of his self-assigned role as trouble-shooter.

The one thing that did trouble Larry was his apparent inability to develop what he viewed as important friendships within the organization. The relationships he had developed with his peers, while enjoyable, did not satisfy Larry's thirst for influential contacts. He was impatient to develop a cadre of supporters among the people who he perceived were actually making things happen.

Unwilling to wait long enough for such friendships to evolve, Larry began to take the initiative. This was not an easy thing for Larry to do. His apparent aloofness masked a fundamental shyness that rendered social situations uncomfortable. Nonetheless, he decided to give a cocktail party and to invite thirty of the supervisors and managers he most admired. Only two of the trainees were invited. "After all," he reasoned, "they are already my friends; they do not require courting."

The party was a disappointment. Only half of the persons he had invited chose to come, and most stayed only a short time. Larry sensed that he was still an outsider, and that troubled him. He redoubled his efforts to get to know the decision-makers.

He began to seek opportunities to be of help to people. His greatest success in this area occurred when he overheard one of the supervisors talking about the difficulties he was having with a statistics course. Larry offered his assistance. The offer was enthusiastically accepted. Larry had managed to make a friend in court.

Larry's eagerness on the social front began to pay off. His ambition to stand out as a shining star among the trainees was not coming to fruition, however. On the contrary, Larry was trying too hard, and, in the process, he was antagonizing both his peers and the vice-president of administration.

Hoping to challenge the trainees, Wendell Gladhand had established a task force, a special project involving six of the trainees. The team was charged with doing an analysis of the competition.

Larry was fortunate to be appointed to the task force. Once appointed, he was determined to make the work of the team a success. For a week prior to the first meeting of the task force, he stayed up late every night, studying all the articles he could find on the competition. By the time the task force convened, he had formed a number of opinions as to the required scope of the study, and the hypotheses that should be tested.

His behavior during the first meeting can only be characterized as offensive. He assumed the leadership role and began issuing directives. The other team members initially complied, taking notes and appearing to accede to their self-appointed leader. Their compliance was short-lived, however. Before the first meeting ended, one of the members challenged Larry's right to rule.

"Just a minute. Who gave you the right to tell us what to do? Who do you think you are? You act like you think you are better than the rest of us. Why, when you gave that big party, you didn't even bother to invite most of us. You think we didn't notice? Well, we did. You are no smarter than the rest of us, Larry. How many of the rest of you are content to follow Larry's orders?"

A complete silence fell over the room. Most of the participants were clearly uncomfortable, with expressions of discomfort ranging from the shuffling of bodies on squeaky chairs to a nervous tapping of pens on the table. No one looked Larry or his antagonist in the eye.

Eventually, one of the trainees broke the silence. "I think we should start over. Larry is to be congratulated for having prepared so thoroughly. Joel, you deserve credit for your attention to our process. I, for one, would like to see this team function as a committee of equals. I think the leadership role should shift, based on expertise. But our leader should not act like a boss or a schoolteacher. No, this should be a committee of equals."

The speaker succeeded in temporarily diffusing the hostility between Larry and Joel. But, lacking a clear definition of the process, the group floundered. Larry was reluctant to antagonize his peers further by taking charge. He went too far in the other direction, keeping his ideas and opinions to himself. Politeness became the norm, as members avoided the vulnerability and visibility inherent in the leadership role.

In an attempt to compensate for the weakness of the task force, Larry attempted to do the entire project alone. In his fantasies, he envisioned himself rescuing the committee from certain embarrassment and, as a result, gaining the respect and friendship of the other team members. A week before the group was scheduled to make its presentation, Larry unveiled his study and his conclusions.

The reaction of the rest of the group members was mixed. A few were relieved that the task force had a product to show. Many, however, were not grateful. Some seemed to be flatly uninterested. Others were antagonistic, devoting their energies to finding the flaws in Larry's argument rather than attempting to understand his approach and his conclusions.

That the work of the task force was the product of one man became obvious during the presentation. The vice-presidents listened with interest, and then began asking questions. Only Larry had the answers to their questions.

After the presentation, Wendell Gladhand asked to meet with Larry. Larry expected praise. Instead, he was chastised for his inability to function as a team player.

"Larry, your presentation was thorough and raised a lot of key issues. Had I not known the other team members, I would have believed that you were the only one with brains in the room. However, I do know their capabilities. That they were completely uninvolved in the presentation, and unable to answer the questions, indicates to me that you unilaterally took over the job of the team. Further, you obviously did so in such a way as to preclude the involvement of the others in the development of the project."

Larry attempted to defend himself, explaining that the other members had refused to get involved. But Gladhand was not interested in explanations.

"Larry, we created the task force for two reasons. We did want the competitive analysis. But more importantly, we wanted to give you trainees the experience of working as a team. All of you are accustomed to working alone, and to competing with each other. The business school environment seems to breed that kind of behavior. Well, we don't work that way here. You did not function as a team player, Larry. I suggest you work on that."

Larry took the advice to heart, and tried valiantly to behave as a member of the organizational team. Believing that his display of expertise created more problems than it solved, he attempted to mute his natural desire to function as an intellectual leader. He stopped challenging or openly disagreeing with others' points of view. He stopped attempting to lead, and began accommodating the implied or expressed wishes of others. But the role of follower was unnatural for Larry. Sensing that his behavior was forced and not authentic, others grew suspicious of him.

As Larry's tension mounted, he began to make mistakes. While rotating through one of the departments in the video disc division, he got careless and unintentionally erased some critical footage. No one had observed Larry when the accident occurred. It would have been possible for Larry to deny any responsibility for the mishap.

Larry did not do so. Instead, he approached the director of the unit and confessed his mistake. He expected to be criticized or even fired. Much to his surprise, he received praise instead.

"Larry, I am glad that you came to me. In the first place, it might have taken us a week or more to discover the erasure. Then we would have had a real crisis on our hands. Mistakes do happen. We all understand that. It is to your credit that you had the courage to admit your involvement. I hope that you learned something from the episode."

Larry had indeed learned something. *He had learned that it is acceptable to be fallible; and, he had learned the value of honesty.* Unfortunately, his newly learned lesson did not help him resolve the dilemma he faced several weeks later.

He inadvertently discovered that one of the other trainees had been making multiple copies of the software that the company ordered for evaluation purposes. The trainee in question had been selling the copies to others outside the firm. As coincidence would have it, one of the buyers had been a classmate of Larry's. They ran into each other at a bar and began discussing their respective jobs. When Larry mentioned Software Systems, his former classmate told him of the software "blackmarket."

For several days, Larry tried to forget what he had heard. He did not want to further antagonize his peers by being the one to tell tales. And he had been cautioned to be more of a team player. On the other hand, he had learned the value of honesty, and believed it was dishonest to fail to reveal what he knew. It seemed to Larry that silence was tantamount to complicity in the crime.

Not knowing what to do, Larry called Bill. It was too early for their "strategy" session, but timely in terms of Larry's need for both nurturance and advice. Bill advised Larry to go to the vice-president of administration and tell him what was going on, but without naming names.

Gladhand was visibly upset by Larry's news and, at first, refused to believe him. "Now you've gone too far. You gain nothing by implying that another trainee is displaying this kind of disloyalty to the company. You are far too ambitious for your own good, Larry."

Fortunately for both Larry and the company, the "blackmarket" was discovered shortly after Larry's abortive attempt to see that justice prevailed. One of the supervisors approached the vice-president of administration with the same information as Larry had attempted to provide. Because he was a supervisor, with no apparent hidden motive, Gladhand listened. A few weeks later, the guilty trainee was caught in the act of peddling the copies.

Larry was elated when Gladhand approached him and apologized for doubting both his word and his motivation. The apology marked the beginning of several weeks of success for Larry. His attempts to dominate the case team forgotten, and the results of his study remembered, Larry was asked to do a special study on market receptivity to a product the company was considering introducing.

Larry voluntarily involved another trainee in the project, and urged that they share the actual presentation. Word began to get around that Larry was OK, and that earlier suspicions were unfounded. Further, the presentation was a complete success. Larry had begun to earn a reputation as a rigorous analyst.

It may be that success went to Larry's head, and made him forget that he was still a trainee. On one of his assignments, Larry was invited to sit in during a presentation to a client. The supervisor's intent was to give Larry an opportunity to observe a direct client interaction. Larry misunderstood his role, and acted not as an observer, but as a spokesman for the corporation.

The supervisor did not expect Larry to speak during the meeting. He was furious when Larry not only spoke, but actually dared to disagree with statements that had been made by the supervisor. It did not matter that the client agreed with Larry. Nor did it help when the client complimented the supervisor on the company's ability to attract such fine young talent. On the contrary, Larry's intervention into the meeting infuriated the supervisor.

Larry was to discover that he had made a strategic mistake when he met with Gladhand for his performance review. The organization did not expect their trainees to be trouble-shooters. Trainees were paid to learn, not to be visible. Larry had not yet "earned his stripes." Until he completed basic training, he was not invited to comment on the officers' behavior or on the institution they had created.

Gladhand was charged with delivering the message to the overeager trainee. "Right now, you are paid to learn, not to make waves. We expect you to spend the bulk of your time listening. A lot of people think you have a chip on your shoulder. Just because you have your M.B.A., you are no better than others around here who had to learn the business the hard way. I suggest you maintain a low profile for awhile. You are very bright. Some of your work has been of excellent quality. That does not compensate for your abrasive approach, however. You will be of no use to us if you persist in antagonizing your co-workers and your superiors. Your behavior in the meeting with the client was inexcusable."

Larry tried to remind Gladhand that the client had appreciated his comments, but Gladhand was not going to be dissuaded from his critical point of view.

"The issue is not whether you were right or wrong. That is beside the point. You were presumptuous in speaking at all. When you disagreed with your supervisor in the presence of a client, you broke a cardinal rule. Remember, Larry, you are a trainee. At times, you act like you think you are president of the company."

Badly shaken by his performance review, Larry called Bill and asked if they could get together a few weeks earlier than planned. Sensing the distress in Larry's voice, Bill agreed to meet him for golf and dinner that weekend.

By the time Saturday arrived, Larry had gotten over blaming himself for his organizational mistakes, and had turned his anger toward the company.

"I am not going to be part of an organization that puts people in little boxes and stifles their creativity. I have been doing the best job that I can, and what do I get for it? Criticism, that's all I seem to hear, criticism. I think people are threatened by me. Well, if they're so cowardly and so set in their ways, then forget it. I want no part of it."

Bill let Larry vent his anger for awhile, empathizing with Larry's frustration, and sensing that Larry's impatience and apparent arrogance, coupled with his intellect, had gotten him into trouble.

Larry finally calmed down, and began to recite the events that had characterized his tour of duty as a trainee. Omitting nothing, he told of the party and his efforts to make friends with the organizational decision makers. He spoke of the many evenings he had spent with one of the supervisors helping him pass a statistics course. And he told of his superlative performance, in completing first the competitive analysis, and then the market receptivity study.

"Why, I even uncovered a blackmarket in software, and alerted the company to the plot! And I have one of our major clients literally wrapped around my finger."

Bill enjoyed Larry's recitation of his heroic feats and his successes. He knew, however, that trainees are generally paid to learn, and to integrate themselves into the organizational culture. A trainee, almost by definition, cannot be a hero. Dramatics and high visibility moves during the trainee stage tend to get the individual labeled as a trouble-maker.

"That's the good news, Larry. Now, tell me about the bad news. Explain to me why you were criticized during the performance review."

With some difficulty, Larry told of the problems he had experienced in getting along with his peer group. It was clear that, while he understood their antagonism, he felt misunderstood, unappreciated, and unfairly treated.

"So, I gave a party and didn't invite them. Big deal. They probably wouldn't have come, anyway. It was not the social success of the season. The competitive analysis I mentioned; well, that was supposed to be the work of the task force, and I guess I took over prematurely. To this day, I believe that if I had not jumped in and done the job, it would not have gotten done. We all would have suffered as a result. All I got for my efforts was criticism for failing to act like a team player.

"As for my ability to impress a client with my insights, well, that backfired too. To make my point, I had to disagree openly with my supervisor. I guess his ego couldn't handle that.

"As far as the software blackmarket goes, well, the vice-president of administration, Gladhand, thought I was trying to get ahead by destroying the reputation of another trainee. I didn't even mention any names! That was really unfair. There was nothing in it for me. I should have kept my mouth shut!

"The only honest mistake I made was to accidentally erase some footage. I confessed my sins and was forgiven. At least that manager has an open mind and is willing to give me a chance."

They played the remaining holes without further discussion of Larry's predicament. Only when they were seated in the dining room did Bill begin to counsel Larry on the approaches he had taken.

"Larry, you simply assumed that others wanted to hear your opinion. In rendering opinions about the operations of the company, you stepped beyond the bounds of the role of "trainee." In effect, you failed to live up to the expectations people had of you because of your role, your position. That offended your supervisors and triggered the negative performance review.

"To make matters worse, you aggravated some pre-existing negative stereotypes about M.B.A.s. Much of your behavior confirmed the belief that young people with M.B.A.s are impatient, overly ambitious, and willing to step on the toes of others to make things happen.

"In both of these instances you suffered from lack of *position power. Position power is the power of role, and of the expectations people have and the assumptions they make because of the formal and informal roles a person fills.*

"Position power can expand or restrict an individual's opportunities to act, to influence situations. Women were historically expected to be passive and emotional. These role expectations restricted them in their ability to climb the corporate ladder. Happily, that is changing.

"As a trainee within Software Systems, Inc., you are restricted. Trainees are expected to maintain a low profile, to learn and to accept the status quo.

"Similarly, the role of M.B.A. affected your ability to get a fair hearing for your ideas. It was simply assumed that your intent was to function as the corporate show-off.

"Position power can, however, provide a useful source of leverage. People generally grant a great deal of power to people who fill such roles as king, president, or general. Regardless of the individual's ability to lead or to rule, power is conferred because of role alone. *The advantage of having position power is that people comply without resentment.*

"The Viscount Morley, I believe it was, said it all: 'Success depends on three things: who says it, what he says, how he says it; and of these three things, what he says is least important.'

"All of the roles we fill affect our ability to influence. We can control some of those roles, such as our organizational roles. When we get promoted, we typically enjoy a change in role that opens up additional opportunities to influence others.

"You made *position power* work for you when you earned the informal title of 'market analyst' by expressing an interest in special projects, and then performing well on those projects. People will subsequently expect you to have a deeper understanding of the

*"I will have the senior-executive businessman's lunch, and Hooper
here will have the junior-executive's businessman's lunch."*

Drawing by Gahan Wilson; © 1983
The New Yorker Magazine, Inc.

market than do the other trainees. That role label will probably stand you in good stead.

"The biggest disadvantage of relying on position power in this day and age is that we can't be certain that the desired response will occur as others question whether 'rights and privileges' can be assumed according to role."

"Well, I would happily give up the position power, or rather the lack of power, that comes with the role of trainee," said Larry.

"That will happen in short order. And when it does, you will find that you have a great deal more formal power than you now enjoy. *Formal power is conferred upon an individual by the organization.* The point at which it is conferred generally involves a promotion into a role which carries with it not only position power but also an increase in the power to reward and to coerce.

"The role of trainee brings with it little or no position power, or the right to influence because of the role we fill. Nor has the organization conferred upon you reward power, or the ability to persuade others because of your ability to grant such rewards as raises, promotions, etc. And, you have not been given the right to use coercive power, or the ability to deprive others of things they value if they fail to do your bidding."

"So, in effect, I have no power and no way of getting any until I finish with the training program. That is a pretty grim picture. Why, I was more influential in graduate school. At least, as a student, I had the right to challenge and to question."

"I can understand your frustration, Larry, but it would be a mistake to assume that you are totally without power, and that you cannot build up a power base, even as a trainee. Admittedly, you are not likely to gain any formal power while you function as a trainee. But you can certainly work on building up your informal power bases.

"*Informal power is the power of friendship, or trust; the power of expertise; and the power of image, or presence.* These kinds of power cannot be conferred. They are a function of the person, and can be earned by taking steps to inspire trust, to build respect, and to project a persuasive image. Nothing in your present situation precludes you from working on developing these kinds of power.

"In fact, you have already begun to enhance your power as an expert. You did so when you made the effort to serve on special projects that provided an opportunity for you to show that you have strong analytical skills. *To make a conscious attempt to show people what you can do, and the relevance of what you have done, is a good strategy.*

"I'm afraid, though, that you haven't done yourself a favor with regard to building the power of friendship. You did a number of things that created a climate of mistrust and put interpersonal distance between you and others. Failing to invite your peers to the party was a bad move, as was your behavior on the task force.

"I like your choice in suits, Larry. You dress well, and carry yourself well. That provides a certain measure of presence power, or the power of image. And, never minimize the importance of image. As Publilius Syrus put it, 'A fair exterior is a silent recommendation.'

"Since the most important thing for you to do at this point in your career, Larry, is to establish a power base, I suggest we focus on that right now, and leave the subject of influence strategies and power plays for another time."

"To affiliate with the most powerful unit in the organization is to increase immediately your position power. You have three months in which to select the division and department you want to join. Because position power is important, and because you are already off to a bad start in that area, I suggest you use the time during the next three months to determine which organization within Software Systems is the most powerful. Answering these questions should help you do so."

Bill's questions to Larry were as follows:

1. What work group or unit is perceived to be most vital to the ability of the organization to solve those problems it feels are critical?

2. What work group or unit is perceived to be most vital to the organization's ability to respond to key opportunities?

3. Which work group or unit is the least dependent on the resources of other groups in terms of its ability to reach its objectives?

4. On which work group or unit do many other work groups rely in order to reach their objectives?

5. Which unit or work group is thought to be most important in terms of grooming someone to assume a top leadership role?

6. In which work group or unit has the organization invested a significant amount of money?

7. Which work group or unit is perceived to be the most difficult to replace or replicate?

8. Which work group has the smallest margin for error; in which area are mistakes the most costly?

9. Which work group or unit has the greatest degree of control over information?

In response to Larry's puzzled look, Bill told him that the questions represented the nine areas that determined the power of one work group over another. He pointed out that affiliation with the most powerful work group carried with it the greatest measure of position power, as well as other forms of leverage.

"You've had some turbulent times as a trainee, Larry. Let's see if we can devise a strategy to make your first line job more productive. Answering these questions is a beginning."

Larry thanked Bill for the day, and gathered up the notes he had made during dinner.

LARRY'S NOTES

Three Kinds of Formal Power (Conferred by the Organization)

REWARD: The ability to provide something of value to the other.

COERCIVE: The ability to punish, or to deprive the other of something of value.

POSITION: The power of role and the expectations associated with the roles we fill.

ADVANTAGE: Compliance without resentment.

DISADVANTAGE: Lack of certainty that desired action will occur as the other person questions "rights" and "privileges."

Three Kinds of Informal Power (Earned; Not Conferred)

EXPERT POWER: The power of respect gained as a result of what we know and what we can do.

FRIENDSHIP: The power of trust.

PRESENCE: The power of image.

As they parted, another thought occurred to Bill. He shared it, hoping to rekindle Larry's enthusiasm.

"I've been there, Larry. We all have. Don't dwell on your mistakes. The key to success is putting your energy into learning from your mistakes. Do that and you'll soon be miles ahead of the rest of the pack."

3

Crown Princes
and Manipulators

BY MONDAY MORNING, Larry was recommitted to the pursuit of his dream. He had a strategy, a mission, and was eager to find the answers to Bill's questions. It amused him that, in doing so, he would be behaving as a trainee is expected to behave, devoting his energies to learning about the inner workings of the corporation. In actuality, he was working on a strategy for enhancing his visibility; that was *not* expected trainee behavior!

Larry began his search for the answers to his questions with the director of strategic planning, George Foresight. Given his role, George would have the most information about the organization's key problems and opportunities.

Larry called George a few times, but his calls were never returned. Attempts to schedule an appointment through Foresight's secretary were equally unsuccessful. Again, Larry began to feel like a second-class citizen, fettered by his trainee status.

He was expressing his resentment to his supervisor friend over lunch one day. As luck would have it, the supervisor knew Foresight well.

"You got me out of a jam when I was struggling with that statistics course. Now, it's my turn to be of help to you. Foresight and I play racquetball several times a week. In fact, we have a game scheduled for this evening. I'll take care of it."

And take care of it he did. Early the next week, Foresight called Larry and suggested that they meet for lunch. Larry eagerly accepted, certain that by the end of lunch, he would have the answers to all of his questions.

Larry failed to appreciate that in order to answer many of the questions, Foresight would have to reveal some highly sensitive information. And he had overestimated his ability to convince Foresight that he could be trusted to maintain a confidence. Foresight's initial reaction to Larry's list of questions was polite but uninformative.

"Yes, those are all very good questions. I suppose we could all benefit from giving more thought to them from time to time. I can see you are very intent on making a name for yourself in this organization. I applaud your ambition. The company needs eager, dedicated people like yourself. Tell me, what other interests do you have in life?"

Larry responded as briefly as he could, hoping to turn the conversation back to an analysis of the organization. "Golf is a real favorite of mine. I play a little tennis and, occasionally, some racquetball."

Foresight apparently preferred discussing racquetball as opposed to the corporation, for he began telling Larry tales of matches won and lost. Larry had no choice but to feign an interest he did not feel.

Dessert had arrived before Larry succeeded in bringing the conversation back to his questions. Scanning the list, Foresight chose to comment only on the relationship between the software and video sides of the house.

"I can answer question three and, I suppose four. 'Which work group is the least dependent on the resources of other groups?' and 'On which work group or unit do many other work groups rely?' The Video Disc Division is very dependent on the Software Division for sales. Almost without exception, video discs are sold as part of a package containing both software and video. The video component is almost an add-on. Software, on the other hand, is often sold without the video component. I would say, then, that the Software Division enjoys the greatest degree of independence with regard to its ability to reach its objectives.

"The same relationship holds true with regard to question seven, 'Which work group is perceived to be the most difficult to replace?' The systems personnel would be harder to replace than would people on the video side of the organization. That is simply a result of the demand for systems expertise within corporations today.

"With regard to margin for error, again the software side of the house prevails. Actually, the Simulations Department, run by Reginald Sterling, has the smallest margin for error. This is particularly true when it comes to the programs developed for the government. An error there would be disastrous for the company.

"As for information flow and control, again software wins over video. But, then, that should be obvious to you. I mean, the systems people write the programs that store the information."

Foresight then asked for the check, effectively ending their conversation. Wanting another opportunity to talk with him, Larry suggested they get together again later in the week. Foresight declined, claiming that he had a very busy schedule. Persisting, Larry suggested they get together that weekend for a racquetball game. Much to his surprise, Foresight accepted the invitation.

Larry had not played racquetball in over two years. To describe his game as "rusty" would have been overly kind. Wanting to impress Foresight, Larry arranged to practice every night that week. There were times when the stiffness in his muscles was so intense as to make him wonder whether the effort was indeed worth it.

They got together Saturday as planned. Larry's game was passable. While Foresight won, Larry at least made him work for the win. After the game, they decided to share a beer or two. Again, Larry tried to introduce Software Systems, Inc. into the conversation. His effort met with only limited success.

"Don't you ever think about anything else? Your dedication borders on the obnoxious. Seriously, I am a little discouraged about the company, or actually about my role in the company, and don't particularly enjoy talking about it."

Hoping to learn more, Larry said, "I don't understand. You've got the ear of the top man. You're in a position to make things happen. That's a lot more than I can say."

The comment succeeded in provoking an unusually open response. "Whatever you do, don't go into strategic planning, or into any staff job for that matter. I feel like a student, not like a viable part of the management team. I make a recommendation about a merger or acquisition, only to have it ignored. We are pouring a shameless amount of money into research and development, and putting far too few dollars into getting the products that we do have out into the marketplace. But will the company listen to me? No.

"It's different when the CEO is around and available. But lately he has been too busy for me to approach him. Anyway, if I keep asking him to fight my battles for me, he is bound to lose respect for me. At any rate, I, like you, suffer from lack of power. I am regarded as a staff person whose job it is to do studies and make recommendations and to then sit back and simply hope that the line managers choose to act on those recommendations."

Larry empathized with Foresight, hoping that this sudden openness would continue. But Foresight had already said more than he had wanted to say. His discomfort obvious, he abruptly changed the subject, asking Larry about his social life.

When Larry volunteered that his social life was practically nonexistent, Foresight suggested that Larry join his party that evening.

"The woman I have been seeing has a friend visiting her from out-of-town. I had planned to take the two of them to dinner tonight. Why don't you join us?"

Larry accepted and was glad that he had. The evening was enjoyable; so enjoyable, in fact, that the foursome decided to get together again on Sunday. By the end of the weekend, Larry and Foresight had built the foundation for a strong friendship. In spite of the dramatic difference in their status within the organization, they had begun to experience each other as peers. The once reticent Foresight was now far more willing to help his friend get the answers to his questions.

Only a few weeks after their initial meeting, Foresight shared the following with Larry.

"The greatest problem facing the company is its inability to penetrate the corporate software market. We've got a competitive edge in the retail outlets and in the educational area, but our corporate sales efforts are inadequate.

"The greatest opportunity facing the company is related to its greatest problem. There is a real need out there for computerized strategic planning tools. Corporations pay millions of dollars to consultants who apply their formulas and recommend changes in product portfolio, competitive strategy, and the like. Well, many of the tools used by the consultants can be programmed to enable the corporation to consider a variety of contingencies as it plans.

"Because the corporate market is far less price sensitive than the retail market, our profit margins would be considerable. And there is no decent product out there. The market is ours for the taking."

Larry asked Foresight to name the units in the company which were in the best position to gear up a corporate sales effort, and which were most likely to be involved in the development of financial planning tools for the corporate market. Foresight responded that the Business Systems area, and, in particular, the finance unit, should, in his opinion, oversee the development and sale of the product.

Larry carefully noted down everything that Foresight was saying. Perhaps Larry's trust in and reliance on his judgment touched Foresight, for he made himself vulnerable as he volunteered news of an impending power play.

"Let me hasten to add, Larry, that what you have just heard is simply my opinion of how the organization should respond. It may not happen that way, however, if it happens at all. You see, Reginald Sterling, the director of software simulations, is attempting to make a case for putting the financial planning model in his area."

Larry had heard the legends about Reginald Sterling. A lot of people in the company were afraid of him. Few trusted him, though many admired his capabilities. He shared what he had heard with Foresight.

"While I haven't had a lot of direct dealings with Reginald," Larry said, "I hear that he plays hard, and plays for keeps. There is no such thing as neutral ground as far as Reginald is concerned. Either you are his ally or his enemy. Thus far, I am fortunate enough to be neither, but I suppose that won't last forever."

"It's not likely that it will," agreed Foresight. "You are not the kind to keep a low profile. No, Reginald will soon begin to regard you as a threat. He wants it all. He'll step on anybody to get it. And he's quite powerful. He's got Willit, the VP of software, on his side. More importantly, Reginald and Buck, the chief financial officer, have formed what they regard as a mutually beneficial alliance.

"Buck and I have never gotten along. As you may or may not know, I have developed and still control a very sophisticated financial planning model. We use it in this company. I believe it could constitute the prototype for our product offering.

"For the past six months, Buck has been trying to convince the CEO that control of the model should be in his area. You see, access to the model gives me a chance for some visibility with the board of directors. Buck would love to have the opportunities I have to make those presentations. The only reason he hasn't won so far is that the CEO is in my corner. But, as I said before, you can only lean on someone else's power for so long before they begin to tire of it or to feel that you can't pull your own weight.

"There, now, I have definitely said too much. If you breathe a word of this to anyone, and I do mean anyone, I will never trust you again. I only hope it will help you make your decision about which unit to join."

In the weeks that followed, Larry continued to seek the answers to his questions. He learned that others disagreed with Foresight's definition of key problems and opportunities. No argument, however, was as convincing as Foresight's had been, and he decided to take the response of the strategic planner as his answer. And he learned more about Reginald Sterling and the power he was able to wield.

Reginald was in charge of the Simulations Department of the Software Division. As the most visible of the software directors, Reginald was clearly the most powerful individual at his level.

It was with relief that Larry discovered that the organization's most significant speculative investment was not in Reginald's department, but in the Research and Development area. Only weeks later did he discover that the bulk of the funds budgeted for R and D activities were in response to Reginald's request for development of a simulation for space shuttle passengers!

Larry was thorough and effective in his search for the answers to Bill's questions on position power. Unfortunately, his search for the answers so preoccupied him that he failed to pay enough attention to his ongoing activities, and found himself caught in a dangerous power play.

Larry's earlier dispute with Joel, the trainee, resurfaced. (Joel was the individual who took exception to Larry's attempt to take charge of the competitive analysis task force.) Apparently Joel never forgot, or never forgave Larry, for he finally succeeded in putting Larry in an extremely awkward position.

As the time neared for the trainees to identify their job preferences, and for the supervisors and managers to indicate their trainees of choice, the competition between the trainees intensified. It is perhaps for this reason that Joel chose this time to manipulate Larry into a situation in which he could only lose.

Larry was an easy target. Given his desire to enhance his friendships within the organization, Larry was very willing to help others whenever possible. Joel was no exception. On the contrary, given their historic disagreements, Larry would have taken almost any opportunity to ease the tension that continued to exist between them. When Joel asked for assistance in doing the mathematical analysis for a presentation, Larry readily agreed.

Nor did he withdraw his offer when he learned that the presentation was for Reginald Sterling. After all, he reasoned, Reginald is part of the organization, a key part, and helping him is helping the organization. He did not appreciate that, in the process, he would be hurting his new found friend, George Foresight.

One day, while they were working on the presentation, Joel called in sick. He pleaded with Larry to try to gather some information that was essential for the presentation. Knowing that he could get the information from Foresight, Larry agreed.

While Foresight accommodated Larry's request, he cautioned Larry that the figures were tentative, and that they required checking and confirmation before they could be released to anyone of significance. Larry agreed to respect Foresight's wish that the data remain in the hands of the trainees.

When Joel returned to work, Larry gave him the data, but asked that he agree to use it only to form tentative conclusions, and that he share it with no one, including Reginald Sterling. Joel gave his word, and appeared extraordinarily grateful for Larry's help. Larry returned to his own work, and his own search for the answers to Bill's questions, dismissing the entire episode from his mind.

A few days later, Foresight called Larry and demanded that he come to his office. He was irate, believing that Larry had abused their budding friendship. Apparently the unconfirmed data had found their way first to the desk of the chief financial officer, and then to the desk of the chief executive officer. Buck, the chief financial officer, was attempting to use the inaccurate data as ammunition to prove that Foresight was unreliable and incapable of properly managing the financial planning model.

Larry had to work very hard to convince Foresight that he had been an unwitting pawn in one of Reginald's games. The bond of trust they had begun to establish was severely weakened, however. It was to take months before Foresight would be as open with Larry as he had been in the past.

Larry was so shellshocked by the experience of first being manipulated and, then, by Foresight's anger, that he resolved to refocus his attention on the routine projects that constituted the work life of the trainee and to continue to find the answers to Bill's questions in as inconspicuous a way as possible.

He began by working on the question of, "Which work group is thought to provide experience essential to grooming people for leadership positions?" Larry started asking questions about the background and career progression of the CEO, the COO, the CFO, and the vice-presidents. He was chagrined to find out that no one in the top spots had come from a marketing background. It appeared that his first professional love was not regarded as central to the ability to guide the company. It became clear that experience in the technical aspects of the business was regarded as important. The majority of the organization's leaders had either a systems or engineering background.

Larry gave a great deal of thought to all of the information he had collected in response to Bill's list of questions. The time had come to indicate his preference with regard to a permanent assignment.

The responses to the nine questions indicated that Larry should seek a position somewhere in the Simulations Department of the Software Division. If he did so, he would be reporting directly to Reginald Sterling. That troubled Larry immensely. Reginald had manipulated him into betraying a friend, and he could not forget that.

Nor did Larry believe that Reginald's power would last. A war was being waged within the corporation, and it was not clear who would prevail. It was entirely possible, in Larry's opinion, that Reginald would one day betray his own allies, and manipulate himself right out of a job.

If that happened, reasoned Larry, then development of the commercial financial planning product would occur in the Business Systems area of the Software Division. That area would then be the most important to the organization's ability to solve a key problem and respond to a significant opportunity. Thus Larry decided to join one of the three units in the Business Systems Department.

The Financial unit, the area which developed software in the financial area for the business community, clearly offered the most position power. The fight over the planning model, and the concept of using that as a prototype for a major corporate release, gave the unit a great deal of visibility. However, to join that unit was risky. If the decision was made to put the model under Reginald, then the financial area of the Business Department would either report directly to Reginald, or be reduced to a shadow of its present capacity.

The second unit in the Business Department was the management development unit. This unit was charged with the development and marketing of programs on leadership. The primary market was

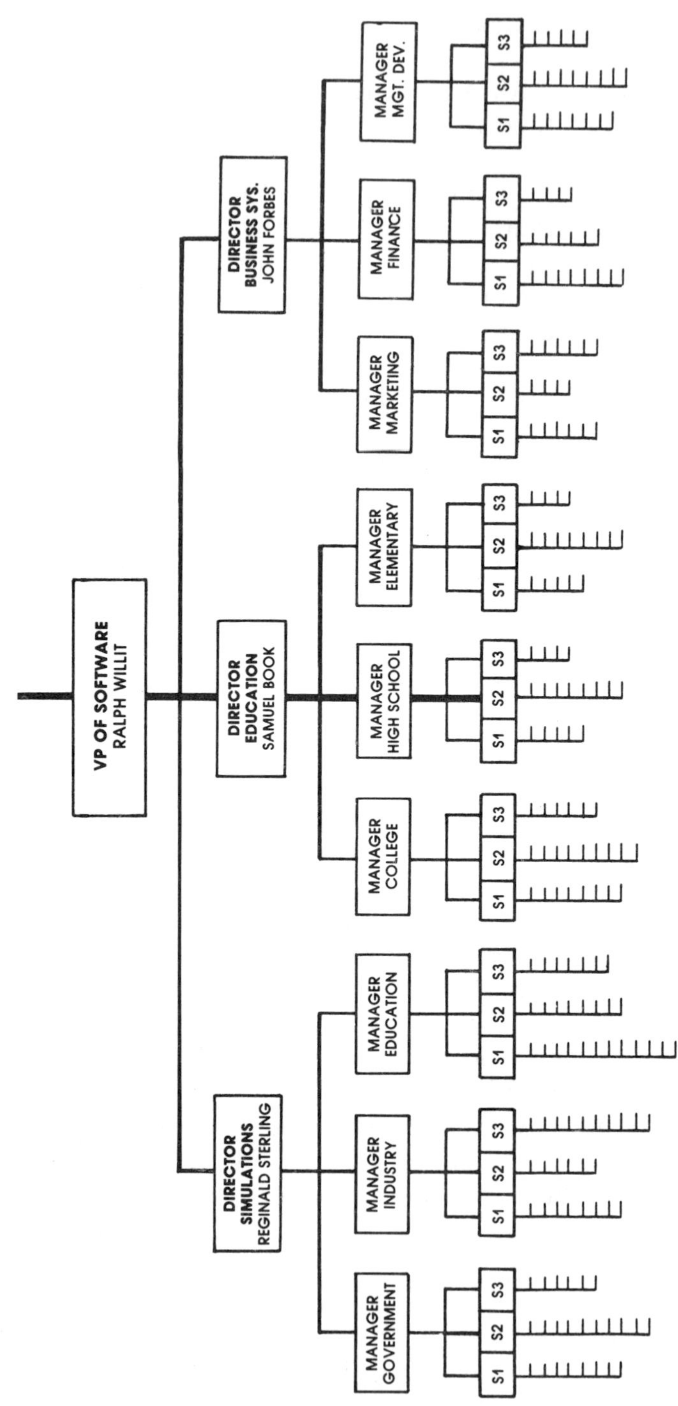

VP OF SOFTWARE
RALPH WILLIT
DIRECTOR BUSINESS SYS. JOHN FORBES
DIRECTOR EDUCATION SAMUEL BOOK
DIRECTOR SIMULATIONS REGINALD STERLING
MANAGER MGT. DEV.
MANAGER FINANCE
MANAGER MARKETING
MANAGER ELEMENTARY
MANAGER HIGH SCHOOL
MANAGER COLLEGE
MANAGER EDUCATION
MANAGER INDUSTRY
MANAGER GOVERNMENT
S1
S2
S3

training directors in corporations. Membership in that area would confer very little position power. Its performance was stable and acceptable, but it did not have the attention of top management.

The third area was marketing, responsible for programs on the subject of marketing for corporate clients. Products included such programs as "How to Develop a Brand Image," "Product Differentia-tion," "Understanding the Competition," and "Establishing a Cus-tomer and Service Orientation."

Small business owners were the primary buyers of these pro-grams. Sales growth had been dramatic in the last six months. Due to its contribution to the bottom line of the corporation, that area was receiving increasing attention from top management.

Not wanting to risk having an eventual reporting relationship to Reginald Sterling, and hoping to use his knowledge of marketing while enhancing his technical knowledge of the design process, Larry elected as his number one choice the position of supervisor of design for the marketing unit, in the Business Department of the Software Division. His second choice was supervisor of marketing in the management development unit. His last choice was supervisor of marketing in the finance area.

A few days later, Larry was elated to learn that his first choice had been granted. He called Bill, and invited him to a celebration lunch. He also asked Bill to begin thinking about strategies for increasing position power when the role itself afforded little. That was Larry's way of informing Bill in advance that he had allowed other factors than position power to influence his decision.

After listening to Larry's description of his search for the answers to the nine questions, and of the other events that had transpired during the search process, Bill began his evaluation.

"It sounds as though you made some progress with regard to attitudes toward M.B.A.s. By maintaining a relatively low profile and proving that you are capable of performing in a reliable, consistent way, you have probably begun to convince others that you, and others like you, are not necessarily overambitious, arrogant, and abrasive.

"And, in spite of the fact that it backfired, your attempt to build trust with your peers was commendable. In the long run, you may even be glad that you attempted to help Joel with the presentation.

"Using your friendship with the supervisor to get Foresight's attention was also a nice piece of work. In effect, what you were doing is using the power you had over one person to get to someone over whom you had no leverage. *We can make indirect use of* either *the formal or informal power of others.* In this case, you used *indirect informal power.* And it was very nicely done.

"You are also to be congratulated on the way you established a friendship with Foresight. It was very smart of you to suggest that you play racquetball, even if it did cost you a few nights of physical pain. And it was a good idea to agree to escort his lady friend's friend. Yes, nice work."

"That wasn't all strategy, Bill. Oh, it was in the beginning, but I quickly grew to like the guy. The friendship is important to me for its own sake, not just because George can help me make things happen in the company."

"That, Larry, is the only reason your strategy worked! People have a way of knowing when gestures of friendship are insincere. *Trust begins to build only when people are honest about their feelings and their intent. To do otherwise is to manipulate.*

"You did allow yourself to get manipulated, Larry. Had you been more alert, you would not have fallen into Reginald and Joel's trap."

"You are right on that score. How could I have been so stupid? So gullible?"

Larry's question was rhetorical. He did not really seek an answer. Bill chose to comment anyway.

"Larry, you have been exposed to a true organizational power play. Organizations can become highly political animals. Hidden agendas can abound, particularly during times of intense competition. A great deal of organizational energy goes into constructing and playing the kind of political game that you have witnessed."

"How do I avoid getting involved in that kind of situation again? I mean, if politics play such an important role in organizations, maybe I better learn to be as devious as possible."

"Larry, you were manipulated. Joel had a hidden agenda, one that he did not share with you. If we stop and think about requests that others make of us, we can often sense the existence of an ulterior motive. Sometimes it is only a gut feeling that something is amiss. Other times the nature of the relationship has been such that the request is unnatural.

"In either case, if you sense you are being manipulated, then the safest thing to do is to confront the would-be manipulator. All this requires is a straightforward statement that you feel uneasy and why. That forces the other to reveal what he is doing and why.

"In no event should you try to outmanipulate the manipulator. How do you feel about Joel at this point?"

"I doubt I'll ever trust him again."

"That, Larry, is the price you pay for being caught in a manipulation. It is too high a price to pay. But let us get back to the present. I am uneasy about your choice of assignment. It provides no more than a moderate degree of position power."

"You are right, but I think in the long run it will be worth it," Larry replied. "I'm clearly in the right division. Software is more powerful than the video side of the business. And I will be getting the technical experience that is regarded as the key to the ability to assume a leadership position in the corporation.

"While no funds are being invested in the function at present, I believe that a request for funds would be honored, given the unit's contribution to the bottom line. While the unit per se is not perceived as being directly relevant to the organization's key problems and opportunities, it is part of a department that is key, or could be key, depending on how the dispute between Reginald and Foresight evolves. With regard to information flow, well no one seems to have an edge on that."

"That, Larry, is the other mistake you made; assuming that information is less important than it is. Had you placed a greater value on the importance of information, you might even have refused to give those figures to Joel, and avoided damaging your friend's reputation.

"Larry, someone always has an edge in terms of information flow and control. *Information is power.* It can be used to reward others, or to coerce others. It can make careers, or break careers. And it can be a political football. Rarely does information flow simply as a function of the need to know.

"I'll give you an example. At one nuclear plant construction site, the Quality Assurance people are the last to know about anything. As a result, they are constantly 'discovering' that design changes have been made after the work is already in progress. It is too late to discuss the changes or to negotiate conflicting opinions. As a result, the Quality Assurance people feel they have no choice but to resort to issuing a stop work order; an order that stops operations at a cost to the taxpayer of one million dollars per day!

"But I don't want to belabor the point. Larry, the important thing to remember is to pay close attention to information flow and control.

Only if you do so will you be in a position to understand who is exercising what kind of power in the organization. That is as important as the kinds of power you are able to exercise.

"It seems that, having opted for a work group which can confer only a limited amount of position power, it is important for you to understand how to go about applying what I call the *Crown Prince Strategy* for enhancing your position power base. *Implementation of the Crown Prince Strategy requires either changing your role, or changing people's expectations about the roles you currently fill.*

"The same organizational characteristics we have already discussed are relevant. *To enhance the position power associated with a given role, it is important to change perceptions of the importance and relevance of the group as a whole to the organization's ability to solve problems.* This may require taking steps to encourage or enable the organization to redefine what it perceives as problems.

"An organization that suffers from a weak market position may define its 'problem' in a number of ways: as inadequate sales efforts; as poor pricing strategies; as a function of inferior product quality. To focus on sales efforts is to enhance the visibility and importance of the Personnel Department, which selects and trains the sales force. To focus on pricing is to potentially highlight the importance of strategic planners or financial personnel who study the pricing practices of the industry. To emphasize product quality is to shift attention to the engineering and manufacturing side of the house."

As usual, Larry was quick to respond. "All I've got to do, then, is to get the organization to redefine its problem as Reginald Sterling."

"I have a feeling, Larry, that the organization regards Reginald as one of its opportunities. *A second tactic supporting the Crown Prince Strategy is shifting the organization's definition of its opportunities.* This can be done by studying the market to find an attractive niche that is not being pursued by the competition.

"And, of course, *it is always a good idea to attempt to get in a position to control the resources that you need to reach your objectives.* That is what Reginald is attempting to do; to minimize his dependency on others by taking control of the financial planning model. Buck's interest in getting ahold of the model for internal use is essentially the same.

"Another tactic, one which we have already mentioned, is *attracting investment.* The group has got to conceive of a project that the organization would want to fund, and to then convince top management that the work group is uniquely qualified to realize a significant return on that investment.

"People like to see their investments pay off. It is hard for any of us to make the decision to cut our losses and declare an investment a poor one. When an organization has poured a lot of money into a group, it wants to see that group succeed. As a result, it will provide that group and its members with special advantages."

"Bill, it seems to me that only people who are already in a powerful position can use the Crown Prince Strategy. New members of the firm can't redefine the firm's opportunities or problems, for example. Nor will I be in a position to request investment dollars for some time to come."

"You'd be surprised, Larry. Why, even in the course of doing a market analysis, you have an opportunity to influence the organization's perception of what constitutes key problems and opportunities.

"Your analytical efforts and task force work have, I am sure, begun to change the organization's expectations regarding the role of 'trainee.' Perhaps in the future the company will regard trainees as a resource to be used, and not simply as people to be trained."

"I'm afraid I don't derive a lot of comfort from the thought that I'm going through all this pain for the sake of tomorrow's trainees. I must say I am glad those days are gone. Next week, I begin what I regard as my first real job. Am I ever ready!"

SOFTWARE SYSTEMS, INC.

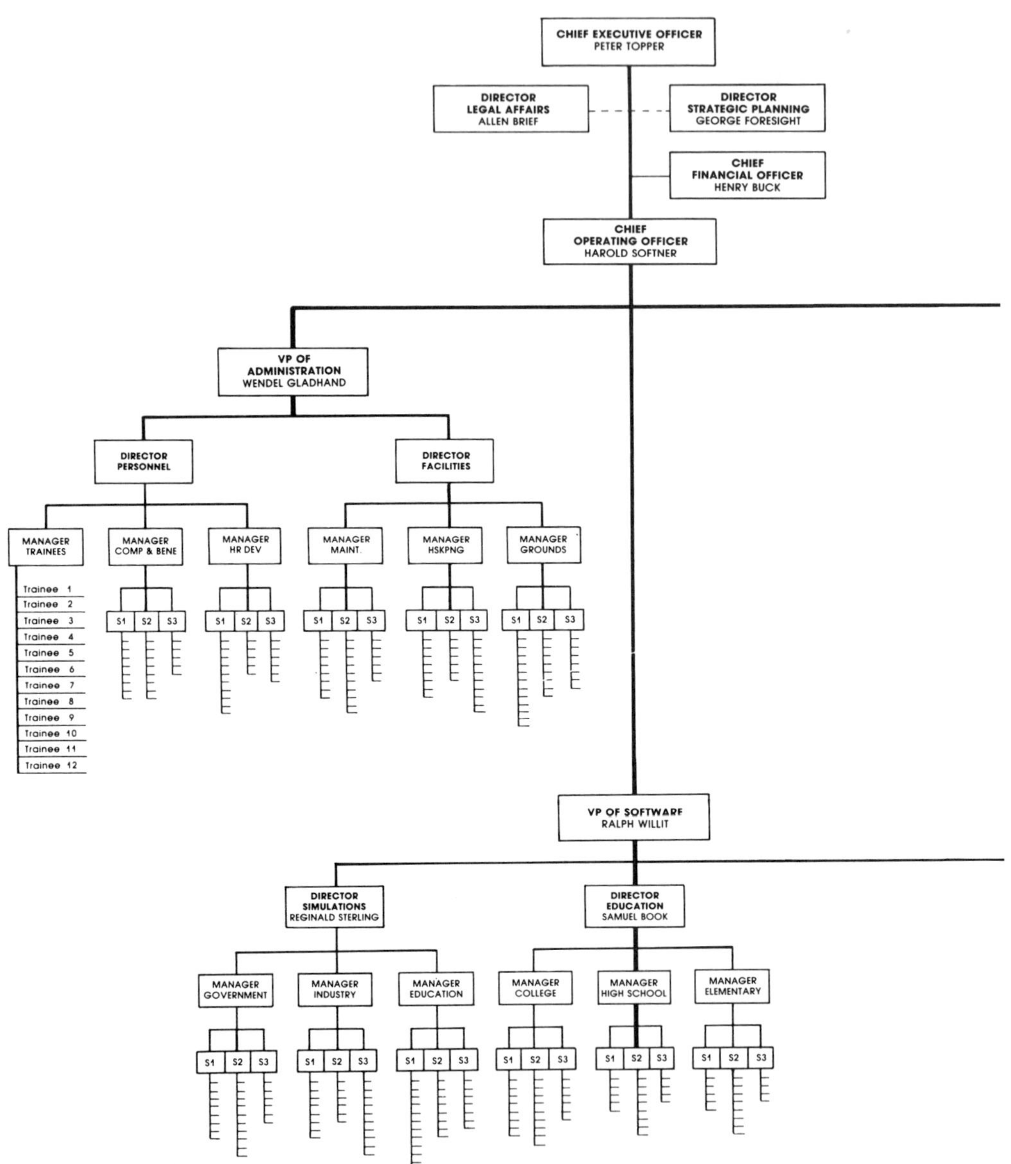

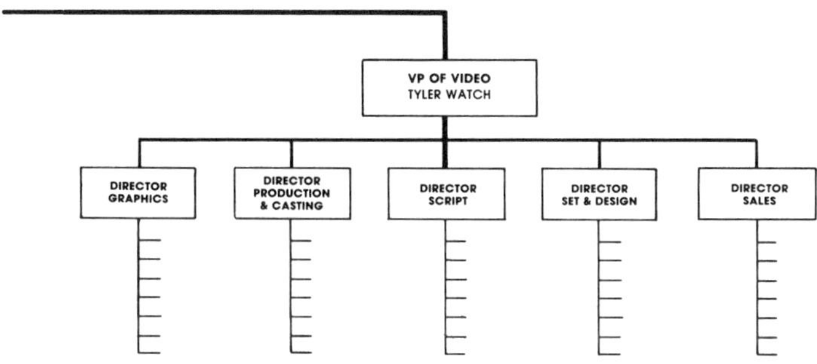

VP OF VIDEO
TYLER WATCH
DIRECTOR GRAPHICS
DIRECTOR PRODUCTION & CASTING
DIRECTOR SCRIPT
DIRECTOR SET & DESIGN
DIRECTOR SALES

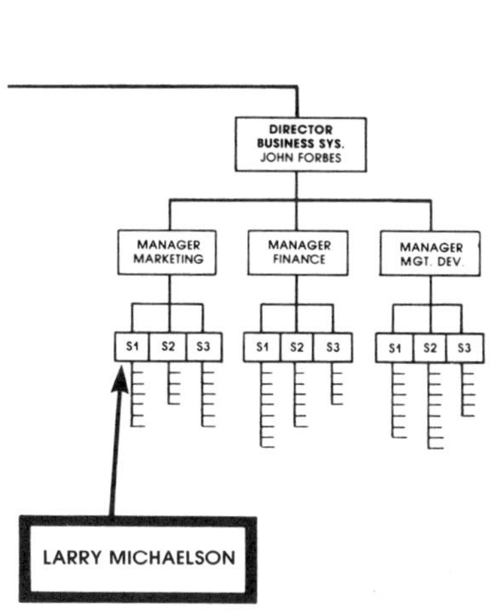

DIRECTOR BUSINESS SYS.
JOHN FORBES
MANAGER MARKETING
MANAGER FINANCE
MANAGER MGT. DEV.
S1 S2 S3
S1 S2 S3
S1 S2 S3
LARRY MICHAELSON

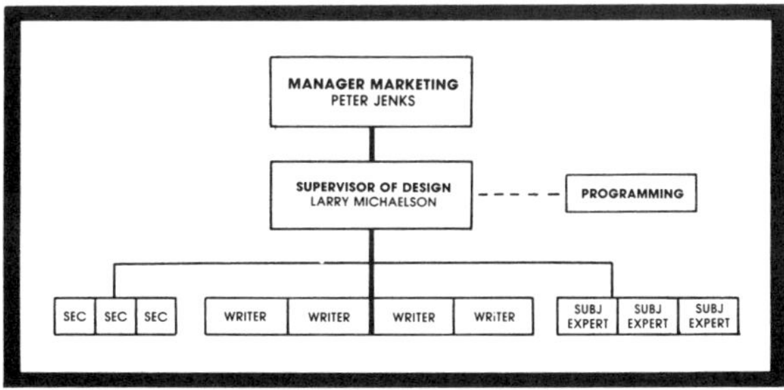

MANAGER MARKETING
PETER JENKS
SUPERVISOR OF DESIGN
LARRY MICHAELSON
PROGRAMMING
SEC SEC SEC
WRITER WRITER WRITER WRITER
SUBJ EXPERT
SUBJ EXPERT
SUBJ EXPERT

LARRY'S NOTES

- Trust is very difficult to build and very easy to destroy.
- Manipulation involves the pursuit of a hidden agenda.
- If something seems amiss, because of the history of the relationship, or due to a gut feeling, then stop and confront the other. Otherwise, you risk being manipulated.
- Manipulation destroys trust; it is risky.
- Do not try to outmanipulate manipulators; both will end up losing.
- Information is power.
- Never assume that just because people have a need to know that they will know.
- The indirect use of power (formal or informal) occurs when one person relies on the power of a second person to influence a third person.
- Tactics for using the crown prince strategy to build position power...
  Change either the role itself or the expectations
    —Change perception of key problems and opportunities
    —Attract investment
    —Find out; get in the information loop
    —Try to get control of the resources you need to reach
      your objectives and minimize dependency

4

Carrots and Sticks and a Supervisor's Dilemma

IT WAS WITH a combination of anxiety and excitement that Larry approached his first day on the job as a line supervisor. The opportunity presented Larry with the need to face many new situations. He had never been in a position of formal authority over others and now had to supervise four writers and three secretaries. Further, he was to share with the other design supervisors in the department the responsibility for overseeing the work of six programmers. Finally, it was up to him to make sure that the subject experts, hired on a consulting basis by the company, were performing their job of checking the content of the programs for technical accuracy.

Larry's anxieties were exacerbated by his lack of technical knowledge. As he walked the last block to the office, he wondered how he was supposed to distinguish good from poor performance when he knew so little about programming! Giving himself a psychological pat on the back, he reminded himself that he had always been a rapid learner and would be able to master the essentials in a short period of time. Why, he had even installed a computer at home so that he could learn programming at night.

He worried, too, about his ability to wield the clout that he would have to wield in order to introduce the necessary degree of rigor and discipline into the unit. During his tour of duty as a trainee, Larry had rotated through the unit and witnessed a degree of disorganization that troubled him even then. While the unit's sales had been strong, Larry doubted the trend would continue, given the inefficiencies in design procedures. Eventually operational problems would affect the ability of the sales personnel to deliver the product as promised.

"At least," thought Larry, as he entered the building, "I do understand marketing. I'll know when both the writers and the subject experts are performing. And, as for the secretaries, well, they are easy to supervise."

Only one or two of Larry's employees were at their desks when he arrived. On the one hand, he was disgruntled to find that their level of commitment was so low that they did not choose to come to work early. On the other hand, he was grateful for the opportunity to go to his office, and get comfortable with his new environment before having to make his first move as a supervisor.

Larry had planned to call all of his subordinates together, introduce himself, and motivate them with a little speech about how they all had an opportunity to work together to make the unit the best design area in the company. Hoping to break down any resistance and minimize the formality and the distance between himself and his staff members, Larry had planned on asking for their suggestions on ways in which the unit might run more smoothly. Of course, he already had a plan in mind, but he would save that for later. He knew from his management courses that people like to believe that they have been part of the decision-making process.

With some trepidation, he waited for the magic hour of 9:00 A.M. when, presumably, everyone would be at their desks. At 9:05, he looked through the glass that separated him from the rest of the unit, and saw that two of the three secretaries, and two of the four writers were at their desks. One of the secretaries was polishing her nails. The other was reading a book. The writers were engaged in a conversation which must have been amusing, for their talk was interspersed with a great deal of laughter.

At 9:15, the other two writers appeared. After saying hello to the others in the department and nodding at Larry, they both sat down at their desks and opened their newspapers. None of the programmers were to be seen; even the chairs of the two programmers who were housed in the unit were conspicuously vacant.

Stepping out of his office, Larry walked up to the desk of the nearest writer, introduced himself, chatted for a few minutes about current events, and then inquired about the missing programmers. The answer to his question disturbed him a great deal.

"Oh, all the programmers are in a meeting with the manager of the finance unit. I doubt they'll get out of there before noon. This happens all the time. Getting a programmer to work on a marketing project is like trying to break a CIA code. It's close to impossible."

One of the secretaries then told Larry that his new boss, Peter Jenks, was on the line. Jenks requested Larry's presence in his office. Their meeting was brief in duration but significant in terms of its impact on the approach that Larry was to take with his people.

Jenks stated very clearly that he expected Larry to triple the productivity of the unit almost overnight. That Jenks believed in hard-line supervisory practices was evident in his comments.

"The people in your unit have gotten away with murder for the past year. Why, even the manufacturing people complain that the designs are never done on schedule. And I am sick and tired of paying subject experts who do not turn in their critiques on time. I expect you to deal with the problem.

"So, to make sure it happens, I want you to submit productivity figures on a weekly basis for the next few months. It is not that I don't trust you. I have no reason to trust you, and no reason not to trust you. I do know that there is a great temptation to try to do things to befriend employees. Good supervisors rarely win popularity contests. Remember that. Why, few of my people like me. However, all of them respect me."

Jenks' message was clear. Larry was going to have to be even more heavy-handed with his people and with the subject experts than he had intended. Oh, he had planned to introduce tighter time control procedures, and to make it clear that he expected results. His boss had insisted that he document productivity increases. That would entail a significant shift from what people in the unit had learned to expect.

Within a week, Larry introduced time sheets, and a system of merits and demerits. Taking a lunch break longer than forty-five minutes would earn the culprit two demerits for every fifteen minutes of tardiness. Failure to hand in time sheets also resulted in demerits.

Merit points were earned by submitting a design, a program, or text ahead of schedule. The suggestion of a procedure to make the work of the unit more efficient also earned the suggestion donor merit points.

Merits and demerits affected not only the performance review, but also the amount of bonus paid at year end. (It was company policy for the supervisors to suggest how bonus dollars would be distributed.) They also impacted on less formal rewards, such as the opportunity to take time off for personal reasons, or the right to take a computer home on weekends.

Within two weeks, Larry met with all of the subject experts and informed them that times had changed, and that he would not tolerate missed deadlines. To reinforce his point, he reminded them that he had a great deal to say about which consulting contracts were renewed and which were canceled.

It was more difficult for Larry to control the behavior of his programmers. They reported to three supervisors. Larry's promises of rewards held only mild interest, and his threats of punishment did not seem to frighten them. They submitted willingly to his insistence on time sheets, knowing full well that the majority of their attention would be devoted to other areas within the department.

Larry's experiences as a trainee had taught him the difference between compliance and commitment, and he knew that his people complied with, rather than believed in, his new procedures. Hoping to create an environment of support, he explained that the new procedures were not his idea, but a response to a mandate from higher-up. That did not seem to help.

Behavior did begin to change, however. Employees began to arrive on time in the morning. The two-hour lunch became the exception, rather than the norm. The time sheets indicated that a lot more activity was occurring within the unit. Larry's boss seemed content.

However, Larry knew better. He realized that productivity had not improved. The increase in activity disguised the decline in results. Larry pondered the situation and decided that the problem lay with the programmers.

Appreciating that mandates and directives were not going to work, Larry decided that the only thing he could do was to convince the programmers that working in the marketing area represented not only an opportunity for growth, but a significant professional challenge.

In order to do so, Larry had to think of a challenging product idea, and learn to speak the programmers' language. He devoted nights and weekends to his self-appointed task. He read all of the computer journals and used every available opportunity to talk to people in the field.

His relationship with the programmers improved markedly.

They seemed to appreciate the interest that he took in their field, and to respect the fact that he understood and could even use the jargon of their trade. When Larry suggested that they develop a program that relied on artificial intelligence, their interest was obvious.

"That's fantastic, Larry. We were wondering when one of you fellows would catch on. That's where the action is. People want the computer to appear to be human, superhuman. They want the machine to understand the meanings that they attach to words and concepts. Is a "heel" a part of the foot, or an individual of questionable integrity? The user wants the machine to know the answer. That's artificial intelligence, and what a challenge it represents! Talk about user-sensitive. Why, with the use of artificial intelligence, we can make a program that is user-proof! It takes money, Larry. I mean you don't develop that kind of program overnight."

Larry had created a potential monster. He had gotten his programmers excited about something that he barely understood. Yet gaining their commitment required that he seek funds for the project. There were days when Larry wished he had taken a nice, safe staff job in Personnel. There were other days when Larry viewed the challenge with excitement and enthusiasm.

He asked his programmers to help him refine the idea, and they willingly complied. In the process, they got more involved with marketing issues. They learned to respect Larry's expertise, as he learned to respect theirs.

Unfortunately, his newfound camaraderie with the programmers did not extend throughout the unit. The quality of the material produced by the writers worsened. The secretaries seemed to take longer and longer to produce error-free documents. In spite of his stated open-door policy, no one approached Larry. On the contrary, they seemed to try to avoid him.

Larry was puzzled. After all, he was trying to turn the unit around. His efforts were designed to benefit everyone. But no one outside of the programming group seemed to understand this. He felt lonely and misunderstood much of the time.

Then something occurred which made him furious. One of his writers called in sick. Needing to check on the status of a project, Larry went through her papers. To his dismay, he discovered that the bulk of the material on her desk had nothing to do with company business. Scanning the sheets, he discovered that the writer had been working on a novel.

Larry's anger was not triggered by the manuscript per se, but by the obvious intent to deceive. The manuscript pages had been carefully concealed under work-related copy.

Larry took the writer's manuscript, planning to confront her with it whenever she chose to return to work. He did not have to wait long. She returned the next day.

Observing her as she approached her desk, Larry noticed with pleasure that she was disconcerted when she discovered that the piles of paper on her desk had been moved. As she searched for her manuscript, her panic was visible. Larry watched for a few moments, and then went out and asked the anxious writer to come into his office.

Holding up the manuscript, he said, "I suppose you are looking for this. You know, Sheila, whatever is written on company time is company property. Suppose we publish some of the more inflammatory anecdotes in the company newsletter. Or maybe we can come out with the first sexual how-to software. Or perhaps the appropriate home for the work is the trashcan."

With that, Larry dropped the manuscript into his wastebasket. Sheila cringed, and pleaded with him to return the manuscript to her. Satisfied that in the future she would devote business hours to business, Larry softened a little.

"I never had any intention of destroying or of keeping your manuscript. Actually, it is rather good. I mean, the pages that I happened to see while looking for your copy are, well, they command attention."

Larry then handed the unnerved woman her manuscript. As she turned to leave, he added, "Sheila, I did not see any reference to the novel on the time sheets you have been submitting. I expect them to be accurate in the future."

Defensive, Sheila tried to remind Larry that her performance was good, and that neither he nor the prior supervisor had ever found fault with her work.

"And, as regards the time sheets, they do not reflect the number of nights and weekends that I devote to this organization. I have never and will never cheat this or any other organization, and I resent your implying that I have done so."

An assertive individual by nature, Sheila gave full vent to a lot of pent-up frustration. She accused Larry of treating his employees like children.

"Merits and demerits, really. The last time I had to tolerate this kind of system was when I was in the fourth grade."

Then, suddenly remembering her place relative to Larry's, she blushed and apologized. Larry, to his credit, attempted to allay her anxieties.

"Sheila, I appreciate your willingness to speak so honestly. I wish more people in the unit would do so. I do not enjoy playing the role of military commander. Perhaps I have gone too far, and been overzealous in my attempt to control productivity rates around here. I will think about what you have said. I would also ask that you think about what I have said. While I cannot fault your performance, I cannot sanction your using office time to work on your book. That would establish a precedent. The other writers are not as talented as you, and seem to require that I introduce some discipline into their work habits."

Sheila left, feeling that it was unfair for Larry to impose restrictions on her simply because the other writers couldn't meet performance standards. Larry, however, felt that Sheila and he had reached an understanding. He gave no further thought to her comment about being treated like a child.

He did, however, decide that it would be a good idea to introduce more motivators into his system. When another of the writers asked for permission to leave early for several weeks in order to attend a class, Larry agreed. When one of the secretaries indicated that she was dissatisfied with the word processing program she was using, he authorized her to select and purchase another program that was more to her liking. As a result, her performance improved dramatically.

Larry found it more difficult to manage the subject experts. They seemed unimpressed by his power to block the renewal of their consulting contracts. Accustomed to the laissez-faire style of the former supervisor of design, they continued to ignore deadlines.

One of the experts, in particular, was the source of great frustration for Larry. A nitpicker by nature, the expert inevitably found a number of things to criticize in all of the material sent to him. His tendency to regard all errors or flaws as of equal significance drove the writers crazy. When Larry attempted to point out the impact of his behavior, the expert simply shrugged his shoulders and said, "You pay me to find flaws, and I find them. It is not my fault that your people create substandard products."

Substandard products, indeed. Larry prided himself on being an expert in marketing theory and technique and knew that their product designs were the best on the market. He would have preferred to do away with the subject experts entirely, utilizing instead his own knowledge base to ensure the quality and accuracy of the material.

Larry made this suggestion to his boss, only to be told that the use of subject experts was company policy, and was not subject to question. "Your job is to manage the subject experts, not to challenge the necessity of their involvement."

Believing that he lacked the authority or the power required to manage the efforts of the subject experts, Larry began to tolerate their existence, no longer attempting to influence their behavior. The experts continued to annoy the writers. Frustrated, the writers' performance began to slip. In response, Larry continued to enforce productivity standards through an ever proliferating system of merits and demerits, rewards and punishments.

Meanwhile, Larry began to seek funding to support the artificial intelligence project. The first hurdle was Jenks, the manager of marketing programs. Initially, Jenks was not at all interested in pursuing the idea.

Cutting short the conversation, he had said, "You have a job to do, and that job does not include distracting yourself with fancy new programming notions that have nothing to do with the business at hand. Leave technological experimentation to the Research and Development Department."

Jenks did not seem to understand, or want to understand, that Larry was not proposing an entirely new product. The application of artificial intelligence would improve all of their products. In the past, the company had often invested funds in order to enhance product quality.

But Larry could not get Jenks to listen. Finally, his frustration level got so high that Larry decided to bypass Jenks and go directly to the director of the Business Systems Department. Larry was prepared to embarrass Jenks, if need be, in order to get a hearing for his idea. Out of courtesy, Larry informed Jenks of his intention.

Apparently Jenks was sufficiently impressed by Larry's threat to reconsider. He told Larry that he would give him one hour in which to present his ideas. Larry agreed to keep the issue within the unit, if Jenks would also agree to have one of the top programmers present at the meeting. Jenks complied with Larry's request.

Larry and the programmer worked hard on their presentation, preparing a tight and logical argument supporting the need to incorporate artificial intelligence into their product line. In order to do so, while still meeting client deadlines, they estimated they would need a budget increase of $100,000 to cover the cost of one additional programmer and a systems consultant.

Jenks was not authorized to grant a budget increase of that size. Approval had to come from the vice-president of the Software Division. Before such approval could be sought, John Forbes, the director of the Business Systems Department, had to endorse the idea.

At the conclusion of the meeting, Jenks agreed to present the idea to Forbes. In response to Larry's suggestion that he be present at the meeting, Jenks stated that he was perfectly capable of bringing the idea to the next level, and did not require Larry's assistance.

Larry had an uneasy feeling that Jenks would misrepresent the concept to the director. He was convinced that Jenks was not at all committed to the idea, and had agreed to the presentation only to discourage Larry from going directly to Forbes.

Larry's fears were confirmed when Jenks called him a week or so later to inform him that Forbes had reacted negatively to the suggestion, and had refused to seek the additional budget authorization.

"It's a closed issue, Larry. I'm sorry. I did all that I could do. You know I'm behind you, don't you? Let's save it until next year. Maybe the system will be more responsive to your idea then."

It was far from a closed issue for Larry. He had begun the project in order to find something to attract and motivate the programming staff. The more involved he got, the more convinced he became that the technique would give the organization's products a true competitive edge.

Believing that the benefits of introducing artificial intelligence went well beyond the marketing unit, Larry began talking about the idea with his peers. He knew that, in doing so, he was potentially giving away the vehicle for attracting programming talent. He put aside his fears by reasoning that what was good for the organization had to be good for him as well.

The other design supervisors shared Larry's enthusiasm over the idea, agreeing that their products would also be markedly enhanced. They, in turn, shared the notion with their managers. The manager of the management development unit was particularly excited about the concept. He suggested that the three units seek the budget increase in tandem, thereby diminishing the power of Jenks to stop the process. Further, he promised to do what he could to convince Jenks that he should take a more supportive stance than he had in the past.

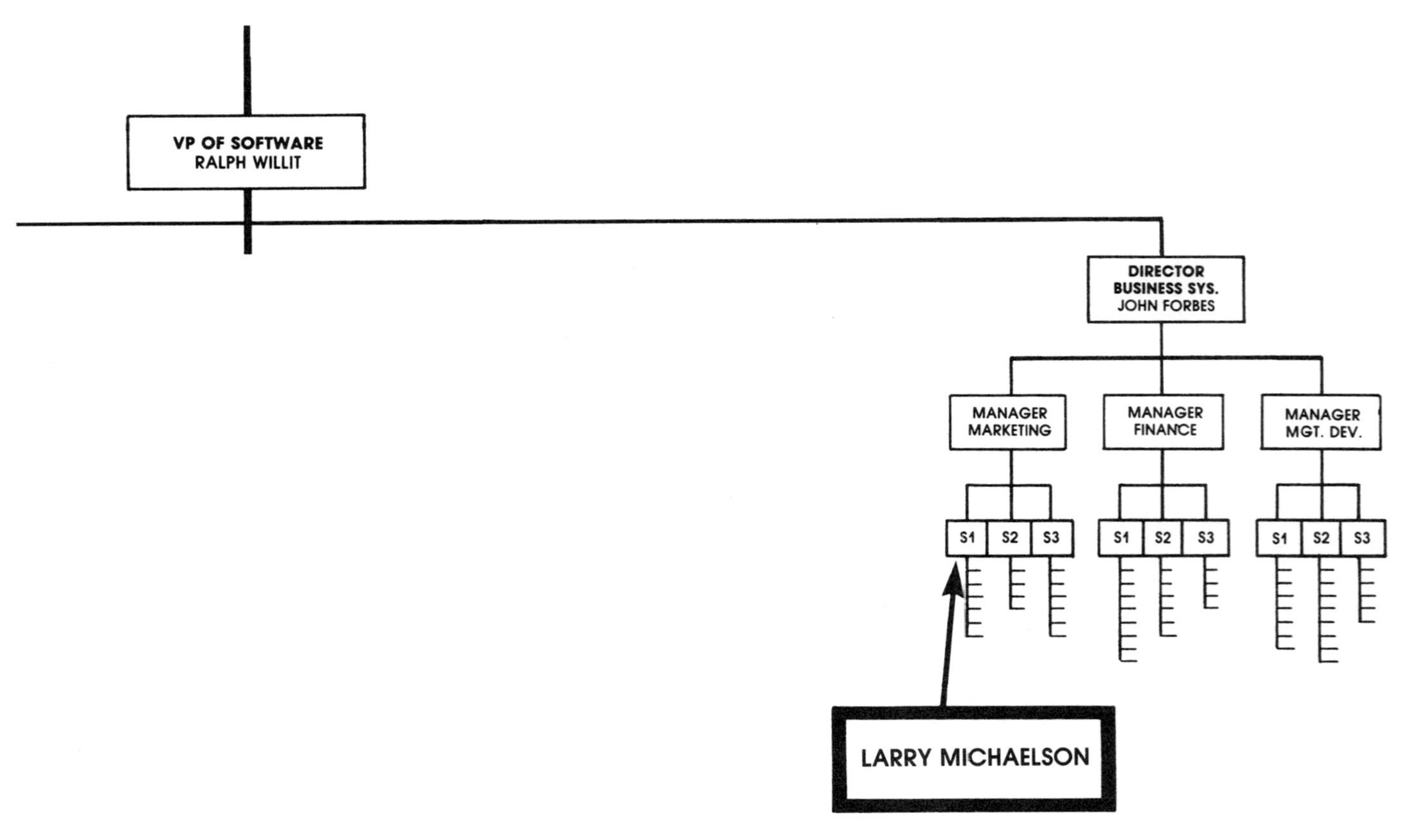

VP OF SOFTWARE
RALPH WILLIT
DIRECTOR
BUSINESS SYS.
JOHN FORBES
MANAGER
MARKETING
MANAGER
FINANCE
MANAGER
MGT. DEV.
S1
S2
S3
S1
S2
S3
S1
S2
S3
LARRY MICHAELSON

He was apparently successful in his efforts, for within a few weeks, Larry was asked to deliver the full presentation personally to the director of the Business Systems Department.

As he prepared to do so, Larry realized that he needed to know what Jenks had already said and not said about the concept. He did not want to be redundant; nor did he believe that Jenks had done justice to the concept during his conversation with Forbes. Further, Larry appreciated that he was in a position to potentially embarrass his boss. While, in some ways, he would have enjoyed doing so, he did not believe that creating an adversarial relationship was in anyone's best interest. As it was, Jenks had been angered by Larry's refusal to drop the issue. Their working relationship was far from comfortable.

Perceiving that Larry could embarrass him, Jenks arranged an invitation to the presentation. Presumably, if worse came to worse, he could pull rank and stop Larry from saying things that would put him in a poor light. With something akin to a look of vengeance on his face, Jenks informed Larry the day before the presentation that he would be attending the meeting.

Jenks' power play came as no surprise to Larry. Ready with a strategy, Larry asked Jenks to describe to him the content of Jenks' earlier meeting with the director.

"It is my hope that, as a result of the meeting, Forbes will have a greater degree of respect both for our function and for us, as individuals. I know that you are annoyed with me for continuing to discuss the concept after you told me to drop it. I understand also that I have put you in an awkward position with your peers. I regret that I had to do that. At this point, I would like to design the presentation in such a way that your position is enhanced, as well as my own."

Jenks seemed to be taken off-guard by Larry's straightforward approach. Few people dared to speak to him in that way. The barriers he erected between himself and others generally discouraged such honest communication.

After a few moments of dreadful silence, Jenks said, "OK, Larry. I appreciate your honesty, and I understand your position. I suggest we begin anew, both with regard to the project and our working relationship. I confess that during my discussions with Forbes, I referred to your project as a 'hair-brained scheme.' If we are to save face, then it will be necessary for you to state that your idea was in its infancy when you presented it to me. I would suggest you then go on to say that refinements since that time have made the idea far more feasible."

Their newly formed alliance, coupled with Larry's confidence and the tightness of his argument, resulted in a highly successful presentation. After complimenting Larry on the work he had done and on the professionalism of the presentation, Forbes promised to give the matter serious thought and to get back to Larry within the week.

Nor was Jenks offended or threatened by the director's intent to communicate his reaction directly to Larry. On the contrary, Jenks was pleased when Forbes said, "And congratulations to you, Jenks, for doing such a fine job of developing your people. That, after all, is a sign of fine management."

Within a few days, Forbes called Larry to inform him that he had gained authorization for the artificial intelligence project. Further, the project was to fall under Larry's supervision. Finally, Larry was to feel free to access *any* programmers in the organization, *including* Reginald Sterling's people.

Feeling victorious, Larry and Jenks treated themselves to a lavish lunch, celebrating what both perceived to be a shared success. Larry devoted the rest of the afternoon to visiting his peers in the other functions. By the end of the day, the entire Business Systems Department was enjoying the promise of great things to come.

The euphoria lasted several days. It was broken only when the manager of the finance unit suffered a mild heart attack and, as a result, decided to leave Software Systems, Inc. and to take a less stressful job.

The manager's departure caused Larry to feel both regret and anticipation. He had learned to value the manager as a friend and ally. On the other hand, he knew that the sudden vacancy would create a promotional opportunity. He did not believe, however, that he would be viewed as a serious candidate, having so recently left the ranks of trainee.

In slightly less than two years, Larry had changed from an overeager trainee into a realistic student of corporate politics and timing. For once, he underestimated his chances. Forbes had been sufficiently impressed with Larry to decide to give him a chance to lead the financial systems unit.

The promotion was contingent, however, on Larry's ability to prove that he could correct what were perceived to be significant flaws in his managerial style. Forbes told Larry that he would be regarded as the "acting manager" until such time as he had demonstrated that he could learn to manage his writers and subject experts. He had three months in which to prove himself. Forbes then went on to state the reasons for his reservations about promoting Larry.

"Larry, one of your subject experts has come to me several times with complaints about you. It seems you do not treat him with sufficient respect, or so he feels. Why, he even said that you threatened not to vote for renewal of his contract if he refused to abide by your rules. Larry, it is not good managerial practice to bully our subject experts, or anyone for that matter. You are a manager, not a military commander."

Larry took advantage of a pause to interject that he knew of whom the director spoke, and that there were extenuating circumstances. "That particular subject expert is a relentless nitpicker, Mr. Forbes. He creates a great deal of unnecessary aggravation for my writers. I feel my job is to protect them from such abuse so that they can be productive."

Larry's defense fell on deaf ears. Forbes was not finished, and went on to say that Sheila, Larry's writer, had requested a transfer out of Larry's area.

In response to the surprised look on Larry's face, Forbes said, "Sheila complained to Gladhand, the vice-president of administration, that you treat your people like children. She claims that she cannot function as a professional under your supervision. Your failure to perceive the extent of her frustration disturbs me. Your people skills need sharpening, Larry."

When Larry left Forbes' office, he was experiencing a strange mix of excitement and dread. Given the war between Reginald and Buck, the new position was going to require far more than a shift in management style. Larry knew that he was quickly going to have to become very adept at managing power, and at recognizing corporate power plays.

Believing that there had never been a more opportune time for a power reassessment and a talk about strategy, Larry called Bill, arranging to get together for dinner a few days later.

After listening to Larry recite the events of the past several months, Bill began his evaluation.

"You have certainly been busy, Larry! I scarcely know where to begin. I guess the most significant aspect of your performance is the use you have made of the *formal power* that the organization granted when they made you supervisor of design.

"As you may recall from our earlier discussions, when an organization promotes someone, the promotion generally is accompanied by an increase in formal power. *Formal power is conferred upon a person, and is made up of a combination of position power, reward power, and coercive power.*

"To use *position power* is to say to someone, 'Do it because I have the right to tell you to do so.' To rely on *reward power* is to say, 'Do it if you want me to give you what you want.' Reliance on *coercive power* projects the message, 'Do it because I will punish you or take away something that you value if you don't do as I say.'

 "The problem is not that you used your new power bases, but that you used them excessively with some of your people. From what you have said, it sounds as though you expected the system of merits and demerits to run the department for you.

"With regard to your writers, and secretaries, and even with regard to your subject experts, you ignored two key rules of power politics: *First, avoid the consistent use of the stick unless you can be around all the time to make sure others are doing what you have directed them to do. Second, be careful of buying work with the promise of a carrot. You may run out of carrots or they may grow stale.*

 "Chances are that Sheila, your writer, was reacting to your reliance on the carrot and the stick when she decided to devote some of her work day to the writing of her novel. I imagine she felt a lot more commitment to that than to the assignments you gave her. The overstated threat of destroying her manuscript, which was certainly coercive in nature, only inspired her to seek a transfer out of the unit.

 "Nor did use of threats and coercion work with the subject expert. You did not diminish his tendency to nitpick or to miss deadlines by reminding him that you had the formal power to veto renewal of his contract.

"You even used coercive power with Jenks in threatening to bypass and go directly to Forbes. He capitulated, allowing you to make the presentation to him and then stating that he would take the idea to Forbes. But he was not committed to the idea and, thus, misrepresented it when he spoke with the director. Had you generated his commitment, chances are you could have saved yourself a lot of time and trouble.

"While coercive power has the advantage of generating rapid compliance under some circumstances, the problems it creates generally outweigh the advantages. *Use of coercion, as you have seen, generates resentment and the desire to withdraw from an essentially painful situation.*

"On top of that, *use of the stick eventually loses even its ability to provoke action through fear.* People get tired of being pushed around, and will eventually elect to take the punishment and suffer through the deprivation rather than continue to be subjected to pain or its threat.

"Nor is reliance on reward power an effective way to generate commitment. *When you try to motivate people to perform through reliance on the carrot, what you get is the desire to get the carrot; not the desire to do the work. Furthermore, carrots or rewards eventually lose their power to motivate performance.* People begin to regard rewards as rights. Try giving people a bonus two years in a row. Then try withholding it the third year. People will rebel; they will cry that they have been deprived of a fundamental right."

Larry had his own example to offer. "I've seen that happen in my unit. I let one of my employees leave early every day for six weeks in order to attend a class. Then when I told the employee that the practice had to stop, you'd think I had slapped him in the face. He didn't remember the favor; only the removal of the favor."

"Gratitude for rewards is short-lived. Rewards do not motivate, except perhaps in the short term. As Tolstoy said, 'The more [that] is given, the less the people will work for themselves, and the less they work, the more their poverty will increase.'

"Far more effective in terms of motivational potential are the informal types of power; the types of power that cannot be conferred, and must be earned by an individual. The powers of friendship and expertise are very effective, as you learned.

"When you let Jenks know that you cared enough about him as a person to want to help him save face, you built the power of friendship and shared goals. That was a superb piece of work.

"You also did an excellent job of building up the power of friendship and shared goals with the programmers. Perhaps it is a good thing that your formal power over them was diluted due to multiple reporting relationships. You were forced to work to gain both their respect and their friendship. All the hours you spent studying computer journals really paid off. I'm sure that simply by learning to use their jargon, to speak their language, you gained a great deal of informal power points.

"You did a fine job of building *expert power,* or the power of what you know, when you delivered a logical, convincing presentation to Forbes. I suspect that it was that expert power base that actually won you the promotion.

"And, it appears that you used *presence power* well during your presentation to Forbes. Your manner of dress, your tone of voice, the overall image you projected all helped to get his attention, and keep his attention.

"That, in effect, is the advantage of using presence power. It gets attention. *The projection of confidence makes people assume you are competent.* The downside is that the use of presence power sets up expectations which must then be met. If your image is that of expert, you better be able to deliver!

PRESENCE POWER OPENS DOORS AND ESTABLISHES EXPECTATIONS

"I'd just like to say, sir, that I always make a bad first impression."

Drawing by Stan Hunt; © 1983
The New Yorker Magazine, Inc.

 "Finally, Larry, you are to be congratulated on your superb use of the *networking strategy* to bring your concept to the attention of the vice-president. *To network is to get yourself in a position to use the power of one person to influence a third person. In effect, to network is to build indirect power.*

 "You really set a dynamic chain in motion when you used the power of friendship with your peers to get them to speak of the artificial intelligence project to their bosses. Their bosses, in turn, convinced your boss. That is a superb example of the use of indirect power.

"In short, the mistake you made was to rely too heavily on the formal power to reward and to coerce. At the same time, you did succeed in building and using the informal power of friendship and expertise, at least with regard to the programmers, and eventually Jenks.

"*It is very difficult to build up formal and informal types of leverage simultaneously. Coercive power clearly gets in the way of building closeness between people. The existence of the power to reward also makes it more difficult to build and maintain trust.* It's a strange thing, but we tend to defend ourselves against people who are in a position to give or withhold what we want and need. The psychologists call it counterdependency."

"Funny you should say that," Larry replied. "That is one of the things worrying me about my new position. A lot of the guys in the finance unit went through the training program with me. They're my friends, or at least they used to be. If they go and start feeling counterdependent, as you put it, I'll lose their friendship. I don't want to see that happen."

"Well, as Disraeli said, 'The depository of power is always unpopular.' Disraeli was referring to formal power. There is not much you can do about the power of your new title, but you can make an effort to avoid the unnecessary use of carrots and sticks in your new position," said Bill.

"With my subordinates, perhaps, but not with Reginald Sterling and his crown prince, Joel. I'll need all the sticks I can gather. I had hoped to stay out of the fray over the financial planning model. Now I will have no choice but to join in and try to get the commercial rendition of the model assigned to our area. If Reginald succeeds in taking the model, then my new title won't mean anything; the unit will become insignificant."

While Bill did not agree with Larry's conclusion that the only way to prevail over Reginald was to use formal power, he did agree to explore with Larry the *Candy Store Strategy* for acquiring reward power, and the *Arsenal Strategy* for acquiring coercive power.

"In order to apply the Candy Store Strategy, you will need to find out what Reginald or the people in his area need or value. Then try to corner the market on those things. It is likely that information could constitute a reward. Or perhaps they will be in need of your artificial intelligence programs. Think of the strategy as stocking the candy store with goodies that Reginald can't resist.

"If you anticipate a battle, then you might also use the Arsenal Strategy. Simply stated, applying the Arsenal Strategy requires that you find out what would threaten Reginald, and then get in a position to apply those threats. Again, the weapon may be information. Or it may be your ability to deprive him of some of his best people due to the opportunities you are able to provide for career growth in your area. Think about it.

"As you do so, remember the concept of using the power of others. Develop connections with people who are in a position to influence Reginald. That may make it unnecessary for you to resort to the use of carrots and sticks."

"Let's hope so. You have convinced me that the use of formal power, while efficient, certainly has its drawbacks. On the other hand, there is a popular quote that may apply: 'Nice guys never win.' It's a complicated business, this business of power and organizations."

Bill left Larry at the restaurant. Larry sat there for awhile alone, attempting to sort through all of the thoughts, strategies, insights, and fears that raced through his mind. On more than one occasion, he scanned the notes he had taken, hoping to find within them a clear path through what he now perceived to be an exciting though occasionally treacherous corporate jungle.

LARRY'S NOTES

Formal Power

POSITION POWER: Do as I say because I have the right to tell you what to do.

> REWARD POWER: Do as I say if you want me to give you the things you want or value.
>
> COERCIVE POWER: Do as I say if you want to avoid injury.
>
> Formal power is efficient, but it does not build commitment.

Reward Power

> ADVANTAGES: rapid action
>
> DISADVANTAGES: desire on the part of the other to do the minimum required in order to get the reward; diminishing ability to influence as the reward is assumed to be a right; feelings of counterdependency get in the way of friendship

Coercive Power

> ADVANTAGES: rapid action; absolute compliance
> DISADVANTAGES: resentment, fear, desire to withdraw from the situation; need for constant surveillance

Avoid the consistent use of the stick unless you can be around all the time to make sure others are doing what you have directed them to do.

Be careful of buying work with the promise of a carrot—you may run out of carrots or they may grow stale.

When we have formal power over someone, it gets more difficult to build informal sources of leverage, particularly the power of friendship.

The power of friendship is built by establishing mutual goals and shared frames of reference (e.g., talking the same language as the programmers).

The candy store strategy for building reward power is this: Corner the market on things that the other values.

The arsenal strategy for building coercive power... gather weapons... find out what would hurt and get in a position to deliver that hurt... get in a position to deprive others of something they value.

Presence Power

> ADVANTAGES: Gets attention; makes people assume you are competent; makes people listen.
>
> DISADVANTAGES: You set up expectations that you better be able to meet!

Remember to keep working on the network, or getting in a position to use indirect power, or the power of others to make things happen.

SOFTWARE SYSTEMS, INC.

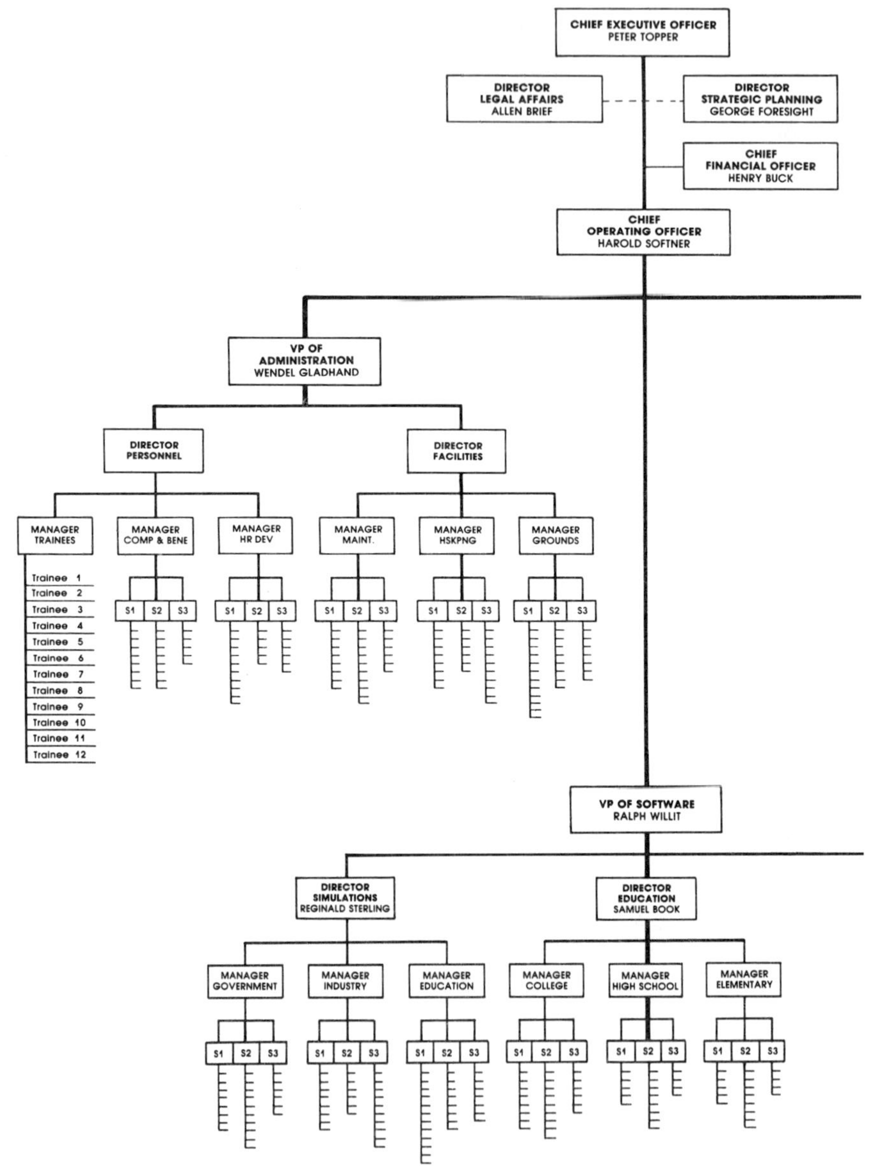

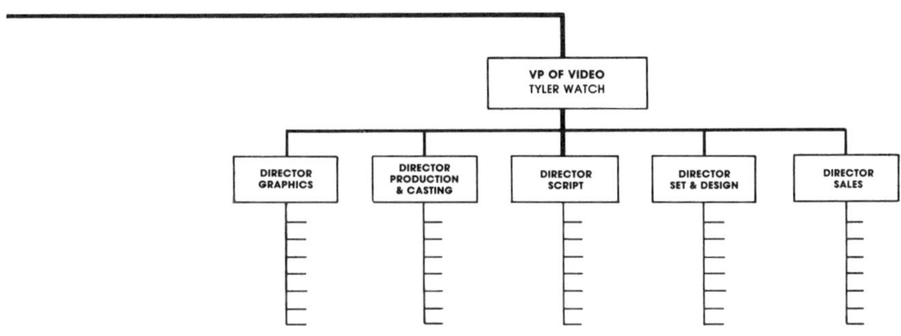

VP OF VIDEO
TYLER WATCH
DIRECTOR
GRAPHICS
DIRECTOR
PRODUCTION
& CASTING
DIRECTOR
SCRIPT
DIRECTOR
SET & DESIGN
DIRECTOR
SALES

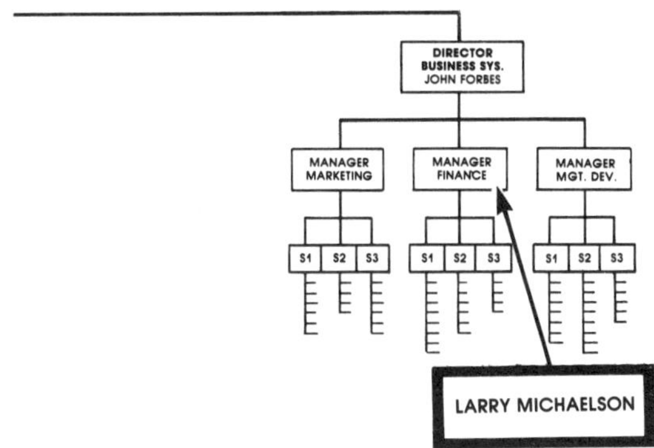

DIRECTOR
BUSINESS SYS.
JOHN FORBES
MANAGER
MARKETING
MANAGER
FINANCE
MANAGER
MGT. DEV.
S1 S2 S3
S1 S2 S3
S1 S2 S3
LARRY MICHAELSON

5

The Manager Misjudges the Power of Friendship and Expertise

LARRY FELT AS AWKWARD his first day on the job as manager as he had the day he assumed his first line responsibility in the organization. That his office was larger and more finely appointed only made him more uneasy. He regretted that the organization had opted for glass office walls, certain that his lack of composure was obvious to all of his subordinates. Subordinates—those were the same people who only days before had been his friends. Now his status was visibly different from theirs. He felt alone, and uneasy.

Larry's uneasiness stemmed from more than the newness of his position. His gut was telling him that he had once again gotten involved in a corporate power play; that he was being the unwitting victim of a carefully concealed manipulation. Yet his rational mind could find no persecutor, no manipulator. Attempting to ignore the gnawing feeling that something was amiss, Larry called his first staff meeting.

Giving what he hoped would be perceived as a special nod to his three closest friends in the unit, Larry opened the meeting.

"Good morning. I expect that it seems strange to you to have me standing here before you. I know that it seems odd to me. I imagine there are also some feelings of resentment in the room on the part of those of you who had hoped to get this job yourself. I hope that we will be able to work through those feelings. The friendships that we developed during our work on the artificial intelligence project are important to me. I am confident that we can retain those friendships regardless of the change in our formal roles."

His introduction finished, Larry sat down and waited for a group discussion to begin. Instead, silence prevailed, broken only by the squeaking of chairs and the clicking of pens by nervous fingers. The group was forcing Larry to assume the role of leader.

Larry continued, attempting to describe the climate that he hoped would prevail.

"Many of you have probably heard of the procedures I introduced during my last job. I'll be honest with you. They backfired. Instead of stimulating greater productivity, I merely succeeded in antagonizing some of my best people. You might say that I learned my lesson the hard way. I do not intend to repeat that mistake.

"I feel very confident of my ability to lead this unit. The subject of finance is familiar to me. I specialized in marketing in school, and after working with the design function in marketing, I have a pretty good feel for the programming side of the house. I do not pretend to be an expert, however, in any of these areas. You are the experts in your own fields. I promise to respect that expertise, and to rely heavily upon your input as I make decisions.

"The first thing that I need to do is to get familiar with the projects on which you are currently working. I will be in my office for the next few days, and urge each of you to find time to come and talk with me both about what you are doing, and what you would like to be doing, or think you and the unit as a whole should be doing. Once you have brought me up to speed on current projects, we'll meet again and, as a group, decide on where we go from here."

Convinced that he had gotten off to a good start with his new team, Larry went to his office, and waited for his people to seize the opportunity to talk with him. It did not happen that way. The hours passed, and no one came to call. As the lunch hour approached, Larry decided he would have to take another initiative.

He decided to focus first on the writers. After all, that group had constituted his biggest problem in the other unit. Going into their section, he found three of his people. Two seemed to be engrossed in a project; a third was shuffling paper in an apparent attempt to reorganize his desk. Larry approached this individual, unwilling to interrupt the train of thought of the others.

"You're Geoff, right? Well, Geoff, how about going down to the cafeteria for a bite to eat?"

Although Geoff agreed, his reluctance was obvious. During lunch, Larry tried to stay away from work-related subjects, attempting to build a personal relationship with Geoff. Their conversation was stilted and awkward. Larry asked questions and Geoff responded, revealing as little as possible.

As their lunch was drawing to a close, Geoff suddenly sat upright in his chair, and said, "OK, Mr. Michaelson. Let's have it. I can't stand sitting here and waiting for the other shoe to drop. I'm sure you've read all of our personnel files, and I'm equally sure that what you read about me wasn't positive. I went through a severe personal crisis a year or so ago, and my work admittedly slipped during that period. Well, things are better now, and I know that I can be a highly productive part of the team. My former boss would never let me or anyone forget that I had once let the group down. I figure you invited me to lunch to tell me that you were going to clean house, and that I had to go."

Larry was about to respond, and to reassure Geoff that his assumptions were totally wrong, when Geoff decided to continue.

"I guess I know what's coming because of what I've heard about you. Sheila told me about the episode over her manuscript. I guess we're all feeling cautious. I may as well say that outright. After all, I have nothing more to lose, do I?"

Larry suggested that the two of them take a walk around the block. As they walked, Larry told Geoff that he had had no ulterior motive in inviting Geoff to lunch. His agenda was simply to get to know his people. He assured him that he had no intention of firing Geoff, or anyone else for that matter.

"People make mistakes, Geoff. What is important is the ability to learn from mistakes. I do not plan to review the personnel files. I want to make my own assessment of people. Let us agree that as of today we start with a clean slate. I will not hang you for your past, if you agree to do the same for me."

Larry and Geoff had done more than reach an agreement that afternoon. They had established a norm of honesty between them. Because Geoff had a lot of friends in the unit, others heard about the conversation, and began to be more open with Larry. By the end of the third day, almost everyone had taken the opportunity to tell Larry what they were doing, and their opinions as to what was working and what needed correcting.

By the end of the week, Larry had formed a clear picture of the operation, and had a strong sense of internal processes that were hindering productivity.

He made a list, intending to call another staff meeting and suggest the formation of a task force to recommend solutions to the problems that he had identified:

- Communications between the programmers and the writers were poor; the writers were not respecting design parameters. The programmers, on the other hand, were not responsive to the difficulties the writers were experiencing.
- Work flow was terribly uneven, with crises interspersed with periods of no activity.
- The customer inquiry service was handled in a very inconsistent manner, depending on who happened to take the call. Standards for customer service did not exist.
- A major custom product was due to be delivered to the client in two months, but unless a miracle happened, it would not be ready.

The next week, Larry called a meeting of the entire unit, and outlined the problems as he perceived them. No one disagreed that the items on the list were key issues. Everyone had comments to offer. Larry found it difficult to regain control of the meeting, and to stop the discussion once it reached what seemed to be a point of diminishing returns as people focused on pinpointing blame rather than on seeking best solutions.

"The writers just have to understand that they are not being paid to develop the great American novel. That's what causes us to get behind and to miss deadlines."

"The programmers ought to spend more time with the customer. Then they would understand what the term 'user-sensitive' or 'user-friendly' means. And they would appreciate that it takes a lot of words to create the kind of program that users can understand."

Delighted that members of the team were finally communicating openly, Larry allowed the conversation to continue. Nor did he interrupt when conflicts arose in the group, or when blame placing and defensive reactions precluded a search for solutions.

The meeting, scheduled to last two hours, consumed the better part of the day. Whatever advantage the group gained in terms of enhanced team spirit was offset by the loss of time and resultant inability to meet the client deadline.

The weeks slipped by, and Larry's anxiety about the deadline began to mount. Unwilling to sacrifice or to even compromise his new-found identity as a participative, democratic leader, he refused to take a more directive stance and mandate that certain actions occur by certain times. Instead, he had a series of meetings with the supervisors of each of the functions, reminding them that time was growing short, and attempting to cajole them into action rather than directing their efforts.

Larry found it necessary to ask for two extensions of the deadline. The first time, the client was only mildly annoyed. When the second extension was requested, the client's annoyance turned to anger. Larry knew that to request a third extension was to jeopardize the entire client relationship. That was out of the question. The client was a major one and did business with all of the departments in the organization.

Meanwhile, events outside the unit began to concern Larry. That old feeling of uneasiness returned, and was fueled by the rumor mill. The "grapevine" was carrying the news that Reginald Sterling had been instrumental in getting Larry promoted.

For weeks, Larry ignored the rumors, unable to find any reason for Reginald to have done such a thing. Given Larry's friendship with Foresight, and the fact that Foresight was regarded as being in the "enemy camp," it was likely that Reginald regarded Larry more as foe than as friend. And Larry had succeeded in getting the mandate to supervise the artificial intelligence project, and to access Reginald's people as needed. It was doubtful, then, that he would have been instrumental in helping Larry rise in the organization unless, of course, there was something in it for him.

Eventually the reason for Reginald's apparently supportive behavior emerged. Knowing that Larry was intensely dedicated to the artificial intelligence project, Reginald correctly perceived that he didn't have a prayer of prying it loose from the Business Systems Division as long as its champion had the time and energy to watch over it.

When the manager of the finance unit resigned, Reginald saw an opportunity to erode Larry's steadily increasing power base. He would suggest to the vice-president of the division that Larry be considered for the promotion. Once promoted, he had reasoned,

Larry would be too preoccupied with the responsibilities of his new position to give the artificial intelligence project the attention it required.

His assumption had been correct. Within a few months, project coordination began to break down. The programmers began pursuing isolated pieces of the overall project, unconcerned about how their work fit in with the work of others.

All Reginald had to do was to approach Ralph Willit, the vice-president of software, and propose that he do everyone a favor by taking control of the artificial intelligence project. When Willit agreed, Reginald walked away not only with Larry's pet project, but with some of his better programmers as well.

All of this occurred at the time when Larry most needed his best people if he was to meet the client deadline. To further compound the problem, Reginald chose that moment to escalate the war over the financial planning model. He clearly intended to act while Larry was down, and when Reginald's chances for victory were the best.

Experiencing pressure from every source, Larry began to get more and more impatient with his people. Unwilling to invest the time required to solve problems in a group setting, Larry began to issue mandates. When the mandates were ignored, Larry became angry. His anger took the form of threats of dismissal and demotion. The atmosphere in the unit shifted from one of team endeavor to one of fear and resentment.

The unit managed to meet the deadline, but the cost in terms of the relationship between Larry and his people was enormous. To make matters worse, the time had come for the decision as to whether Larry would continue as manager of the unit. Fearing the worst, Larry appeared for his preordained meeting with Forbes, the director of the department.

Apparently Forbes had been watching Larry very closley, monitoring, but not interfering with his management approach. He was aware both of Larry's early attempts to function as a participative manager, and of his sudden shift to a more directive, militaristic approach when the pressure mounted.

"Larry, you and I both know that your behavior with your people has swung from black to white, or white to black, depending on how you view it. Your apparent inconsistency has got to be very stressful for your people. It seems that you have confused the notion of leadership based on trust and expertise with a laissez-faire, or 'anything goes' policy. They are most definitely not the same. *A relationship based on trust, and on respect, is built on a very strong foundation. A relationship based on noninvolvement rests on a weak foundation. A strong relationship does not crumble when it is subjected to pressure and temporary measures designed to cope with a crisis."*

Larry was now convinced that his tenure as manager was over. It was with surprise and relief that he heard Forbes say, "But Larry, at least you are trying, and trying hard. I believe you are capable of being a fine manager. However, you must change the way you deal with people.

"You need to listen harder and try to be less evaluative and judgmental. When you're angry or disappointed, say so, without putting down the other person. Sometimes you seem aloof and almost cold. People often have that reaction when they're scared. Work harder on giving others reasons to trust you."

Larry immediately tried to act on Forbes' advice. As a gesture of friendship, he invited all of his subordinates to his home for a party, to celebrate the end of their crisis, and the beginning of a more comfortable work pace and environment.

He tried being open with several of his people, stating how difficult he found it to be warm and available, particularly when under pressure. He told the unit as a whole that he was proud of them, and would defend them any time, at any cost. He tried expressing feelings more openly, in spite of the discomfort he experienced in doing so.

Larry also introduced some operational plans and procedures which were designed to avoid a recurrence of the kind of crisis that had threatened to tear the unit apart. Much to his surprise, he found that his people were relieved to have a plan to follow.

Secure in the knowledge that he was no longer on probation as manager, Larry began focusing some of his energies outside the unit. He began by calling and asking Foresight to have lunch. It had been months since they had gotten together. Larry had even canceled a number of dates for racquetball games with Foresight, finding it necessary to work nights and weekends to meet the client deadline.

While Foresight agreed to have lunch, he seemed quite cool toward Larry. Larry asked Foresight if something was bothering him. Foresight's response was brief but clear.

"I have been feeling used, Larry. You seem to approach me when you want something, and to forget me when your life is going well.

I've gone out on a limb for you several times. Once it nearly cost me the planning model. You seem very ungrateful and, at times, downright unfriendly."

Larry fought the temptation to offer an explanation or defense of his behavior, and, instead, concentrated on listening and understanding. Only after he felt he really understood did he share with Foresight the reasons for his apparent disregard of their friendship.

Their conversation then turned to business. Foresight was very concerned about the continued fight waged by Peter Buck, the chief financial officer, to gain control of the planning model.

"My relationship with Buck has completely deteriorated. It's at the point of open warfare. I have had to forbid any member of my staff from giving any figures to any member of his staff until they have triple-checked the numbers and have gotten a personal signoff from me. Buck is just looking for an opportunity to catch me with an error.

"Further, I have seen the preliminary budget for next year. A lot of money, and I do mean a lot of money, is slated for development of the commercial version of the financial planning model. If I'm not mistaken, the decision as to whether the model will be developed by you folks in Business Systems or by Reginald's group will be made within the next two or three months.

"I suggest we carve out a strategy, my friend, or we are both going to emerge as losers. If Reginald gets the model, then he will inevitably help convince the CEO that Buck should control the internal use of the model."

Together they mapped out a strategy. Foresight would work with Larry's staff to familiarize them with the existing model and the underlying program. That would give them an edge over Reginald's people who had seen only an occasional printout.

At the same time, Larry would use his existing client base to assess their interest in having a financial planning simulation as opposed to a program that would diagnose the client's actual financial position, and enable the client to input data to test the outcome of various investment strategies. If need be, he would convince them that such a product would be far more useful than a simulation designed to educate and train the user to become a better financial planner.

Finally, they decided to augment the weapons at their disposal by gathering data which would indicate that the company's investment in building a program for space shuttle passengers was not likely to generate a decent return. The decision to abandon the space shuttle program would presumably free resources which could then be invested in development of the financial planning model.

Their arsenal would be further stocked by the information Larry felt he could gather from one of his programmers who had chosen to follow the artificial intelligence program into Reginald's unit.

"I know that guy. He'll never survive under Reginald. He's a real maverick, and likes to do things his way, according to his time table. I'm sure that, by now, he is regretting his decision to transfer into Reginald's area. Let me see what I can find out. If I'm right, Reginald in mismanaging the artificial intelligence project. If we can prove that, then we'll be in a good position to make a case against his taking on yet another project."

Content that they had covered all the bases, Foresight and Larry devoted their time and energy to familiarizing Larry's people with the model, and to getting in a position to undermine Reginald Sterling.

An opportunity presented itself for Foresight to speak about financial planning models at a Young President's Association luncheon. He accepted the invitation, and then turned over the assignment to Larry, suggesting it would be a good idea to begin to build Larry's credibility as an expert in the area. As part of their strategy, they had the speech typed and disseminated to the top management group.

Meanwhile, Reginald was busy rearming. Having stripped the Business Systems area of many of its good programmers, Reginald did not need to request additional personnel to cover his next year's objectives. He knew that Larry would have to get an authorization for additional people if his area was awarded the job of developing the financial planning model.

Explaining the situation to his friend and ally, the chief financial officer, Reginald convinced Buck to issue the directive that there would be no additions to staff in the coming year. The only way to get additional people was to arrange to borrow persons from other areas that were temporarily underutilized, or to respond to requests for transfers initiated by individuals who were unhappy in their present positions.

Larry and Foresight both realized that the staffing freeze would require that they seek additional talent from the Video Disc Division. The video people tended to operate in a vacuum, unaffected by the political power plays that characterized the Software Division. Having no reason to ally themselves with the Sterling-Buck team, or with the Michaelson-Foresight team, they enjoyed an unusual degree of organizational neutrality.

The video area did not enjoy much organizational power, however. This was the source of great frustration to Tyler Watch, vice-president of the Video Division. Believing that the video disc represented the technology of the future, he was frustrated by its lack of visibility in the corporation. Given his interest in the production process, however, he had done little to promote sales. His continued reliance on the software salespeople to sell video as an "add on" perpetuated the image that Tyler found so offensive.

Larry and Foresight were unaware of this, however. Neither had ever taken the time to develop a relationship with Tyler Watch.

Larry had had a few conversations with Roger Arnell, the manager of video graphics. He had sought Arnell's advice while he was still supervisor of marketing design. Pleased at being asked to render an opinion, Roger had been very helpful.

Not knowing where else to start, Larry tried to make an appointment to see Roger. He was more than a little surprised when Roger's secretary responded that Roger's calendar was full, and that he could not see Larry for another week or so. Surprise changed to suspicion when the secretary went on to inform Larry that Reginald Sterling was consuming all of the time and talent they had available.

Larry could not believe that it was sheer coincidence that Reginald was making extensive use of Arnell's services at this time. On the contrary, Larry knew that Reginald preferred using the services of an outside graphics firm.

Sensing that the war had gotten out of hand, Larry decided that it was time to involve his boss, Mr. Forbes. After all, Forbes and Sterling were on the same hierarchical level. Perhaps Forbes could help. At the very least, Larry reasoned, he needs to be informed. Forbes listened to Larry's story, holding his comments until Larry had finished.

"Larry, your awareness of organizational politics amazes me. While I am pleased that you are sensitive to what is going on in the company, I must admit that I am a little dismayed by your obvious involvement in the problem. You have a unit to manage, and an important one at that. I am concerned that you may not be devoting enough time and energy to your primary responsibility.

"I think it is important that I share with you my perception of what is going on in this organization. Normally, I would not talk organizational politics with a subordinate, but I respect the fact that you have come to me, presumably to keep me informed. For that reason, I will be more open with you than I would otherwise be.

"When Reginald convinced Willit, the vice-president of software, that the artificial intelligence project belonged under him, I initially felt that a piece of my turf had been taken away from me. I guess we are all alike in that sense; we all want to protect what we regard as our turf. Anyway, I fought the decision for awhile, before I realized that it was in the best interests of the organization to move the project. You were overwhelmed with your new responsibilities, and the other managers in Business Systems did not have the competence to handle the project."

Forbes looked at Larry, seeking a reaction. Artificial intelligence had been Larry's baby. It would have been only natural for Larry to resent Forbes for not fighting harder to keep the project in the department.

Larry did not feel betrayed; on the contrary, he was glad that the project had been moved; glad because his sources had informed him that very little progress had been made since Reginald assumed control.

He told Forbes that little progress had been made on the artificial intelligence project, and suggested that Reginald's poor performance in this area might constitute just the argument they would need to convince the organization that development of the financial planning model belonged in Business Systems, and not in Reginald's area.

Forbes did not share Larry's delight that Reginald had let the artificial intelligence project slow down, pointing out to Larry that the organization had to stay on top of the latest technology, and that the entire organization, including Business Systems, would suffer if that were not the case. Nor was he pleased that Larry was spending his time attempting to influence the decision over the planning model.

"Look, Larry, calm down and concentrate your efforts on your unit. Trust me to do what needs to be done in terms of convincing my boss that the development of the planning model belongs in our area. I firmly believe, Larry, that Reginald is his own worst enemy. One of these days, he will maneuver himself right into a corner."

Larry looked at his boss, hoping that Forbes would elaborate on the meaning behind his last statement. That Forbes was unwilling to do so became obvious as he rose in order to escort Larry to the door.

Larry was nearly out the door when Forbes added, "By the way, Larry, Jenks dropped a comment the other day that leads me to believe that the two of you are not on the best of terms. Pay attention to your relationships within the department, Larry."

With that, Forbes allowed the door to close, leaving Larry very puzzled. What did Jenks have to do with anything? Why, he had scarcely given a thought to the man since he had left the marketing unit. He had called him once, to inform him that he needed additional programming support. Jenks had assured him there was no problem in providing it.

His mind spinning with thoughts of corporate intrigue, and unanswered questions, Larry decided that it was time for a talk with Bill, and was pleased when Bill issued him an invitation to dinner.

Bill suggested that they modify their approach and that Larry do a self-appraisal after reflecting on the strategies he had been using.

"I would give myself a high rating with regard to building all three types of *formal power:* Reward, Coercive, and Position Power. The promotion to manager increased my position power, as well as my ability to grant rewards and deliver punishments.

"My budget authority levels are higher, which means that I can grant bigger raises and bonuses. Because I'm now managing an entire department, I have greater flexibility with regard to assignments. I can move people around more freely between the functions. Assignments, themselves, constitute a potential form of reward or punishment, depending on the nature of the task to be done.

"The only reason I wouldn't give myself a top rating with regard to the building of the *formal power* bases is that I lost the artificial intelligence project to Reginald Sterling. Along with the loss of the project, I lost several programmers. As the size of my empire shrunk, so did my *position power.* To some degree, clout in the organization is a function of the number of people reporting to you.

"At the same time, I lost the ability to assign people to the project. Because that project is so challenging, people regard having the opportunity to work on it as a reward. Therefore, my *candy store* is not as well stocked as it might have been had I retained the project.

"I am doing a good job of implementing the *Arsenal Strategy.* Foresight and I are making a solid effort to amass arms to use in the impending war against Reginald and Buck. Those guys are dirty players; we've got to get them where it hurts. Walking softly with those guys won't work. We've got to carry a big stick."

Larry then described how he had infiltrated Reginald's camp, as one of the programmers expressed the willingness to provide information which would prove that Reginald was not managing the artificial intelligence project.

"To make sure our arsenal is equipped to handle a full-scale war, we are also gathering market data which will prove that the customer is more interested in diagnostic and application software than in simulations. Foresight is gathering information that will convince top management that their investment in Reginald's simulation for space shuttle passengers is not going to pay off. Once we get all of the data, we'll have Reginald where we want him."

While agreeing that Larry's arsenal was impressively stocked, Bill felt the need to remind Larry of the negative consequences of building and using *coercive power.*

"Remember, Larry, as you build coercive power, you are destroying your chances for gaining Reginald's trust. And there are no winners in an all-out war. Everybody loses. As Benjamin Franklin said, 'There was never a good war or a bad peace.'"

Larry was not going to be so easily dissuaded from pursuing his re-armament strategy.

"I think that when it comes to Reginald, I must assume John Paul Jones' position, 'I have not yet begun to fight.' In spite of the negative consequences of using coercive power, I believe it is appropriate in Reginald's case.

"Use of the big stick was far less appropriate with my own people. I regret what I now regard as excessive and inconsistent reliance on the power of the stick, and the power of the carrot.

"I seem to revert to my old militaristic behavior when under pressure. An important client deadline was rapidly approaching. We were shamefully behind schedule, which was, in large part, my fault.

"I had gotten so wrapped up in my desire to be liked, that I forgot to lead the group. Instead of being decisive, I became wishy-washy. For awhile, absolutely no decisions got made. Everybody had a chance to vent their frustrations, and there was a lot of conversation going on, but almost nothing was happening. In focusing all my energies on the people, I ignored the task.

"As the days went by, and the schedule continued to slip, I panicked. Instead of explaining my panic to my people, I simply shifted gears. I started issuing directives. I didn't care at that point about how people were feeling, or even whether or not they liked me as a person. Meeting that deadline was all that mattered. In effect, I stopped using the power of friendship, and started leaning very heavily on formal power."

"And, in the process, you destroyed the trust you had worked so hard to establish," said Bill. *"Reliance on formal clout rapidly destroys trust.* Even the presence of formal power gets in the way of building trust, as we have discussed before."

"There is no doubt about it. It's a shame, too, since I had been doing such a good job of building and then using the power of trust and friendship," replied Larry.

"Right from the beginning, I let my subordinates know that it was my hope that we would learn to work as a team. I did not impose my definitions of the problem on them, nor mandate the solutions. I asked for their input, and let them influence the decision process. I even shared my feelings with a few of them, though I find that really hard to do.

"And I managed to build a solid relationship with Geoff, the writer. I let him know that I cared about him, and that I would not hold his past against him. I think he feels he can trust me."

"Larry, it sounds as though you have begun to master the *Fraternity Strategy* for building the power of friendship. Mastery of this strategy is essential, particularly in today's organizations. As organizational complexity increases, the need for coordination increases. Coordination by fiat becomes less and less workable as specialization intensifies, and as functions and support services proliferate. *Cross-functional loyalties and friendships often make the difference between a manager who can make things happen and one who cannot."*

Bill then offered Larry the following tactics for implementing the Fraternity Strategy:

- Identify what you have in common with the other person; look at activities, goals, and life values.

- Look for ways in which you and the other person can help each other.

- Make a deal with the other person and live up to it.

- At all cost, avoid winning at the other's expense.

- Develop a shared language, or create other "symbols" to remind yourself of your common bond. Think about the fraternity handshake, or tee shirts that team members wear. These are all devices used to build the power of friendship.

- Actively listen to the other person, and check to make sure you understand his or her feelings and point of view.

"All of these tactics help to build trust, and trust is really the foundation, the basis, of the power of friendship. *The power of trust begins to build between people as they come to realize that they have something in common; that they are after the same things in life; or, that they face common obstacles.* The degree of power increases as these persons begin to appreciate that, through joint effort, they can increase the likelihood that they will achieve their shared objectives.

"Once the foundation is laid, we must strive hard to nurture trust. *Trust is terribly difficult to build, and frighteningly easy to destroy.* We really trust only those persons who are available to us, and who are open with us about their feelings as well as their ideas. We trust those who understand us because they take the time to listen. Most importantly, we trust people who are straightforward in terms of putting out their true agenda. We do not trust manipulators. And we trust people who are consistent, people whose words and actions project the same message over time.

"Of course, there are disadvantages to using the power of friendship. In expressing your feelings, you make yourself vulnerable. And you must expend a lot of energy to maintain trust. Nonetheless, I think the effort is worth it," Bill concluded.

"As I said before, Bill, I really blew it when I shifted gears on my people. They have to perceive me as one of the most inconsistent managers around. If I had not let the schedule slip so badly, I would not have had to adopt strong arm tactics."

"You never had to do so, Larry. I would suggest that what really happened is that you failed to rely heavily enough on your expert power, at least in the beginning. I suspect that your people would have willingly adhered to your scheduling suggestions because they respected your managerial and planning skills. But you were too busy trying to be everybody's buddy, and overly reluctant to advise that they pursue a single course of action.

"I would give you a negative rating for your overuse of the involvement influence strategy. *To involve others is to rely on the power of friendship or expertise to engage in a problem-solving discussion with others.* Everyone exerts influence over the process. Outcomes and approaches and best responses are not predetermined. Participative management and the involvement strategy are one and the same. *Involvement inspires commitment; on the downside, it takes a lot of time.*

"In your case, you relied inappropriately on involvement as a strategy when time constraints would have argued for a greater use of the enlistment strategy. *To enlist is to rely primarily on the power of your expertise to convince others to behave in a certain way.* You did not make enough use of that strategy, forcing you to be directive, or to require fixed behaviors and to support those demands with promises of rewards and threats of coercion."

"You're right. Now, I am using my expert power, and making it clear that I expect certain things to be done in certain ways. My people are responding, and yet I do not sense that they view me as a dictator, or as a person to be feared.

"Yes, I sense that they respect my expertise now. That wasn't always the case. I had to prove to them that I knew something about programming, finance, and marketing. Now I'm faced with convincing people *outside* the department that I'm an expert.

"I think I'm doing a good job of that," Larry continued. "I would give myself a high rating on the building of expert power. My staff and I are busy not only enhancing our expertise regarding financial planning models, but we are publicizing that expertise through speeches and articles."

"Nice; that's very nice, Larry. You are obviously naturally adept at implementing the Look-What-I've-Done Strategy for building expert power. In effect, you are creating opportunities to let people know what you know, and what you can do.

"And you're doing it well. You are getting *visibility*; disseminating the text of your speech was a stroke of genius. You are also *displaying competence* in the area of expertise; at least the review of your speech would indicate that it was competent. You're doing all of this in an area that is regarded as *relevant to a pressing problem or opportunity.* At least I assume the organization still believes that it should introduce a commercial version of the model."

"Absolutely, Bill, that's what all the intrigue is about. Getting hold of that model; getting the assignment to develop the commercial version is the biggest carrot the company has held out for a long time."

"Then, as I said, Larry, you get a lot of points for building expert power in an important area. The trick now is going to be effecting a balance between reliance on the power of friendship and the power of expertise. Finding such a balance is important both with regard to your own people, and others in the organization.

"That, by the way, is no minor accomplishment. *The two forms of power can conflict with one another. Experts are, by definition, different from the nonexperts whom they counsel. Yet friendship, or the power of trust, is based on a sense of similarity or identification between people.*

"The other thing you are going to have to do, Larry, is to intensify your networking efforts, getting in a position to indirectly use the power of others. It may be that, by doing so, you will not have to rely so heavily on your arsenal as you attempt to prevail over Reginald and Buck."

"I agree that I have paid little attention to building indirect power. I was so preoccupied with meeting that client deadline and developing new relationships with my team, that I stopped working on the development of contacts in the larger organization.

"I did use indirect power, or the power of another, however, when I got Geoff to convince the other members of the department that I could be trusted, and that I wanted to listen to their viewpoints."

"I would suggest, Larry, that you consider relying indirectly on the power of Forbes with regard to your dealings with Reginald. In the first place, he told you to stay out of the fray. In the second place, Forbes and Sterling are peers, hierarchically speaking. It would be a lot safer to network through Forbes; use his power over Reginald, as opposed to continuing to move in the direction of a head-to-head collision with Reginald."

"I don't have a lot of faith in Forbes' ability to stop Reginald. Reginald is in bed with Buck, and Buck wields a lot of formal power. I am glad that I talked to Forbes, however.

"At least I leveled with him, and let him know of my interest in the planning model. He'll never be able to say that I didn't warn him, either. I think I even built a little friendship power that day. We are after the same thing, after all. It's only our approach that differs. I could tell that Forbes trusted me; he talked quite openly about his perception of organizational politics."

"As I hear it, Larry, you are pleased that your boss trusts you, and yet you are still planning to ignore his suggestion that you focus on your unit, and leave the business of organizational politics to him. I'm not at all convinced that that is a good idea."

Larry was convinced that he had to continue to stock his arsenal, and attempted to defend his position. "Look, I am not manipulating anyone. I told my programmer in Reginald's unit exactly why I wanted the information. Nor did I try to manipulate my boss. I was very straight with him. As for the gathering of information, well, my agenda and Foresight's couldn't be more obvious. I am not trying to outmanipulate the manipulator, as you would say it. I am simply getting in a position to protect myself, and I am keeping my eyes and ears open so that I never again fall prey to one of Reginald's manipulations."

"You are very angry, aren't you?"

"You bet, I am, Bill, and I have good reason to be."

"Have you tried expressing your anger to Reginald? Have you sought to identify some shared goals? Have you tried building at least that degree of understanding? Have you tried to influence Reginald through your expertise? No, the answer is no. You are preparing for war and, in the process, almost guaranteeing that war will happen.

"Use the Fraternity Strategy to build trust and the Look-What-I've-Done Strategy to build expert power. You can always revert back to stocking your arsenal, Larry. It is not as easy to move in the other direction. Once you have played your formal power card, you cannot start a game of hearts."

In reviewing his tactics, Larry perceived how dramatically different his strategy had been with Reginald from the strategy he used with others whom he regarded as friends and allies. While Bill had not convinced him that it was safe to disarm, he had made him at least reconsider his heavy reliance on coercive power.

During the weeks to come, as the drama with Reginald unfolded, Larry would frequently consult the notes he had taken that evening.

LARRY'S NOTES

- *Look-What-I've-Done Strategy to Build Expert Power*
  —Keys are visibility, competent performance, and relevance to a pressing problem or opportunity.

- *Fraternity Strategy for Building Friendship Power*
  —Identify shared goals; talk the same language; listen actively; never win at the other's expense; make contracts and live up to them; show you care.

- *Friendship Power,* while inspiring commitment to you as a person, requires that you make yourself vulnerable and that you work to maintain trust. These are potential disadvantages.

- *Involvement* builds commitment, but it takes time; when urgency is an issue, consider *enlisting,* or asking for a fixed response on the basis of expertise.

- *Possible to balance Expert* and *Friendship* power, but is difficult because expert power sets up a distance, while friendship power is based on a sense of similarities between people.

- *It is always possible to stock the arsenal,* to rearm; having done so, it may not be possible to build friendship or expert power.

6

Noble Networks and Managerial Maneuvers

BILL HAD SUCCEEDED in muting Larry's almost fanatical desire to "get" Reginald Sterling. After thinking about their conversation over the weekend, Larry decided to tread more softly, focusing on making himself look good as opposed to making Reginald look bad.

He began with his own work unit, determined to create a culture and climate that was so positive that talented people from other areas would request that they be transferred into his unit. He began by rethinking the way the department was structured. It had always operated as a functional hierarchy, with a supervisor in charge of design, another in charge of manufacturing, etc. Larry thought it quite possible that this segmented structure was compounding the communications problem between the writers and the programmers, and between the marketing people and the manufacturing specialists.

Knowing that any restructuring or realigning of job functions would threaten someone's turf, and therefore engender resistance to a change, Larry decided to establish a task force to consider restructuring the unit. All the functions in the department were represented.

After deliberating for three weeks, the task force approached Larry with a recommendation that the department be reorganized to reflect customer accountabilities, rather than functional responsibilities. Believing that account-specific reporting would make everyone more sensitive to the market, Larry enthusiastically agreed. Account-specific teams were formed, with each team having a representative from each of the functional disciplines.

The job of supervisor was abolished. Instead, the team itself was charged with making compensation decisions, dividing the work, and dealing with marginal performers who were not meeting the group's standards regarding quality or quantity of output. Leadership in the group became a function of expertise, not role. The ability to wield formal power became less important than the ability to communicate in a persuasive fashion.

The teams competed with one another for sales dollars. The competition was healthy, however, motivating everyone to both understand the customer, and to maintain good customer relationships. Customer inquiries received prompt attention. Referrals increased, as satisfied customers recommended that others approach the organization for existing software or the development of customized products. The schism that had existed between the marketing and sales people healed, as sales personnel realized that their compensation was dependent on production, and as production people realized their welfare was inextricably tied to the success of the sales staff.

Innovation and creativity flourished. Enjoying their work, people began coming early and staying late. Word began to spread throughout the organization that Larry's department was the best place in which to work. With the exception of one disgruntled supervisor who resented the dissolution of his empire, no one requested a transfer out of the function.

A number of requests were made for transfer into the department. It came as no surprise to Larry that several of these requests were from the programmers who had followed the artificial intelligence project into Reginald's area.

While the reorganization introduced vitality into the department, it also created problems of product and design coordination. Programmers on different teams competed with each other, refusing to share information or programming ideas. Realizing that duplication of effort was an increasing problem, Larry reconvened the task force and asked them to recommend a solution.

The result of their work was a modification of the incentive system. Part of each person's compensation was to be based on the performance of the department as a whole. Product development teams were created that cut across the account-focused teams. These teams, in turn, introduced the notion of core modules, or program segments that could be used in a variety of products, thus decreasing the time it took to create or modify any of the department's programs.

Their innovativeness did not stop there. Wanting to ease the work of the writers, and to make the writers' output more immediately usable by the programmers, the programmers created what they called an "authoring system." The system was a computer program which asked the writers a series of questions. In typing their answers into the computer, the writers were actually helping to create the final product.

Given the increases in productivity, several members of the department approached Larry and said that they had time on their hands, and wanted to use it to begin development of a prototype of the financial planning model. Larry agreed to let them pursue the prototype, under the condition that commitments to customers and existing product development schedules be honored.

With his unit essentially managing itself, Larry felt free to reapproach his boss and to seek permission to continue with activities designed to increase the likelihood that the Business Systems Division would be assigned the development of the commercial planning model.

"Some of my people are working on the development of a prototype. Much of the effort is occurring on their own time. I saw no problem with letting them proceed. For my part, I want to devote some of my energies to a market study; finding out what the market needs with regard to computerized financial planning tools, identifying market segments, studying the competition, and the like. Of course, Foresight is already working on this, but I feel that I have something to contribute, particularly in the marketing area."

Pleased with the performance of Larry's unit, Forbes agreed to let Larry devote resources to the study. He imposed the same condition that Larry had imposed on his people. "Just don't let your other work suffer; don't lose sight of existing business in an effort to predict the future."

Larry was about to leave Forbes' office, when Forbes called him back, asked him to sit down, and said, "By the way, I am pleased with the way you have kept your nose out of organizational politics. For awhile there, I was afraid that you were going to create a lot of unnecessary trouble for all of us.

"Patience has paid off, Larry. As I think I told you, I suspected that Reginald might turn out to be his own worst enemy. Well, it looks like that is exactly what has happened.

"Reginald did a really dumb thing. Apparently, he panicked when people started requesting transfers out of his area in order to join your unit. Instead of trying to learn from the situation, he tried to pull up the drawbridge. He approached Willit, the vice-president of software, and claimed that you were luring his people away with false promises.

"Well, that prompted Willit to look more closely at our department and at Reginald's. Willit was quite impressed when I described your organizational experiment. I showed him one of your latest products, and described the core module design approach you have adopted. His reaction was very positive.

"Then Willit took a close look at Reginald's operation. Instead of innovation, he found a rigid adherence to routine, and a complete lack of any exciting new products. As you no doubt remember, Willit was pretty excited about the artificial intelligence concept. When he saw how little progress had been made, he got quite upset.

"The upshot of the whole thing is that Willit wants to meet with you to discuss applications that your core modules and authoring systems might have in other parts of the division. Yes, even in Reginald's area. I suggest you call him and make an appointment. Rest assured, I will not feel bypassed. I am delighted to help you get the credit that you deserve."

Larry thanked Forbes, thinking to himself that he hoped that one day he would be as fine a manager as Forbes. He told Forbes that, while he would appreciate having an audience with Willit, it was really one of his programmers who deserved the credit for the concept.

In the end, several members of Larry's area made the presentation to Willit. Willit, in turn, was sufficiently impressed to request a repeat of the presentation to a broader audience. The audience was to include Reginald as well as his managers and supervisors.

Larry had mixed feelings about the opportunity. In some ways, he would have preferred keeping Reginald in the dark. He feared that, during the presentation, Reginald would devote all of his energies to finding fault with the concepts.

Larry's fears were unfounded. Reginald did not even attend the presentation, claiming that he had a prior commitment with a major customer. In his stead, he sent Joel, Larry's adversary, as his representative. Surprisingly, Joel behaved himself, asking only an occasional question for clarification. Larry knew, however, that the story had only just begun. He waited anxiously for Reginald's reaction.

He did not have long to wait. A few days later, Joel called Larry and suggested that they get together for lunch. While Larry could think of no reason to spend time with Joel, he agreed to meet him. His curiosity outweighed his dislike for Joel.

Joel was excessively polite. Sensing the inauthenticity in Joel's behavior, Larry was alerted to the possibility that the lunch invitation was part of another manipulation, another power play. Deciding that he could not be victimized if he listened a lot and said little, Larry let Joel talk.

Joel expressed his regret over their inability to form a friendship, and stated that he wanted to begin again. He told Larry that he had a lot of respect for him, and was eager to work on building a better relationship. Reminding Larry that they had come from the same "trainee" class, Joel urged that they try harder to support one another's efforts.

Impatient with Joel's dishonesty, Larry confronted him. "Look, Joel, I don't have any reason to trust you; on the contrary, I have a number of reasons to distrust you. The kind words you are expressing today do not make me feel any differently. I may be wrong, but I sense that you are here as an emissary of Reginald's, and that you have something on your mind other than establishing a better relationship with me."

At first, Joel pleaded innocence. Larry stated again that he was suspicious of Joel's motives. Eventually, Joel confessed.

"OK. Reginald did suggest that I meet with you. I guess he thought he would be compromising his position if he called you himself. He is a director, and you are just a manager. I'm not even a manager. I'm functioning as Reginald's administrative assistant. That position doesn't even appear on the chart. I think I made a real mistake when I agreed to take the job. I don't see any future in it."

Larry relaxed a little, believing that Joel was finally being honest. Joel continued to talk, revealing more and more about himself.

"Reginald treats me like a prince; anything I want, I get. What I am beginning to realize, however, is that I am paying a tremendous price for his devotion. In the first place, he expects me to report to him on anything and everything I hear, whether fact or rumor. You're right in maintaining a silence with me, Larry. I'd have to report anything you said. If you say nothing, then I'll have nothing to report.

"Needless to say, no one trusts me. I feel completely isolated. Because of my isolation, I'm not learning much. Oh, I learn from Reginald. In fact, he seems to really respect my expertise, but then of course he would. I'm turning into a parrot; when Reginald listens to me, he hears his own biases being confirmed.

"I guess your presentation really made me think about all of this. You have managed to do some really exciting things since you joined the company. I made the mistake of thinking the way to climb the corporate ladder was to latch onto someone else's coattails, riding with him to the top. Reginald apeared to be a likely candidate. I mean, he is powerful, or he *was* powerful.

"He is losing his grasp, however. His strong-arm tactics are backfiring, and he knows it. Now he's been directed to adopt some of your systems; unless, of course, he can prove that they are no good. Let me warn you, Larry, Reginald would love to prove that you are the resident Don Quixote, pursuing windmills on company time."

Having shared his frustrations, Joel then revealed his true agenda, or what Larry perceived to be his true agenda. His voice shaking, Joel told Larry that he was going to request a transfer into Larry's unit, and that he wanted his support.

Completely surprised by Joel's request, Larry said that he would think about their conversation, and get back to Joel within the week. Sensing that Joel's plight represented an opportunity, Larry wanted time to talk with Foresight. Foresight immediately perceived the opportunity.

"What you may not know, Larry, is that the vice-presidents are voting in two weeks about the disposition of the financial planning model. I've got an idea as to how we can capture the vote of Tyler Watch, the vice-president of the Video Division.

"In order to get Watch on our team, we have to show him how he will benefit. What he needs most are sales. Until now, he has relied heavily on Reginald's group to sell simulations with video components. If Reginald were to get the financial planning model, then he wouldn't have the time to sell as many simulations, would he? On the other hand, if we get the planning model, Reginald will have to sell harder than ever to maintain decent profitability levels. It is not in Watch's best interest for Reginald to get control of the model.

"You've taken a giant step in terms of getting Willit on our side.

The grapevine is carrying the news that your management systems are a reflection of pure genius. I'm still concerned, though. You see, Reginald has long enjoyed the role of Crown Prince. Willit is not pleased with him at the moment, but that may be temporary. To be on the safe side, we need Softner in our camp.

"Larry, I think I know how to curry favor with Softner. I understand that the Video Division is about to shoot a program on financial planning. I am going to suggest to the director of casting that you would be superb in the role of financial planner. You are conservative in manner and dress while, at the same time, being able to project your voice. The video folks are over budget already, and would love to avoid having to pay an outside actor.

"The real payoff for us does not lie in doing a favor for the video people, however. It lies in developing a relationship with Raymond Wilkes. Wilkes is scheduled to make a guest appearance on the video. Raymond is our chief operating officer's son's father-in-law. Get to Wilkes, and we'll get to Softner. Softner has tremendous respect for Wilkes. If you succeed in impressing Wilkes with your understanding of financial planning models, word will surely get back to Softner."

Hoping to render their strategy fail-safe, Larry suggested that there might be a way to undermine any attempt Reginald might make to gather votes. They decided to try to make use of the power Joel was able to wield with Reginald.

Appreciating that they would have to risk revealing their hand, they nonetheless viewed the potential gain as being worth the risk. Joel would be told that Larry and Foresight had gathered a lot of information that would embarrass Reginald and that they were prepared to use that information unless Reginald agreed to tell Willit that he thought the financial planning model belonged in the Business Systems Division.

At first, Joel resisted the idea. The thought of challenging Reginald and suggesting that he withdraw from the battle unnerved Joel. After all, Reginald was a fighter. He viewed organization life as a series of win-lose events, and he did not like losing. Larry tried a number of different approaches, first leaning on his expertise, and then trying to entice Joel with carrots, before reminding him of the rod.

"Joel, I have given a lot of thought to your predicament. I think I know a way out of it for you, and am willing to help if you will do something for me."

"Just name it, Larry."

"Tell Reginald that it is in his best interest, and in the best interest of the organization, to allow the Business Systems area to develop the commercial version of the financial planning model."

"I agree that it is in the organization's best interest, but I doubt I can convince Reginald that it is in *his* best interest to lose the model. Reginald thinks in terms of empires. The area that gets the model gets money, people, and visibility."

"It is in Reginald's best interest because the cost of not supporting Business Systems is the release of certain information that will both embarrass Reginald and damage his reputation within the firm."

"Saying something like that to Reginald is like waving a red flag in front of an angry bull. It's an invitation to battle. He's not going to surrender on the strength of simple innuendo, either. What kind of information do you have?"

Larry told Joel that he preferred not to go into detail about the information at his disposal.

"It sounds as though you don't trust me, Larry. I've already told you that I am ready and willing to shift my allegiance to you. Reginald is going to want to know what information you have."

"Tell him you don't know, but you have reason to believe it is both comprehensive and accurate, and that, if released, it would reflect negatively both on his abilities as a manager of people and on his judgment with regard to the investment of company funds."

Joel was silent for a few minutes, obviously visualizing a conversation of this nature with Reginald, and considering the impact.

"I can't do it, Larry. Reginald would think that I have already joined the enemy camp. I would lose all leverage over him before getting a commitment from you. That's too risky for me, Larry."

"No risk, no gain, Joel. Think of it another way. If we get control of the model, that increases our need for high calibre people such as yourself."

"But what if you don't get the model?"

"What you don't seem to understand, Joel, is that Reginald is not going to get the model. If you refuse to help us now, opting to remain in Reginald's camp, your reputation will suffer along with his. As his empire shrinks, so will your chances for becoming an influential member of the firm."

Joel finally agreed to attempt to convince Reginald that it was in his best interest to urge that the model be assigned to the Business Systems Division.

The outcome of Joel's conversation with Reginald was mixed. While Reginald did not surrender, neither did he announce his intention to engage in open battle. Sensitive to Willit's pro-Larry attitude, Reginald decided that he must at least appear to be cooperative. He would suffer the appearance of surrender in order to buy time in which to prepare his counterattack.

Reginald told Joel that he favored a compromise; Business Systems would control the development of the diagnostic and application segments of the product, while he would oversee the development of the simulation components. This would make it possible for him to stay sufficiently involved to enable him to spot an opportunity to once again tip the power scales in his favor.

Forewarned by Joel, Larry and Foresight developed a strategy to block the compromise. Their plan was to get Forbes, Larry's boss, to suggest to Willit that Softner, the chief operating officer, should be kept informed of the organizational innovations in Larry's unit that were drawing so much attention.

Once aware of the changes, Softner presumably would be open to the idea of having a cross-functional team operate as a profit center as it developed and marketed the commercial planning model. Larry had proven his ability to manage such a team, while Reginald had not. Further, assuming that Softner bought the idea, several of Reginald's simulation designers would be assigned to the unit. Reginald's defeat would be compounded by the loss of people.

Larry and Foresight spent a great deal of time together during the ensuing days, fine-tuning and modifying their strategy. Larry's debut performance as an actor went very well, as did his discussion with Softner's son's father-in-law.

Foresight was able to get to Tyler Watch, and felt that Tyler understood the benefits to the Video Division of assigning the development of the model to Business Systems.

Forbes agreed that Softner needed to be kept informed of the organizational innovations in Larry's area, and convinced Willit to brief Softner prior to the meeting on the disposition of the model.

Everything seemed to be going according to plan. They had not given sufficient consideration to Wendell Gladhand, the vice-president of administration, however. Nor had they anticipated that Larry's former boss, Peter Jenks, would present a problem.

Crediting himself with Larry's success, Jenks felt that Larry owed him at least the courtesy of a continued effort to maintain the friendship. In Jenks' perception, Larry had abandoned him once Larry knew Jenks could do Larry no further good. In short, Jenks felt used.

That, in itself, might have posed no problem. Unfortunately, Reginald had been kept fully informed by Joel, and knew that Larry and Foresight had failed to court Gladhand, the vice-president of administration. Further, he was aware of the friendship that existed between Jenks and Gladhand.

It was a simple matter for Reginald to get Jenks to convince Gladhand that Larry's rapid rise in the Business Systems area was bad for the trainee program.

"You're setting a precedent, Gladhand, an unfortunate precedent. Why the trainees today are an aggressive, overconfident, impatient, ambitious bunch. Larry was lucky; he was in the right place at the right time. But future trainees will learn about his promotion rate, and expect to be given the same opportunities. When you can't deliver, you'll be saddled with a group of demotivated, frustrated trainees. Your whole program could fall apart, Gladhand. If Larry is given the opportunity to manage the financial planning model project, the situation will just get worse. I suggest you argue that the assignment belongs in Reginald's area."

Their allegiances formed, the contestants entered the arena the day of the meeting. Conflict was inevitable. Softner, a man who had assiduously avoided conflict and political games throughout his career, grew increasingly uncomfortable as debate turned into accusation.

Gladhand fought hard for Reginald, making a convincing argument that a project of this size required tested managerial talent. Willit appeared to be ambivalent, arguing one moment for Business Systems, and the next for Reginald. Historic loyalty to his former crown prince clashed with the respect he had only recently developed for Forbes, and for Larry.

Tyler Watch expressed the belief that the project entailed far more than the ability to construct a simulation, and that it, therefore, would require more input from Business Systems personnel than from the organizations' experts in simulations. Lacking conviction, however, Watch did not argue forcibly.

Confused by the conflicting arguments, and uncomfortable with the adversarial relationships that had developed, Softner decided to favor neither Business Systems nor Simulations. Instead he announced he was going to form the new division of Special Projects. The as yet to be named vice-president of the division would be brought in from the outside. An outsider, Softner had reasoned, would be objective, not contaminated by the political allegiances that Softner found so disruptive.

Larry was appointed director of special project marketing in the newly formed Special Projects Division. Reginald, whose performance did not warrant a promotion, was to be offered the position of director of development. Foresight was to function as a consultant to the group.

Borrowing Larry's idea, Softner announced that the Special Projects Division would operate as a profit center, with the compensation of individuals to be based on the financial performance of the whole unit. Further, the continued existence of the division was to be dependent on the performance of the financial planning model. No other projects would be funded or even considered until the division had demonstrated its ability to design, produce, and market the model.

Larry and Foresight were ambivalent about Softner's decision. The idea of having to share the limelight with Reginald was disturbing, and detracted from their enthusiasm over the opportunity the new division would afford Larry. They were consoled only by the fact that they would now have an opportunity to work together, thereby lessening the likelihood that Reginald would be able to assume control of the project.

At no point did they anticipate Reginald's next move. Reginald turned down the job, and convinced Softner that Joel was the man for the position.

Larry was horrified by what he perceived to be a miscarriage of justice. Calling Foresight on the telephone, he said, "Joel doesn't know what he's doing. He lacks technical skills. He has been Reginald's lackey for so long that all he knows how to do is play games, vicious games. And to think that I had begun to trust him! He used us, George, and now we have to work with him. Why, I think I'd prefer to have to work with Reginald. He may be a snake in the grass, but at least he is consistent. Joel is nothing more than a wind sniffer, changing his allegiances depending on the direction in which the political winds are blowing."

Upset that he had once again been victimized by a corporate power play, Larry called Bill, suggesting that it was time for a talk.

They got together that evening and, as always, Larry began with a recitation of the events that had transpired since their last meeting. In spite of the fact that Larry now had a tremendous opportunity, he was not pleased with the outcome, and was very harsh on himself with regard to his inability to block the involvement of first Reginald and then Joel in the new division. Bill disagreed with Larry's assessment, concluding that Larry's strategies had been basically sound.

"To begin with, I do not share your perception that you failed to manage the power dynamics that have been occurring. On the contrary, I believe that you have done a superb job. I mean that, both with regard to your own work unit, and the organization as a whole. Let me start with a comment about the way you have been managing your people.

"You seem to have found the perfect balance between reliance on *expert* and *friendship* power, and are responding simultaneously to the needs of your people and the demands posed by the task.

"You avoided excessive reliance on formal clout, and you also made it impossible for others in the group to play win-lose games. *Involvement* became the norm, not the exception.

"Yet you did not abdicate your responsibilities. You structured the teams in such a way that your staff remained aware of schedule pressures. In effect, you took advantage of the benefits of involvement and minimized the potentially negative effects of schedule slippage due to lengthy problem solving discussions.

"I am most impressed, however, by the way you *networked* to get in a position to use the power of others indirectly. Your use of *indirect power* was superb.

"Using the power of Foresight's contacts (his network), you got yourself in a position to appear as an expert alongside of the chief operating officer's son's father-in-law. That was a stroke of genius. I know it was not your idea, but at least you had the sense to go along with it. As a result, you enhanced your own expert power base.

"I might add that the power of your *presence*, your image, undoubtedly made the episode a success. You continue to carry yourself well, to dress well, and to project enthusiasm. Those are all key elements of *presence power*."

"In effect, you did a very nice job of applying the *Public Relations Strategy* for building presence power. You projected an image of *competence* and *confidence*, using your physical posture, your eyes, your dress, and your tone of voice. By standing erect, dressing like an executive, making good eye contact, and making your speech interesting through a clever use of tone and silence, you let people know you were *there.* You became a definite presence. Yet, in doing so, you were not overbearing or obnoxious. You were, in effect, charismatic.

"You followed the advice of an impressive French duke who said, 'To succeed in the world, we do everything to appear successful.'

"But let us return to your use of the power of others, or of your *indirect power.* Another nice piece of work was using the power of friendship with the programmer who had moved to Reginald's area to gather information which could be used against Reginald. In effect, you used the power of another to stock your arsenal. While I am glad that you never had to use those weapons, I do begin to understand why you felt it necessary to be prepared for the worst.

"What most impresses me, however, is the way in which you used the existing hierarchy to gain visibility first with Willit, and then with Softner. You leveled with your boss, gaining his trust. Then you performed beautifully, creating a team of innovators who came up with the idea of core modules. That move alone enhanced your expert base. The performance was visible, your competence was obvious, and the potential benefits to the overall organization were clear.

"Equipped with a nice dose of *friendship* and *expert* power, you then used that power to get your boss to arrange a presentation of your concepts to the vice-president of the Software Division and, later, to the chief operating officer. To have them then use *their* position, reward and coercive power to direct Reginald to listen to you was masterful. You manipulated no one in the process, and yet you managed indirectly to use every kind of power base in the book.

"The one thing for which I would fault you was the fact that you ignored your boss' warning that Jenks was upset with you. By the way, I would be too, if I were Jenks. Once you and he got over your initial difficulties, he gave you every opportunity to show what you could do. Then you were promoted to his level. That, in itself, could have been threatening. But you compounded the problem. You ignored him, thereby destroying any trust and sense of friendship that had been developed. *The power of friendship erodes if efforts are not made to maintain it.*

"The other thing you did which caused you trouble also had to do with Jenks. You apparently dismissed him as a key actor because he was not on the vice-president level. You did not consider the fact that

THE FORMAL ORGANIZATION CHART DOES NOT ALWAYS DEPICT WHO
REALLY MAKES THINGS HAPPEN

*"I'm afraid you've come to the wrong man. I'm only the titular
head of this organization. The real chief is in an underground
bunker in Idaho with an unlisted phone."*

Drawing by Stan Hunt; © 1984
The New Yorker Magazine, Inc.

he could influence Gladhand's vote with regard to the disposition of
the planning model.

"Larry, it is important to remember that the formal organization
chart, the official hierarchy, does not always accurately depict who
does or who could make things happen in an organization. *You must
never lose sight of the informal organization chart; the patterns of influence
that are based on informal power, and on linkages between people.*

"Finally, you did allow Joel to manipulate you. Your trust in him,
and your consequent willingness to discuss your strategy with him,

was misplaced. I must say, though, that I suspect I would have done the same thing if I had been in your position.

"I would, however, give you a high score on your avoidance of the temptation to manipulate others. The last time we talked, you implied that you were going to try to outmanipulate Reginald. That could have been disastrous. You have put my fears at rest. You are turning into a fine student of organization power dynamics.

"But, lest you get overconfident, as you begin your new assignment, remember the words of Machiavelli, 'There is nothing more difficult to take in hand, more perilous to conduct, or more uncertain in its success, than to take the lead in the introduction of a new order of things.'"

Larry left Bill feeling a great deal better about himself, and the way he had managed both his people and others. The brevity of his notes indicated to Larry that, indeed, he had begun to master organizational power dynamics. It had taken almost four years. He felt ready to take the risk of introducing "a new order of things."

LARRY'S NOTES

- Balancing reliance on *friendship* and *expert power* leads to effectiveness regarding both people and task.

- *Presence power* helps build expert power; people listen, in part, because someone projects an image of competence and self-confidence.

- The *Public Relations Strategy* for building *presence power* is to
  (1) Put forth an image of competence and confidence by
     —Standing erect
     —Making good eye contact
     —Dressing the part
     —Making your voice interesting through effective use of tone, emphasis, silences, etc.
  (2) Let people know that you are in the room, without being overbearing or obnoxious.

- Trust or friendship power erodes if efforts are not made to sustain it.

- Never lose sight of the informal organization chart, the patterns of influence that are based on informal power and linkages between people.

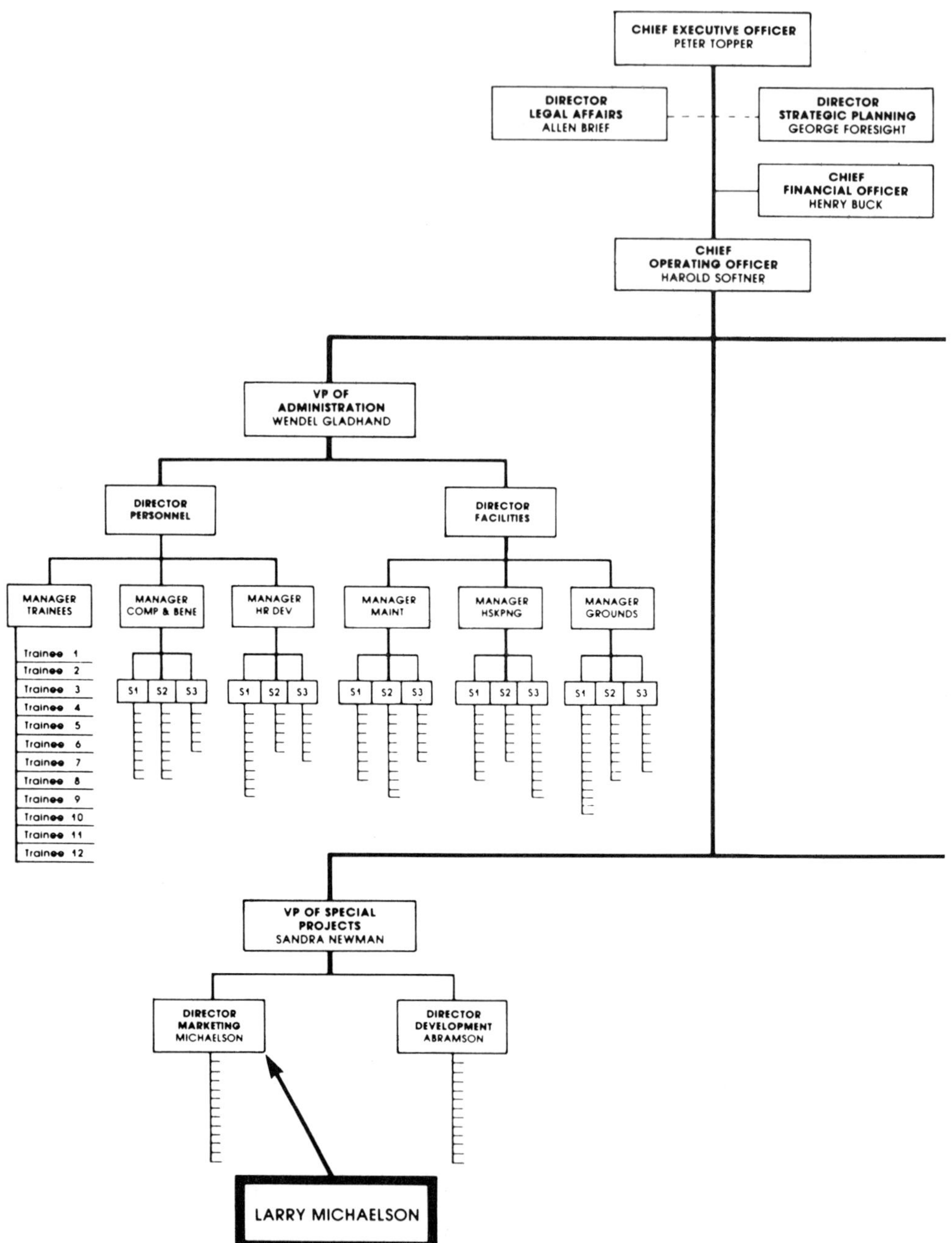
CHIEF EXECUTIVE OFFICER
PETER TOPPER
DIRECTOR
LEGAL AFFAIRS
ALLEN BRIEF
DIRECTOR
STRATEGIC PLANNING
GEORGE FORESIGHT
CHIEF
FINANCIAL OFFICER
HENRY BUCK
CHIEF
OPERATING OFFICER
HAROLD SOFTNER
VP OF
ADMINISTRATION
WENDEL GLADHAND
DIRECTOR
PERSONNEL
DIRECTOR
FACILITIES
MANAGER
TRAINEES
MANAGER
COMP & BENE
MANAGER
HR DEV
MANAGER
MAINT
MANAGER
HSKPNG
MANAGER
GROUNDS
Trainee 1
Trainee 2
Trainee 3
Trainee 4
Trainee 5
Trainee 6
Trainee 7
Trainee 8
Trainee 9
Trainee 10
Trainee 11
Trainee 12
S1 S2 S3
S1 S2 S3
S1 S2 S3
S1 S2 S3
S1 S2 S3
VP OF SPECIAL
PROJECTS
SANDRA NEWMAN
DIRECTOR
MARKETING
MICHAELSON
DIRECTOR
DEVELOPMENT
ABRAMSON
LARRY MICHAELSON

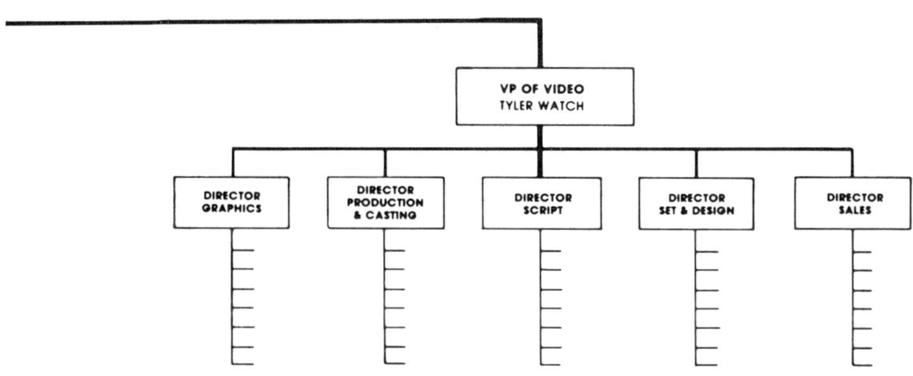
VP OF VIDEO
TYLER WATCH
DIRECTOR
GRAPHICS
DIRECTOR
PRODUCTION
& CASTING
DIRECTOR
SCRIPT
DIRECTOR
SET & DESIGN
DIRECTOR
SALES

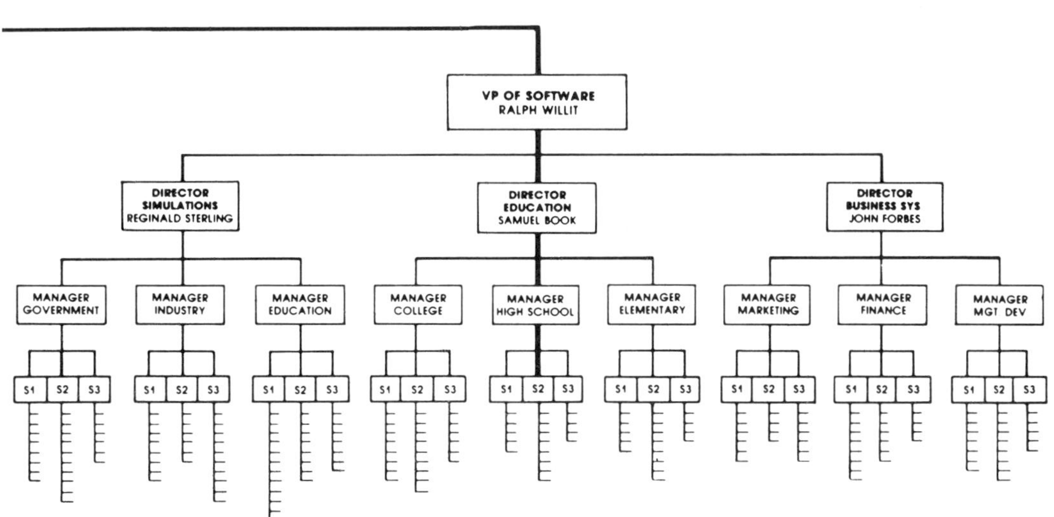
VP OF SOFTWARE
RALPH WILLIT
DIRECTOR
SIMULATIONS
REGINALD STERLING
DIRECTOR
EDUCATION
SAMUEL BOOK
DIRECTOR
BUSINESS SYS
JOHN FORBES
MANAGER
GOVERNMENT
MANAGER
INDUSTRY
MANAGER
EDUCATION
MANAGER
COLLEGE
MANAGER
HIGH SCHOOL
MANAGER
ELEMENTARY
MANAGER
MARKETING
MANAGER
FINANCE
MANAGER
MGT DEV
S1 S2 S3
S1 S2 S3
S1 S2 S3
S1 S2 S3
S1 S2 S3
S1 S2 S3
S1 S2 S3
S1 S2 S3
S1 S2 S3

7

Dares,
Deals,
and Debates

THREE WEEKS LATER, Larry entered his new office, and for the fourth time in his career, began hanging his favorite paintings, and rearranging the furniture to accommodate his work style. As he did so, he puzzled over the fact that the maintenance people insisted on placing desks so that they faced the wall.

He thought to himself, "It must be the technical orientation of this company. It is certainly not a marketing orientation, nor a management orientation. Why, if all our managers spent all their time looking at the wall, or at the desk, they would never understand either the market or the employees. Maybe that's what's wrong around here."

Larry's musings then turned to the way the organization used office space to denote status and title. With each promotion, the size of Larry's office had increased, as had the size of his desk, and of the ficus plant in the corner. "Symbols of power," thought Larry. "How silly it all seems. It's like a game, in many ways."

While Larry did not take the symbols of power very seriously, Joel did. Larry's thoughts were interrupted by the sound of activity in the next office. Getting up and walking out of his office, Larry went to greet Joel, hoping to establish at least a norm of cordiality between them.

Larry found Joel overseeing the efforts of several workmen. One was constructing a mahogany wall unit. Another was hanging a large gilt-edged mirror. A third had removed the dull beige drapes that hung throughout the division. Shutters that had the look and feel of mahogany were being installed in their place. Four lush potted plants were on the floor outside, awaiting placement in the plush office.

Larry was stunned and had to work hard to stop himself from making a derogatory comment. He knew, however, that it was important to begin to develop a better relationship with Joel. Unless they did so, the new effort would suffer. The first few weeks were going to be especially important.

Sandra Newman, the vice-president, was not scheduled to begin for another month. In the interim, Joel and Larry would have to function as a management team, resolving their conflicts, and arriving at decisions both could support. Personal friction would surely inhibit their mutual productivity.

Their first effort would clearly require cooperation, if not collaboration. They had to entice qualified people to leave their present positions to join the highly visible, and yet highly risky, Special Projects Division. The chief operating officer had suggested that they accomplish this task prior to the arrival of the new vice-president.

The job was not going to be easy. Larry knew that the other directors would be reluctant to lose their best people, and would use all the power at their disposal to retain them. Larry wanted to avoid getting in a position of having to buy talent. While the Special Projects Division was well funded, it was Larry's belief that the marketing budget was insufficient and that the funds needed to support the advertising effort would have to come from savings made in other areas, such as staff compensation.

Joel, however, disagreed with Larry's strategy, and favored holding out the financial carrot in order to recruit staff. For days, neither would budge. Then, Larry got an idea. He suggested that they engage in a kind of contest.

"Look, Joel, I know most of the programmers in the company, and those I don't know, I can reach through the people who worked with me on the artificial intelligence project. I'll make a deal with you. You need a total of eight programmers. If I can get four of our best to agree to work for you at their present salary levels, would you agree to work with me to contain the compensation budget and to invest the money we save in the marketing effort?"

Knowing that Larry's network was far more extensive than his own, Joel agreed to the terms of the contest. He expected that Larry would fail, however. Reginald would fight hard to keep his people, putting them all in golden handcuffs, if necessary, in order to keep his staff.

Larry had one week in which to use his informal power (the power of his friendships, his expertise), and the indirect power of his network, to get a commitment from four high quality programmers. The first individual Larry approached said that he would be happy to move *if* he could report to Larry, as opposed to Joel. His reluctance to report to Joel was understandable. Why should he transfer out of Reginald's unit in order to report to someone he viewed as Reginald's puppet?

The second programmer Larry approached refused on the basis of dollars. Larry had more success with the third programmer. At least this individual was interested enough to want to hear more about the proposed product line, and to request an interview with Joel.

Unfortunately, the interview did not go well. The programmer refused to further pursue the opportunity, claiming that he did not appreciate the high pressure tactics Joel had used during the interview.

As tactfully as he could, Larry expressed his concerns to Joel. Unwilling to admit that he had erred, Joel claimed that he had conducted a thorough interview, and had determined that the programmer was essentially unmanageable.

"He's loyal to his profession, not to this company. On top of that, he is very opinionated and arrogant. I got the distinct impression that he would refuse to follow any orders with which he was not in full agreement."

Larry tried to share with Joel all that he had learned about the management of creative people. "You can't play boss-man with them, Joel. It simply doesn't work. If you pull rank, relying on your position, or your formal power, you'll set up a climate that discourages creativity. We're going to need a real commitment from our people and we're not going to get it by using high pressure tactics."

But Joel seemed unwilling, or perhaps unable, to understand the importance of what Larry was saying. His years of operating in the shadow of Reginald had provided him with few managerial role models. He had not had the opportunity to supervise others directly.

Not knowing what else to do, Larry decided he was going to have to approach programmers who so craved a professional challenge that they would tolerate Joel's overly directive style. The obvious source was Jenks' department. His programmers had suffered through the loss of the artificial intelligence project, and then through the budget cut that was affected in order to launch the Special Projects Division. They were good people who had the misfortune of being in the wrong place at the wrong time.

Larry did not look forward to approaching Jenks' people. Jenks would undoubtedly perceive the action as an invasion of his turf. Nor did Larry believe that he could convince Jenks that the "raid" was in his best interest. All that Larry could hope to do was to clarify his motivation in approaching Jenks' people. At the same time, he hoped to better understand what he had done to so antagonize Jenks.

Jenks agreed to have lunch with Larry. Their conversation revealed that Bill had been correct in his assessment of the situation. Jenks did feel that Larry had used him to further his own ends. Larry's failure to maintain contact with Jenks had convinced the man that Larry placed little value on their friendship.

Larry's protestations that he did indeed care about Jenks did not seem to help. Nor did his expression of regret at having to go after Jenks' people.

Still hoping to salvage the relationship, Larry asked Jenks to suggest an approach they might take that would be supportive of both of their objectives. Jenks' response was direct, to the point, and without feeling.

"It appears that we are in a win-lose situation. If you succeed in taking my people, I lose. If you fail to entice them, then you lose. It's unfortunate, but that's the situation as I see it. I will, of course, try to block your efforts."

In the days that followed, Larry pitted his informal power against Jenks' formal authority. Jenks offered his key people raises in exchange for their continued loyalty, even though doing so required that he sacrifice less competent personnel in order to stay within his budget.

Larry, on the other hand, advised the candidates to seize the opportunity to work on the company's most exciting project. Reminding them of his proven ability to provide an exciting work environment, he promised that he would continue to take a personal interest in their professional growth. And he appealed to their interest in the organization as a whole, pointing out how much the Special Projects Division needed them.

Larry actively courted several of Jenks' people. Forewarned about the differences between Joel's style and Larry's, none of the recruits changed their mind as a result of the interview. By the end of the week, Larry had secured a commitment from three of the four programmers. He was certain he would have succeeded in meeting his full quota had Joel been more reasonable, and less dictatorial, during his interview with the first candidate.

Larry felt that he had lived up to the terms of their agreement, and that Joel should agree to let Larry's recruiting and compensation strategies prevail. Joel disagreed, claiming that Larry had actually delivered only three of the promised four programmers.

Both Larry and Joel were convinced that the other had lost the contest. Unable to agree on a winner, they once again found themselves embroiled in a conflict situation. They might have persisted in their deadlock had not a brief conversation with Bill resulted in a compromise.

Bill urged that Larry give in a little, asking Joel to do the same. Joel would give Larry three more days in which to attract two additional programmers. Further, Joel would promise to avoid the high pressure tactics that had characterized some of his earlier interviews. Only if Larry were successful in actually signing up two additional top quality people would Joel agree to use Larry's strategy as they staffed the rest of the division.

Joel agreed to the compromise, and the contest resumed. Knowing he had exhausted his own contacts, Larry approached Gladhand, the vice-president of administration. Gladhand was in charge of personnel development and would presumably have nothing to lose and everything to gain by helping Larry find the right people for the remaining openings.

Gladhand was not receptive, however. When he learned of Larry's agenda, he brusquely stated that Larry should talk with his director of personnel. Larry knew that Gladhand was taking the opportunity to remind him of his subordinate status, and to make it clear that he was not impressed either with Larry or with his recent promotion.

Reflecting on the reasons for Gladhand's hostility, Larry thought of several possible explanations. In setting up his "nonsupervisory" team to work on artificial intelligence, Larry had introduced an innovative peer review system. In doing so, he had departed from the company's standard performance appraisal system. Gladhand may have felt that his professional turf was threatened.

Later, Larry had refused to respond to Gladhand's request that he accept five trainees after their rotational period was over. Gladhand had told him that an overwhelming number of trainees had selected Larry's area as their unit of choice. A few had even indicated that they thought the *only* real opportunities lay in Larry's area. Unwilling to risk losing the investment the company had made in the extensive training program, Gladhand had appealed to Larry.

Larry had agreed to assume responsibility for three of the five trainees, but had flatly refused to expand his training effort to include all five. To do so would have required that he devote too much attention to training, and too little to production. As a result of his decision, one of the trainees decided to leave the company.

Larry had correctly identified two of the reasons for Gladhand's attitude and lack of support. What Larry did not appreciate was that Gladhand was threatened by his lack of control over Larry. Gladhand regarded the trainees as his personal property. Further, he prided himself on his ability to run a systematic operation that could turn out predictable people for predictable jobs.

From the beginning, Larry had refused to fit the mold. He had been overly confrontative as a trainee. As a supervisor, he had antagonized one of the company's most talented writers. Then, switching gears, he had become Mr. Nice Guy, courting favor with everyone in sight. His success had indicated to more recent trainees that it was "OK" to be different, to be a maverick, a deviant. That was the last thing that Gladhand wanted. To Gladhand, Larry was at best an irritant, and at worst, a threat to Gladhand's credibility.

In spite of repeated calls, Gladhand refused to respond directly to Larry's requests for assistance. Instead, he continued to refer him to the director of personnel. Finally, Larry had no choice but to seek the assistance of this individual. Perceiving that the director of personnel was a capable, but slow-moving and indecisive person, Larry had little hope that the required assistance would come in time.

His perceptions were confirmed when the director said that it would take several weeks to identify and talk with suitable candidates. Thus, Larry was thrown back on his own, forced to tap a network that was nearly exhausted. In spite of strenuous effort, Larry was not able to find the two additional programmers in the three days allotted to him.

Larry had lost the contest. He had also lost precious time. To date, he had done nothing to recruit his own marketing staff, focused as he had been on staffing the programming side of the house.

Larry knew that it was going to be difficult to find qualified marketing people within the organization. Because technological expertise had historically been emphasized over marketing skills, few real market experts had been hired. Larry hoped to find people with the natural ability to understand the marketplace, reasoning that specific techniques could be introduced through training.

Moving in his typical sluggish fashion, the director of personnel took a week to provide Larry with the names of six individuals whom he considered to be suitable candidates.

Larry hired three of the candidates the director of personnel recommended. In spite of their lack of marketing experience, Larry hoped that their involvement in the work of the division would enhance both their knowledge of and commitment to the product.

Having done a thorough search within the organization for qualified people, Larry was now free to ask the director of personnel to look outside for the required talent. Knowing that Gladhand liked to oversee personally the hiring of professionals from the outside, Larry was at least assured that he would get an audience with the vice-president of administration.

Gladhand's cordial greeting did not disguise the hostility that he felt toward Larry. Attempting to get the relationship on a better footing, Larry reminded Gladhand that they shared the same goal: to place the right people in the right jobs in a timely fashion.

While accepting that as his objective, Gladhand insisted that Larry's request had a lower priority than several of his other projects. Larry began to realize that Gladhand was using the power of his position to block Larry's recruiting efforts. And organizational policy gave him the right to do so. Directors were precluded from hiring from the outside without the consent of the Personnel Department. Larry knew he would never get such a consent.

As a last attempt to get Gladhand to move quickly on his request, Larry suggested a trade. Larry planned to introduce several innovative personnel practices in his area. After sharing his plans with

Gladhand, he expressed his willingness to avail himself of the services of the presumed "experts" in the Personnel Department to develop the practices and procedures. The credibility of Gladhand and his staff would be enhanced as these organizational innovations became known.

He implied that he would involve Personnel only if Gladhand agreed to treat Larry's request as a top priority item. Remembering the attention Larry received when he introduced the "nonsupervisory work team," Gladhand finally agreed, promising to have at least ten candidates lined up for interviews by the end of the week.

Gladhand lived up to his end of the deal, bringing very qualified candidates to Larry's attention. The staffing process was thus completed several days before the new vice-president assumed the reins of the division.

Larry sought to use the time remaining to get Joel to agree that their primary strategy during the early days of the actual launch was to involve the new recruits in the decision-making process, thereby gaining their commitment to the work of the Division as a whole. It was Larry's belief that everyone, regardless of his or her eventual role in the operation, should have a voice in establishing the environment or culture that would predominate in the division.

Larry's desire to get Joel to agree to ignore hierarchy and position during the launch period was intensified by the promise he had made to several of Joel's programmers to act as mentor and protector regardless of formal reporting relationships. Further, he hoped to avoid conflicts that would stem from establishing two separate cultures, with the team approach prevailing in marketing, and hierarchy prevailing in the product development area.

Joel agreed to the collaborative, participative approach to startup after Larry reminded him that their compensation as individuals was going to be dependent on the performance of the division as a whole, and that, therefore, working relationships would have to exist between people in each of their areas.

Due to personal problems, the new vice-president, Sandra Newman, delayed her official start date. By the time she actually arrived, Larry and Joel had held a number of divisional team meetings, as well as functional team meetings. Roles had been clarified; relationship expectations between the functions had been defined. A spirit of collaboration and of mutual respect prevailed between the marketing and systems personnel. While the scars of previous battles remained, Joel and Larry clashed less often and when they did, they were able to resolve their conflicts more quickly.

Even Gladhand, the vice-president of administration, was happy. Several of his human resource specialists had been involved in the design and implementation of the team development sessions. They had contributed, and they had learned.

Convinced that they had created the foundation for a highly workable operation, neither Larry nor Joel looked forward to having their decisions scrutinized, and possibly reversed, by the new vice-president. They knew little about the incumbent, except that she was female, and had successfully headed the software evaluation department of a major computer hardware manufacturer. Her responsibilities had provided her with an in-depth familiarity with the software industry overall, and with the qualities that differentiated superior from inferior products.

Fortunately, Sandra Newman was both analytically astute and competent as a manager. She was a firm believer in the importance of challenging employees to perform to the limits of their potential. To do so, she advocated the creation of an open work environment characterized by freedom to experiment and freedom to fail. Rather than punishing people for mistakes, she urged that they learn from them.

She was capable of being firm when necessary. Her commanding voice, coupled with a tall stature and pleasing appearance, demanded attention. Confident of her ability to handle events and to master new subjects quickly, she was decisive and assertive. Yet she succeeded in being consistently feminine. Experiencing no conflict between her role as a woman and her role as a professional, she was able to make others comfortable even as she exercised formal power over them. As Larry and Joel were to discover, Sandra Newman was among the most competent of the organization's managers.

Within an hour of her arrival at the office, Sandra requested a meeting, first with Larry, and then with Joel. Her agenda in both cases was to be briefed regarding both present status and future plans.

Larry handled the meeting well, providing Sandra not only with a status update, but also with an historical perspective. Larry believed it was important that Sandra understand the origins and political positioning of the division. Sandra found Larry to be a clear thinker and a persuasive communicator. Her intuition told her that

Larry's desire to be helpful to her was genuine, not a manipulative attempt to curry favor.

Larry did not mention the difficulties he had had with Joel. While he was tempted to reveal Joel's faults, he resisted, believing that to do so would only make them both appear less competent. "After all," he thought, "if someone is able to function at the director level, he ought to at least be able to resolve his own conflicts with his peers."

Joel pursued an entirely different strategy during his meeting with Sandra. He attempted to make himself look good by making Larry look bad. He sought to be a winner by portraying Larry as a loser. In the process, he diminished his own credibility and gave Sandra the impression that he, and not Larry, was the manipulator, the political game-player.

Sandra was sufficiently impressed with their progress to date, however, to give both Joel and Larry considerable freedom in the management of the startup phase of the project. She believed that the time they had devoted to team development was well worth the effort. Larry's market analysis plan appeared to be comprehensive.

While Joel did not seem to have a good grasp of systems, he had managed to build a strong team. As long as Joel was willing to rely on the expertise of his subordinates, Sandra did not anticipate a problem. She decided to keep a close watch on that, however, given Joel's apparent tendency to seek to win at the expense of others.

It was with a feeling that the future was his for the asking that Larry anticipated beginning his study of the potential market for financial planning products. After four years, Larry was doing what he most loved to do, and he embraced the opportunity with vigor. The pains of recruiting and project launch were about to give way to the excitement of startup.

Larry decided that it was an appropriate time to step back and reflect, and to get Bill's reaction to the strategies he had been pursuing. As always, Bill listened with interest. Believing that his strategies had been highly effective, Larry felt no need to be humble or modest as he described his accomplishments.

"In managing to get promoted to the position of director of an exciting and highly visible area, I simultaneously stocked the *Candy Store*, the *Arsenal*, and became the *Crown Prince*.

"Because of my new role, I now have the ability to hand out very challenging assignments and potentially handsome bonuses. I also have the ability to kick people off a winning team, which constitutes a pretty effective form of *coercive power*.

"As for *position power,* well, I've never had it so good. I am heading a new function that is closely watched because the organization has invested heavily in us. That gives me a right to access a lot more information and to succeed, potentially, in a high visibility area."

Bill, however, did not agree with Larry's high rating on the application of the crown prince strategy. He cautioned Larry about the limitations he perceived to exist with regard to his position power.

"Larry, you are a director of marketing in an organization which has never had a director of marketing. If I'm not mistaken, you have managers of marketing and marketing supervisors, but, until your appointment, no directors. And, it sounds as though the other marketing units are really sales units, not dedicated to marketing in the true sense of the term."

"Right. They are really order taking units. But what does that have to do with position power?"

"Because the role of director of marketing is new, people's expectations about what constitutes effective performance are fuzzy. While you won't be constrained by a rigid set of expectations, neither will you enjoy the power that would be associated with your title in an organization which had a better understanding of and respect for marketing."

After a moment of reflection, Larry began to understand Bill's point. He seemed unconcerned, however, confident that he would be able to impress the organization with the importance of marketing. He continued with his self-assessment.

"Well, if I say so myself, I used every opportunity to apply the *Fraternity Strategy.* It worked with my new staff members. We are clear about our shared goals. And everyone seems to feel a strong affinity for one another. I think the feeling of closeness is intensified by the perception that we are a special and highly visible group within the organization.

"The Fraternity Strategy is even beginning to work with Gladhand, the vice-president of administration. At least he has begun to perceive that my organizational experiments are in his best interest. I think that my *involvement* of his people really increased the trust levels between us.

"I guess I didn't do well regarding the Fraternity Strategy given my failure to maintain Jenks' trust. I should have worked harder to maintain contact with the guy.

"I would, however, say that I did a good job implementing the *Look-What-I've-Done Strategy* for increasing expert power. In saying this, I am thinking particularly of my new boss, Sandra Newman. She seemed impressed with my ability to organize a department, to motivate people, and with my market study plan. I would say that I have already gained her respect."

While Bill could not disagree with Larry's assessment of his relationship with Sandra, he argued that Larry's expert power base was probably not as solid as he had implied.

"You have entered a new ball game, Larry. You know that you have expertise in the marketing area, but you have yet to convince others of that. *You are only an expert if others perceive you as an expert.* I would suggest that you have work to do in that area in the months to come. Expertise in one area, such as finance, does not always generalize to other areas, such as marketing.

"I do, however, compliment you for the way you have used the power bases available to you.

"You have been relying very heavily on a combination of friendship and expert power during the staffing and launch phases of the division. I believe that was highly appropriate. You have now inspired commitment to both you as a leader and to the work of the division. People joined you because they believe in you and what you are trying to do, not because you held out a bigger carrot than the others. That will lead to productivity later, for, as Bernard Baruch said, 'The highest and best form of efficiency is the spontaneous cooperation of a free people.'

"However, I think you should pay more attention to building *presence power.* That is my subtle way of suggesting that you need a haircut, Larry."

"So noted, Bill. I need to make more use of the *networking strategy* for building *indirect power, too.* Most of my attention has been focused on my department. I haven't devoted much energy to getting out and meeting people."

Bill, however, did not agree, perceiving that Larry had managed to build a significant amount of *indirect leverage.*

"You did enhance your ability to exercise indirect formal power over Joel. You put a couple of programmers who both like and respect you into Joel's area. Those programmers appear to be key to Joel's ability to develop the financial planning package. All they have to do is to threaten to resign at an inopportune moment, and Joel will have to comply with their wishes.

"Given their expectation that the department will be run according to your style and standards, it is likely that they will use their power to help you persuade Joel to do things your way. You have infiltrated Joel's unit with your supporters, Larry. I know that was not your primary objective, but it was a beautiful strategy nonetheless."

Larry confessed that he had not thought of the ramifications as he placed people within Joel's unit.

"Obviously, Joel did not think of it that way either, or he surely would not have agreed to my recruiting strategy. Joel seems to view every situation in win-lose terms. I guess he learned that from Reginald.

"Well, it is an unfortunate lesson to learn. People who need to get one-up, to prove that they are better than others, tend to be people who undervalue their own worth and are therefore more concerned with how they compare to others than the extent to which they are living up to their own values and realizing their own potential. These people are to be pitied, Larry. Life for them tends to be a never-ending contest; a contest they do not enjoy and cannot win.

"Joel's attitude is likely to continue to be a source of frustration to you, Larry. You are hoping to establish a supportive, innovative climate within the division. A person who plays win-lose games is not likely to encourage such a climate. Such people view power as a finite quantity; to empower someone else is to deprive themselves in some way. When such persons become managers, they tend to impede rather than promote the development of their subordinates. They fear that, as the subordinate becomes more competent, they will lose their competitive edge. If Joel really views power in this way, then you better be prepared for a lot of conflict in the future.

"What I am saying is that you had better be prepared to use all of the types of power at your disposal. Further, I think it is important that we talk about the options available to you as you actually attempt to influence others."

Taking a pad from his breast pocket, Bill drew two axes....

As he did so, he said, "Every time we attempt to influence another, we make two kinds of decisions (consciously or unconsciously). One of the decisions we make is whether to rely on *formal power* (the power to reward, to coerce, or the power of position), or on an *informal power* base (friendship, expertise, presence). As we make

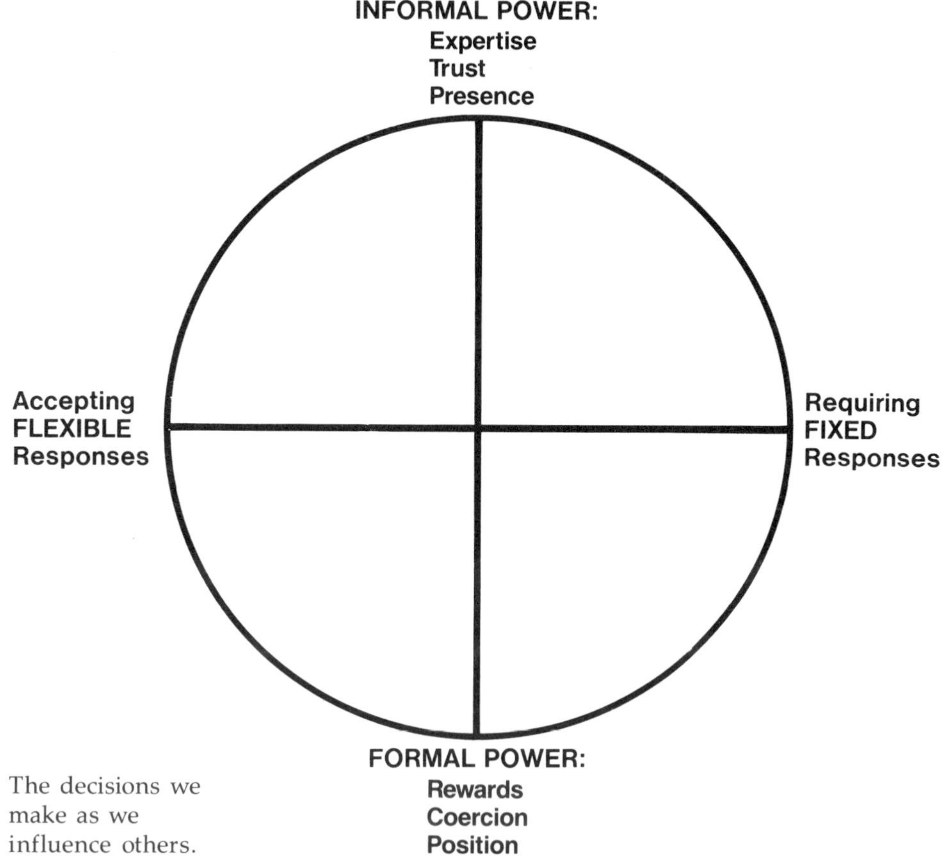

The decisions we make as we influence others.

this decision, we also determine whether to use our own power, or the power of another indirectly.

"The second decision we make is whether we will require a fixed response from our target of influence, or whether we will accept a flexible response. To accept a flexible response is to be open to a range of possible outcomes, or of means to approaching a situation. The second axis can be regarded as fixed versus flexible, or as predetermined versus open. The outcome of the decisions we make in both areas can be described as one of four influence styles.

"To involve someone is to rely on informal power while accepting a flexible response or outcome.

"The strategy becomes clearer when we talk about the tactics that can be used with this approach. *The first tactic is* **sharing,** *or pooling resources, exchanging ideas, to find a solution or an approach that is mutually acceptable.* That is the true problem-solving process.

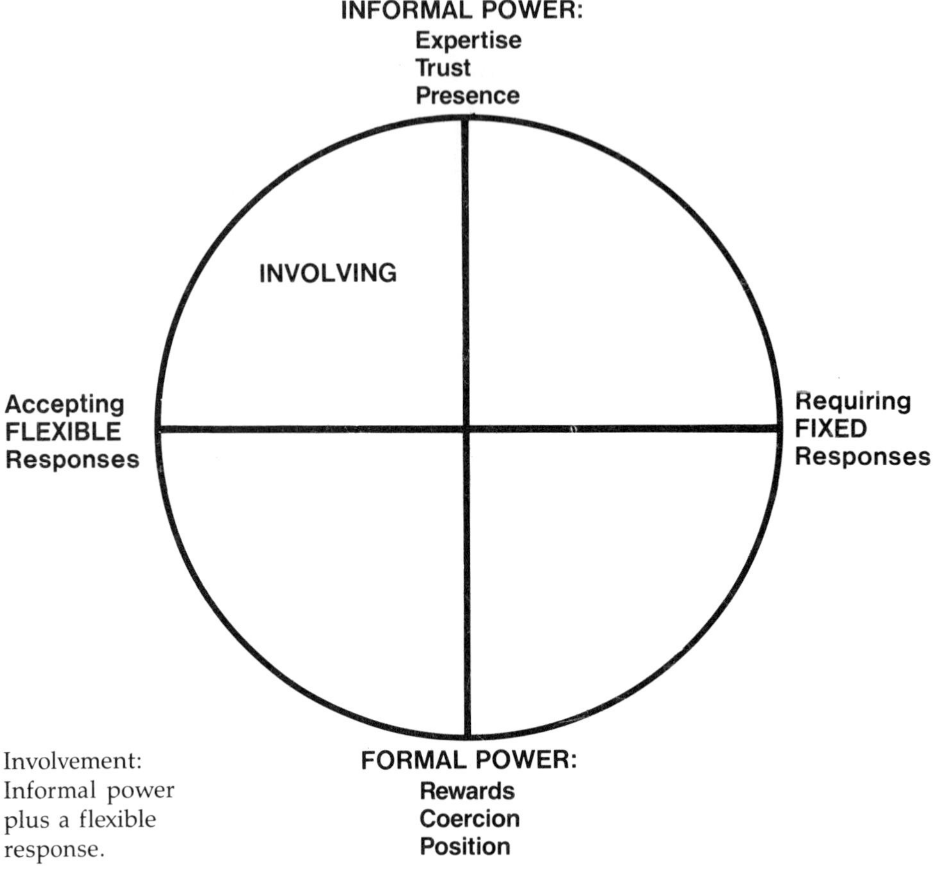

Involvement:
Informal power
plus a flexible
response.

"You did a nice job of using the *sharing* tactic during your team development sessions.

"The second involvement tactic is **enabling,** *or influencing another by offering resources, such as information, contacts, emotional support, and then leaving it to the other to decide what to do with the resources you have provided.* By changing the other's perception or resource base, you influence the outcome to some degree.

"The third involvement tactic is **cooperating.** *It is possible to exert influence over a situation by supporting or accepting the suggestions of others.* In effect, your continued presence affects outcomes. The tactic is subtle, and may amount to little more than keeping your foot in the door while you develop a more impactful strategy, or build a more significant power base.

"From what you have told me, I would guess that you relied heavily on the *enabling* and *cooperating* tactics during your first meeting with Sandra. You *enabled* her to understand the status of the department, thereby influencing her perception. And you *cooperated* with her request for information, thereby affecting her perception of you.

"A second influence option is **enlistment.** *To enlist is to seek a fixed or predetermined response while relying on informal power.*

"You used the enlistment strategy when you recruited your programmers and marketing people. In effect, you were using all three tactics of the enlistment strategy.

"You **solicited** *some on the basis of need.* 'The company needs your help in this area.' People responded to the solicitation because they respected you and your expertise.

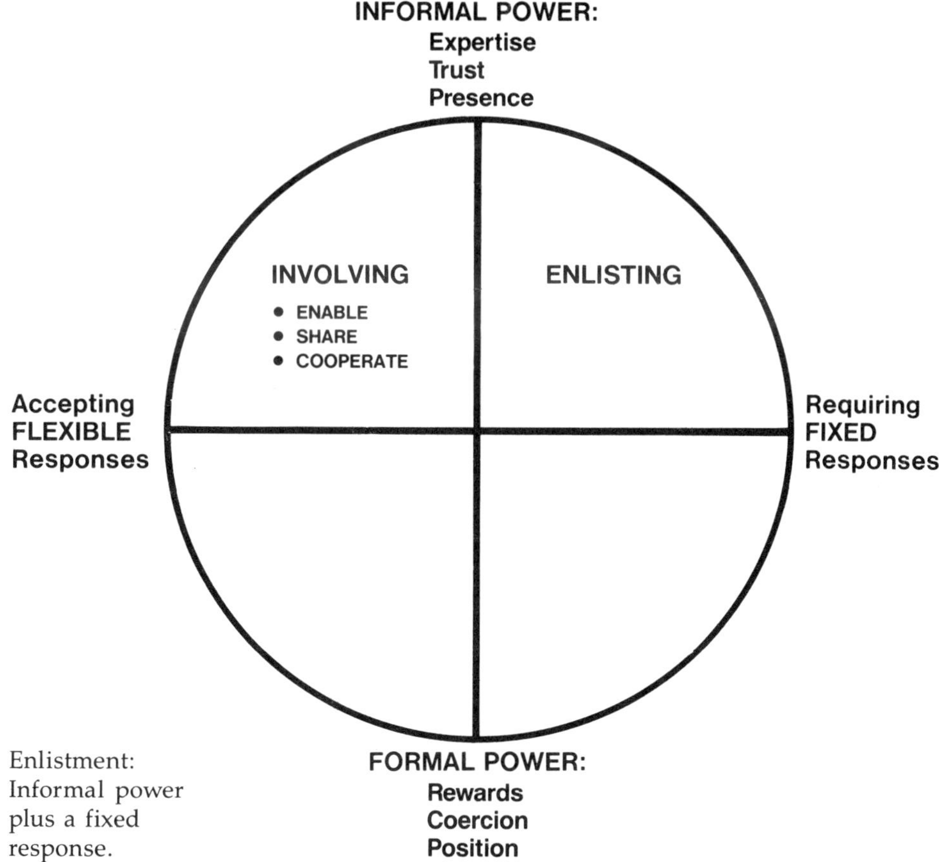

Enlistment:
Informal power
plus a fixed
response.

"With others, you used the tactic of **advising,** or using information to persuade. *'Do as I ask because I have given you good and sufficient reason.'* The power base that underlies this tactic is expert power.

"And, you used the **courting** tactic, which is asking for support on the basis of friendship. *'Do as I ask because you like me, or care about me, and want to see me reach my objective.'*"

"If I understand you," Larry said, "I used enlistment, or more particularly the advising tactic, when I convinced Joel to go along with the team development sessions. I used information, and the strength of my experience, coupled with a reminder that we were dependent on each other for our compensation, to convince him to do things my way during the pre-launch days."

"That's exactly what you did, and since you lacked a formal power base over Joel, and needed his acquiescence to proceed, your choice of both strategy and tactic was excellent."

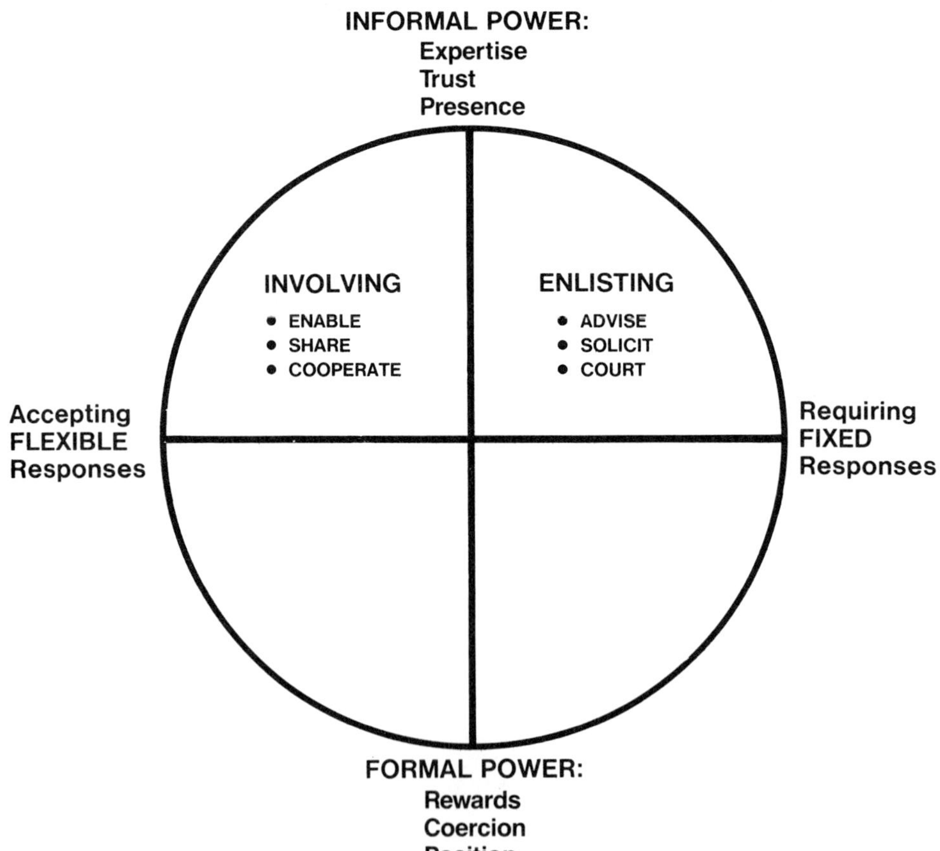

"I tried to use the same strategy with Gladhand, and got nowhere at all. I needed a specific response; namely, that he find me a certain number of qualified candidates by a given date. None of the enlistment tactics worked. He was immune to courtship; unwilling to listen to advice; and even reluctant to admit that my cause was worthwhile. Was I ever uncomfortable in that meeting. I exposed everything, and got nowhere."

"Yes, that is one of the disadvantages of enlistment. You do make yourself vulnerable in the process. I would suggest, however, that the strategy was worth trying. I mean, you didn't know that Gladhand did not perceive of you as either friend or expert. What I'm suggesting is that the strategy didn't work because you lacked informal power with Gladhand. That is precisely why you had to resort to your formal power base, and to become more flexible with regard to your demands. In effect, when enlistment didn't work, you tried the *negotiation* strategy.

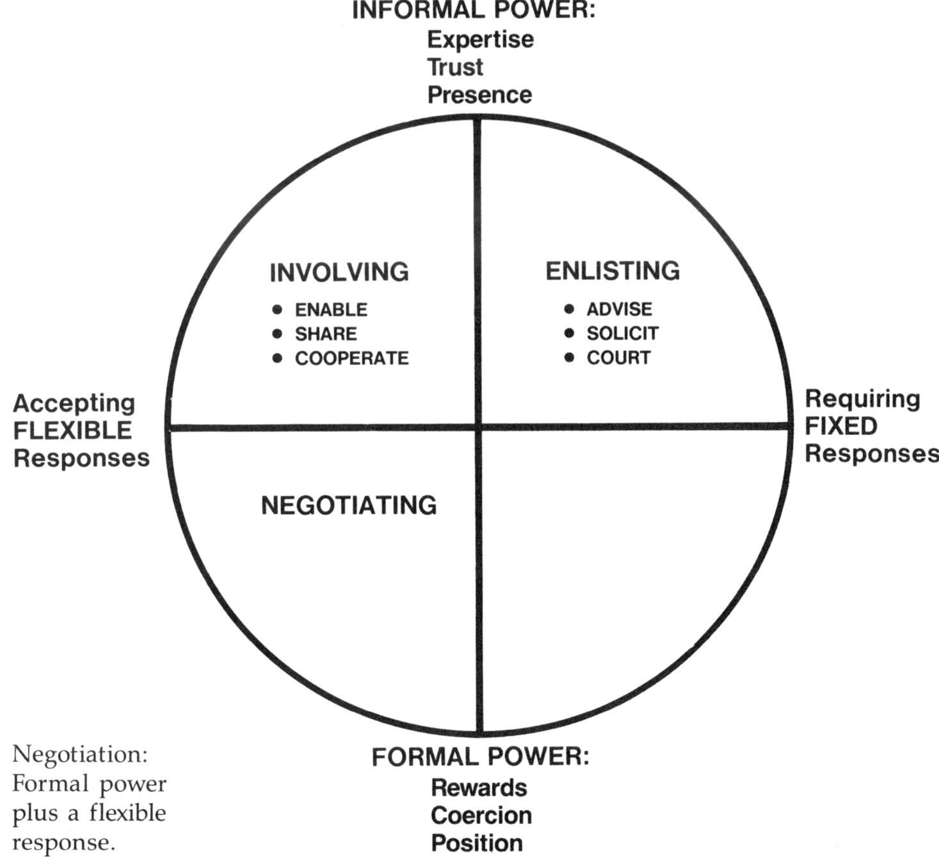

Negotiation: Formal power plus a flexible response.

"*To* **negotiate** *is to rely on formal power. Of necessity, negotiation requires the acceptance of a range of possible responses from another.* When we enter a negotiation, we are uncertain as to how much we will have to give, or give up, in exchange for what we want. To negotiate is to say, 'If you'll do this, I'll do that'; or, 'I'll give a little if you'll give a little.'

"A negotiation can assume any one of three forms. The most satisfying is the **trade.** *As a tactic, the trade represents a win for both parties to the negotiation. There is an exchange of rewards between two empowered parties.*

"You effectively used the trade tactic with Gladhand. You rewarded him with professional visibility in exchange for his willingness to find candidates for you. You both won. As a result, you may have an opportunity in the future to involve Gladhand, or even to enlist his aid. That assumes, of course, that you live up to your end of the bargain."

"I have already begun doing so, Bill. But your point is important. I had not considered that by living up to my end of the bargain, I am at least proving to Gladhand that I am reliable. I guess reliability is an important part of the trust-building process."

"Yes, and this illustrates an important point about power strategies in general. *The most productive influence strategies are those which allow you to enhance your power base even as you are using an existing source of leverage.* When a salesman convinces a prospect to buy, he hopes to simultaneously negotiate a deal, and build the kind of relationship that will insure future sales. But we are getting off the track.

"There are two other tactics that negotiators often use. One is the **compromise.** *When you compromise, you give in to get closer. Since both parties must give up a little, we can say that the compromise represents a lose-lose.* I recommend it only when you accept a loss in the short-term in order to enhance the likelihood of a longer term gain.

"The third negotiation tactic is the **contest.** *The contest is a win-lose tactic.* In essence you are saying to the other, 'There's only one way to resolve this—if I win, you'll do it my way; if you win, I'll do it your way.' It is a useful conflict resolution device.

"You made good use of the contest tactic when you resolved the conflict with Joel over whether you would offer high salaries in order to attract people to the division. Joel wanted to take this route, and you did not. In effect, you said, 'If I can entice a certain number of programmers without offering high salaries, then you will agree to not only implement my strategy, but to allocate the money we save to marketing.'

"As you learned the hard way, *the contest tactic creates more problems than it solves if the rules of the game are not made completely clear to all contestants.*

"You and Joel ended up arguing over whether or not you had 'won' because you had not clarified in advance that he was not to discourage candidates during the interview process.

"The last influence option is **direction.** *To direct someone is to demand a fixed response, and to back up that demand with formal power.* Direction was once a favorite strategy of yours, Larry. That, in effect, was what you were doing when you insisted that your staff follow certain procedures and that they tolerate a very complex system of merits and demerits.

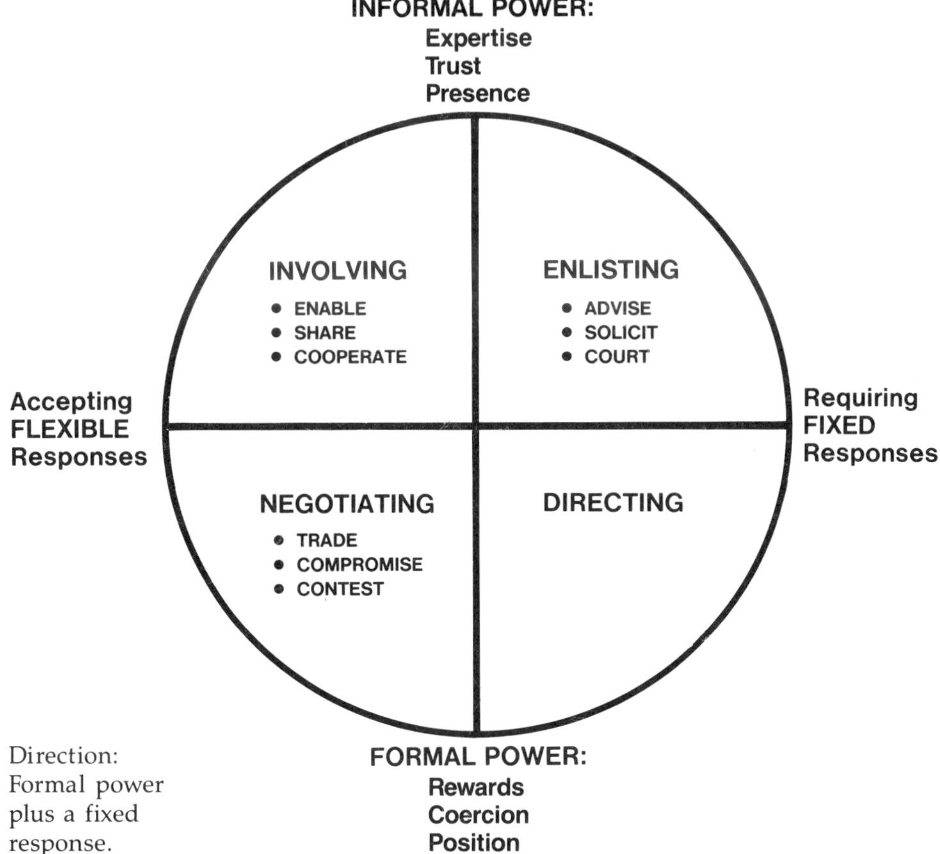

Direction:
Formal power
plus a fixed
response.

"As you did so, you used all of the directive tactics: **ordering, forcing,** and **blocking.** *To order is to give instructions without options,* stating, 'Do as I say because I have the "right" due to my position to tell you what to do.' *To* **force** *is to make demands while discouraging refusal.* The message is 'Do as I say if you want to avoid injury, or because you want to acquire a reward.' *To* **block** *is to prevent others from taking action due to their desire to get something of value or to avoid punishment.*

"Gladhand used his position power to temporarily block your recruiting efforts. Jenks would have done the same thing if he had had the power; as it was, you had the right, or the position power, to 'raid' his people. That, by the way, appears to be the only instance when you used the directive strategy.

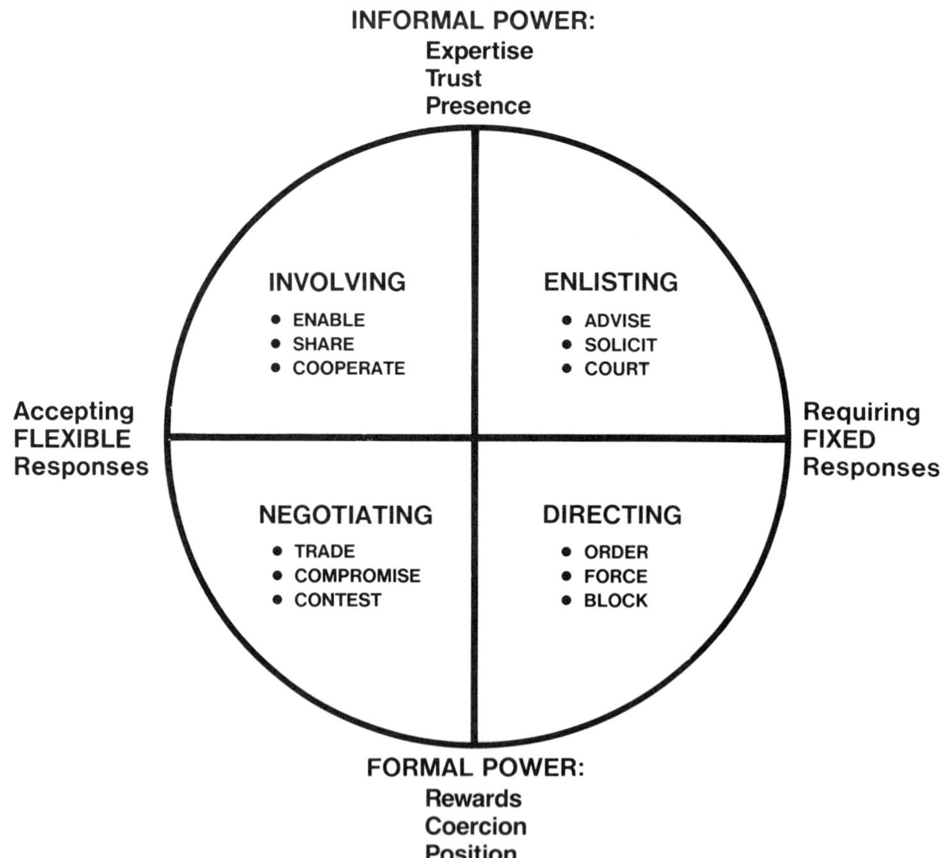

"You forced Jenks to allow you to attempt to persuade members of his staff to join you. Because the organization conferred on you the right to do so, there was little Jenks could do to stop you. Given the essentially adversarial nature of the situation, that is probably the only strategy you could have pursued.

"What particularly pleases me, Larry, is that you have already displayed a great deal of flexibility in terms of your use of the various influence options. You relied heavily on enlistment to recruit your staff. Then, you began using involvement as you brought all the members of the division together for joint problem-solving sessions. These sessions ended with the development of contracts as to who would do what with and to whom. This process required heavy reliance on negotiation as a means of allocating resources.

"You haven't yet used direction with your present staff, but I suspect that you will and you should as the tasks within the division become more routinized, and as the need for more predictable outcomes increases.

"Your continued effectiveness in the future will be dependent on the extent to which you continue to be aware of the influence style options available to you, and of the situations that render one strategy more effective than another. *Flexibility is the key to the effective management of power.* There is no substitute for judgment. As Otto von Bismark said, 'Politics is not an exact science.' Neither are organizational power dynamics; there is no single best way, but only a best way given the situation. That is what makes flexibility and judgment so essential."

Their dinner was over, and Bill left. Larry chose to remain a little while longer, to complete his notes on the night's discussion.

LARRY'S NOTES

Expectations regarding a new role (e.g., director of marketing) are fuzzy; this can minimize position power.

Expert power does not generalize from one area to another (i.e., need to prove expertise in marketing area).

People who view life in win-lose terms perceive of power as finite. Life for them is a perpetual contest; they are always trying to prove they are better than others.

Influence Strategies

<u>Involvement</u>: flexible response; informal power

Tactics: *Sharing*..pooling resources; exchanging ideas
   Enabling...offering resources (e.g. information, emotional support)
   Cooperating....supporting or accepting suggestions of others.

<u>Enlistment</u>: fixed response; informal power

Tactics: *Soliciting*....pointing out need or worthwhile cause
   Courting....relying on friendship and charm
   Advising...using information to influence

<u>Negotiation</u>: flexible outcome; reliance on formal power

Tactics: *Trade*...win-win; exchange of rewards, favors
   Compromise...lose-lose; both give in; sometimes helps to achieve a longer-term gain
   Contest....If I win, we'll do it my way; win-lose; make sure the rules of the game are clear

<u>Direction</u>: fixed response; reliance on formal power

Tactics: *Force*...with threat of coercion or promise of reward
   Order...given the right to do so because of role
   Block....with threat of coercion or promise of reward

Most productive influence strategies allow you to use power and enhance your power base simultaneously (e.g., sales example).

Flexibility is the key to the effective management of power.

8

Shifting Loyalties and Corporate Scapegoats

DURING THE NEXT several months, Larry and his staff devoted ten hours a day to analyzing the market, identifying market segments, and defining the discrete financial planning needs of each of those segments. They conducted surveys, ran discussion groups, attended conventions, and visited the offices of potential buyers. A clear picture began to emerge, a picture that forced the challenging of prior assumptions.

Without exception, all of the persons who had been involved in the decision to create a commercial version of the existing financial planning model had assumed that large corporations were the most viable market. The logic seemed to defy argument. It was the large corporations, after all, who paid billions of dollars to strategic consultants and other financial advisors to tell them how to allocate their resources and adjust their product or investment portfolio in order to maximize their profit and return on investment. Such organizations, it was assumed, would leap at the opportunity to buy a software system costing under ten thousand dollars which would render the consultants and other outside advisors obsolete. Sheer economics would provide the incentive to purchase the product.

Larry had shared these assumptions and, as a result, had initially restricted his market study to large corporations which were known users of consultants. Many executives denied having any interest in the product. Others did express interest, but claimed that they would not view the product as a replacement for the consultants. The assumption that the primary product benefit was cost savings appeared to be invalid.

Larry also encountered a reluctance on the part of the executives he interviewed to explain their reaction to the product. The answers that he got when he asked why they would be hesitant to fire the consultants were frustrating in their simplicity. "We've gotten used to having them around." "The chief executive gets lonely; he can talk to the consultant." "Machines will never replace people."

Corporate strategic planners and financial personnel appeared to be more interested in the product than were their line management counterparts. However, they, too, were evasive when asked to explain their interest in the product. "We're always interested in new toys." "We need to keep buying the latest software in order to justify our investment in hardware." "It would be nice to have all of the formulas in one place." "Our people get bored if they don't periodically get a new program to master."

Puzzled, Larry called Bill, who suggested that their evasiveness stemmed from the power dynamics that were involved. The presence of the consultants affected the balance of power within the corporation. To render the consultants obsolete would significantly shift the balance of power.

The consultants served a purpose that went far beyond their ability to analyze the competition, or the product portfolio, or the investment strategy. Because they were not actually part of the organizations they served, they were not subject to the constraints of the formal hierarchy. It was, therefore, possible for them to say and do things that persons within the system would have perceived as excessively risky. The consultants, who could afford to be objective, were often able to fight for a strategic shift that would never have been implemented given existing power plays designed to protect individual empires and executive turf.

At the same time, internal staff personnel often experienced the consultant as a threat. Strategic planners resented the fact that the consultants were able to command the attention of the chief executive officer. Persons in finance feared that the investment advisors would challenge their investment decisions, thereby diminishing their credibility and expert power within the company. Perceiving of the financial planning model as a way to get rid of the unwelcome outsider, staff personnel reacted favorably to the idea.

The large corporate market began to look increasingly less interesting to Larry. Turning his attention to other areas, he found there was a significant degree of interest among owners of small businesses who needed the tools, and could not afford the consultants.

A chance meeting with an old friend from college who had gone into the insurance business led Larry to speculate as to the need on the part of agents for a personal financial planning model to use with their clients. Subsequent interviews and surveys confirmed the hypothesis that such a need existed. It began to appear that the market for a personal financial planner was greater than the market for the large corporate model.

The implications were enormous. The product would have to be redesigned in order to meet the needs of market segments other than large corporations. Given the price sensitivity of the newly defined markets, the pricing strategy would have to be re-evaluated. A significantly different sales strategy would be required to penetrate the retail as opposed to the corporate market.

The entire division would have to modify its approach. Even the business plan that had been used to attract investment in the division was no longer accurate. Larry faced a double challenge. Not only did he have to influence the market to buy; first, he had to influence the decision-makers within the corporation to shift strategy.

Sandra Newman would have to be convinced. Larry did not anticipate a problem in this area. After all, she had not been part of the original decision-making process, and had no vested interest in protecting the current strategy.

Joel would present more of a problem. Much of the work that had already been accomplished would have to be discarded. Development schedules would slip. Joel would inevitably fear that such slippage would cost him some of his precious status points. Even if he privately agreed with Larry's conclusions, he would never admit that publicly. To do so would be to support someone whom Joel continued to regard as a competitor.

Even Foresight would fight Larry's conclusions. As the originator of the planning model, Foresight had a strong desire to see his "baby" become the leading product of the corporation. So many modifications would be required to satisfy the newly defined market segments, that the "baby" would begin to lose its identity.

Buck, the chief financial officer, would inevitably vote against approving the additional funds required to redesign the product. He had never been supportive of the project, and Larry strongly doubted that he would change his position as a result of this study, or any study.

Softner, the chief operating officer, was likely to keep an open mind. He seemed to like Sandra Newman, and would probably allow her to pursue her chosen course unless doing so put her in direct conflict with the other vice-presidents.

Gladhand, the vice-president of administration, was not likely to be concerned about the shift in direction; unless, of course, he still harbored resentment toward Larry and wanted to use this as an opportunity to make his life difficult.

Watch, the vice-president of the Video Division, would not be affected, and could be counted on to remain neutral.

Willit, the vice-president of the Software Division, could present a problem. After all, the Systems Division competed with the Special Projects Division for resources. Approval of a shift in direction on the part of the Special Projects area would probably trigger the mandate for a budget cut in the Systems area.

Larry decided that first he had to attempt to get Sandra Newman on his side. In planning the approach he would take with her, Larry realized that only two of the four influence options were available to him. He had no formal power over Sandra; nor did he perceive a need to dilute his informal power by attempting to stock his arsenal or his candy store. Convinced that he should rely on the power of trust and expertise, Larry's only question was whether to enlist her support for a predetermined solution, or simply to present the data he had gathered, and work with her to identify next steps.

Feeling the pressure of time and believing that he had already defined the best approach to take, Larry decided to rely on the enlistment strategy. His flow of logic would be so tight, and the presentation of his data so convincing, that the tactic of advising would work. Or so Larry had concluded by the time he was scheduled to meet with Sandra.

Armed with charts, tables of figures, and quotations from potential buyers, Larry presented to Sandra for a full hour and a half. As he spoke, his enthusiasm mounted. Sandra never interrupted to ask a question. Nor did Larry invite questions. He closed with a strong statement that the market they had intended to pursue was not viable, and that the product needed to be redesigned to accommodate the retail and small business markets.

Only then did Larry pause, allowing Sandra to comment.

"You and your team have done a superb job, both with regard to the analysis, and the presentation. I understand how and why you reached the conclusions that you did. And I agree there is probably a market for both the personal financial planner and the small business model.

"I do not agree that the corporate market is as bleak as you portray. My experience has clearly indicated otherwise. While the Fortune 500 or even the Fortune 1000 may be a difficult market to penetrate, I believe there are opportunities within the Fortune 5000 corporations. In fact, until you present me with evidence to the contrary, we will continue with the existing product development plan."

Knowing that Sandra did not expect her subordinates to act as "yes men," Larry continued to argue. However, Sandra remained convinced that their present product strategy was viable, and was unwilling to change her position in the absence of further information.

Discouraged, Larry realized that he had no choice but to devote significant time and energy to the analysis of opportunities that might exist within the Fortune 5000. It disturbed Larry a great deal to see the division devote yet more time and money to a product that was questionable in terms of its ability to satisfy a market need.

Three months later, Larry again scheduled a presentation with Sandra. This time, he was able to rebut her arguments in favor of pursuing the Fortune 5000 market. Sandra finally agreed to reconsider.

Believing Sandra would now fight for a shift in direction, Larry went directly to work on devising the marketing strategy for the two new products. He relied on Sandra to approach Softner and Buck for additional dollars, and to inform Joel that he was going to have to make significant modifications in product design.

Larry knew that Sandra was going to run into resistance. He did not appreciate that she was not sufficiently committed to his strategy to persist in the face of such resistance.

Sandra approached Joel first. Rather than mandate a change in design, she involved Joel, asking for his opinion regarding the proposed change. Joel reacted negatively and, with the help of Reginald Sterling, put together a countervailing argument.

Sandra then took both Larry's argument and Joel's counterargument to Softner, the chief operating officer. Rather than making a strong statement in favor of the shift, she asked Softner to render an opinion that would help her resolve the doubt in her own mind.

Softner was not a man who enjoyed challenging the status quo. Routine and predictability made him comfortable. Schedule changes threatened to disturb the peace of mind that he so valued. It was only because he respected Larry's judgment that he was willing to entertain the notion of a change in strategy.

Softner suggested that Larry present his case to the vice-presidents and all directors who would be affected by the ultimate decision. All would have an opportunity to support or to challenge Larry's point of view.

While Larry was delighted to have the opportunity to speak for himself, he regretted that he did not have much time to gather allies in advance of the vote.

Larry began with his old friend, Foresight. While Larry had mentioned some of his findings early in the research process, Foresight had not been aware that Larry had actually recommended a product modification. It was unfortunate that Reginald Sterling had been the one to alert Foresight to Larry's plan.

"I ran into Reginald in the hall. Taking me aside, he told me that, and I quote, 'Your good buddy Larry is preparing to stab you in the back, my friend. If he has his way, your model will never see the light of day. He's using a lot of trumped-up research and questionable data to attempt to prove that the product won't sell. If I were you, I'd be pretty angry.'"

Larry laughed, assuming that Foresight had dismissed Reginald's comments as nothing more than a feeble attempt to introduce a wedge between the two collaborators. But Foresight was not laughing; he was not even smiling.

"I do not think that you are trying to stab me in the back, as Reginald suggests. On the other hand, I am disappointed in you. It crossed my mind that maybe you don't think your sales staff can handle the big corporate market. Perhaps you are hedging your bet, or covering your ass, and at my expense."

"You know me better than that, George. At least I thought that you did. I have never run away from a challenge. I am not afraid that my sales staff would be unable to handle the professional market. I don't even have all of my salespeople on board. Those who are on board have the sophistication to handle even the most arrogant of professionals or executives. My ability or inability to sell the model has nothing to do with it. I could sell it. I am simply saying that I have discovered a better market; a market that is untapped, and has a much greater potential than the original market."

"Marketing is not a science, Larry. All you really have are hypotheses and biases. I can't buy it, Larry. I don't even need to see your figures to say that. The figures can be misleading. Your sample might not have been representative. The interviewers may have influenced the response simply by the tone they used when they asked a question. You can't convince me, at least at this late date, that you gave the model a fair chance. I will not agree to support you at the meeting. I'm sorry, Larry, but I am still an avid believer in what I thought was *our* project."

Given Sandra's ambivalence, and Foresight's refusal to even consider Larry's point of view, Larry realized that he was not going to be able to rely on "friends in court." On the contrary, it appeared that the deck was going to remain stacked against him. His only allies would be the facts he could gather. Larry thus decided to focus his energies and those of his staff members on creating a comprehensive business plan which would conclusively prove that the organizational bottom line would benefit significantly more from a shift in strategy than from retention of the present strategy.

Larry needed design and production figures from Joel. Getting them, however, required that Larry deny his true agenda, claiming that he needed the information in order to finalize the pricing strategy for the current product. Through carefully phrased questions, Larry was able to get Joel to provide him with the information that he needed.

Larry was then able to create a business plan that indicated that the products he proposed could be out the door and on the market within nine months. The organization would recover its initial investment within eighteen months. By the end of two years, the company would be showing a handsome profit. The financial forecast was significantly more favorable than that which had been generated for the large corporate model.

Larry then began to think about the tone that he wanted to project at the meeting. Hoping to both stimulate enthusiasm, and suppress arguments, Larry decided to adopt a testimonial strategy. It was his intent to invite to the meeting potential users of the personal product and the small business product.

Larry's enthusiasm diminished somewhat when he ran into difficulty convincing credible prospects to put in an appearance at the meeting. Still eager to pursue his testimonial strategy, Larry decided to pay honorariums to prospects for participating in a group discussion of the kind of product that would meet their financial planning needs. A videotape of the discussion would, Larry hoped, stimulate Softner and the others to maintain an open mind.

The outcome of the meeting was a compromise. The group was not willing to turn its back on its investment in the large corporate model. Given the strength of Larry's presentation, however, the group was unable to ignore the opportunities represented by the personal planner. The consensus of the group was to restrict the scope of the original product, eliminating the competitive analysis modules. The resources that were freed would be devoted to the development of the personal financial planner. Development of the small business version was to be delayed.

The decision presented Larry with a number of problems. His marketing strategy would now have to be twofold. The strategy planner was a complex, high-priced product, aimed at the corporate market. The personal planner was priced to attract the owner of a personal computer. Pricing, distribution, sales and advertising strategies had to be different, and yet Larry felt a consistent corporate theme had to be projected throughout the marketing process.

Further, Larry believed that it was important that a consistent theme be projected by *all* of the divisions in the corporation. Accepting the fact that he was going well beyond his formal job description, Larry established as his objective the promotion of a consistent, corporate-wide marketing strategy. He intended to promote the adoption of a common corporate theme and logo. And he intended to do whatever was necessary to get the organization's employees to concern themselves more with the impact of their actions on the customer.

Larry's work plan for the coming year was ambitious. Meeting his objectives required that Joel do his part, staying on schedule and quickly producing demonstration software. For once, Larry was glad that Joel had a tendency to be directive, and to insist that his people file frequent progress reports. Schedule slippage and missed deadlines would undermine the company's image.

Appreciating that marketing could sell only what the development area produced, Larry began to keep a closer watch on Joel's operation. He was very disturbed by what he saw. Joel was having tremendous problems with his programming staff. The better programmers had become so involved with the corporate planner that they did not want to devote time and energy to the personal planner. Still believing that the corporate planner was the more important of the products, Joel had capitulated, assigning the most junior people to the personal program.

In an attempt to compensate for the staffing inequity between the two products, Joel pushed the junior people very hard. Rather than present them with a professional challenge to motivate extraordinary effort, he relied on threats of dismissal.

Frustrated and defeated, one of the programmers resigned. Another threatened to seek a transfer out of the Special Projects Division. Panicking, Joel reversed his earlier decision, and ordered one of the senior programmers to work on the personal planner. The programmer refused. Joel got angry. The programmer responded by giving notice that his resignation would take effect in one month.

Given his intent to leave, the senior programmer had minimal interest in the personal planner. The more junior technicians mirrored his disinterest, and the productivity of the unit as a whole continued to slip. Larry's repeated requests for demonstration software were ignored.

Larry decided that it was time to intervene. He invited the senior programmer to dinner, intending to find out exactly what was going on in Joel's unit. The programmer's comments indicated that technological problems existed, as well as personnel and motivational problems.

"Joel refuses to let us do anything innovative. The end product will be both tedious and difficult for the user to run. To make matters worse, it is likely to be full of bugs. Joel is so budget conscious that he has canceled a number of tests that need to be conducted. I can't allow my name to be associated with a product like that.

"Joel is over his head, Larry. Rather than admit that he should rely on my expertise, or on that of his other systems people, he runs to Reginald. Reginald has encouraged Joel to stand by his decisions, both with regard to the program and the testing cutback."

Hoping to buy a little time, Larry urged the programmer to remain with the company for at least another three months. In exchange for his commitment, Larry promised that, in the event he was unable to get Joel to modify both his managerial and technological approach, he would help the programmer find another position. The programmer agreed to the proposition.

The conversation left Larry with an uneasy feeling in the pit of his stomach, the kind of feeling that he had learned to view as a signal that a power play was in progress. He could not understand why Reginald was encouraging Joel to pursue a strategy that would eventually destroy Joel's credibility. He finally decided that the only explanation was that Reginald wanted to see the Special Projects Division fail.

It all made sense. The Special Projects Division was highly visible; it had become the center of executive attention. Reginald was losing his role as the crown prince. The one certain way of maintaining his claim to the throne was to depose of any other contenders. It appeared that he was willing to attempt to do so even at the cost of sacrificing Joel, his protégé.

The one piece of the puzzle that did not seem to fit was Sandra Newman's failure to insist on the implementation of a thorough testing program. After all, her background was in software evaluation. She, of all people, would understand the importance of making sure that products were free of problems when they hit the marketplace.

Larry speculated that perhaps Sandra was unaware of the testing cutback and possibly of Joel's failure to meet the interim deadlines they had established. She had appeared to be extremely preoccupied during the last several months. The rumor mill carried the news that she and her husband had separated, and that Sandra's personal life was creating a great deal of stress for her as a result.

Larry decided to attempt to solve the problem by dealing with Joel directly. He believed he could use the power of what he knew to force compliance. Joel would not want Sandra to become aware of either the programmer's intent to quit, or of the technological short-cuts that were being taken.

Believing that he had a clearcut case, Larry approached Joel. The meeting did not go as Larry had hoped. He had underestimated the strength of Joel's convictions, and overestimated his own ability to provoke fear. Five hours after they began their discussion, they were no closer to an agreement.

In response to Larry's claim that he couldn't sell if the product was not developed on schedule, Joel countered with the accusation that Larry's people were making false promises to customers.

"The product is going to be a lot simpler, less complex, than we originally anticipated. Yet your salespeople are out there convincing our potential customers that the product will represent the full range of stragetic planning processes. It is simply not true. I will not be held responsible for the siege of customer complaints that will bombard us when we finally fill those orders."

"Joel, we are already behind schedule. You promised me a demonstration disk six weeks ago! If you were so concerned about our reputation in the marketplace, then you would be making a greater effort to maintain production schedules. And you would certainly not eliminate essential steps in the testing process!"

"Larry, the only way I can even come close to meeting those deadlines is by simplifying the product and eliminating some of the tests. Of course, I could request additional resources. Since getting more resources is not a realistic option, I have elected to simplify the product and cut back on testing. I have told you that repeatedly, and yet you fail to modify your sales strategy."

"And I have told you repeatedly that your approach will put us in the position of offering a substandard product. I *know* what the marketplace wants, Joel, and unless we are prepared to respond to that need, we might as well forget this entire effort."

Joel was not convinced. For every argument that Larry offered, Joel had a counterargument.

"Larry, you are not the only expert in marketing around here. I happen to believe that the window for introduction of a product such as ours is very small. If we don't act, and act fast, then the opportunity will be lost. It is more important to get something on the market, than to wait and build a more complex model. You are concerned about schedule slippage. Well, so am I. I am pushing my systems people as hard as I can. They are difficult to manage, and have a questionable level of commitment to this organization."

Larry took this opportunity to inform Joel that his senior programmer was so frustrated that he was looking for another job. In spite of Joel's efforts to hide his concern, Larry could tell that he had finally gotten Joel's attention.

"If I were you, Joel, I would not want to see him leave. His resignation will not only make it impossible for you to meet your production schedule, it will also make Sandra and others question your managerial ability."

"To lose a good man is one thing; to lose a marginal performer is quite another. I thank you for warning me, Larry. Pete is due for his annual performance review. I will make sure that the official record shows that he is not performing. While that may not help in terms of our production schedule, it will protect my reputation as a manager. You have been very helpful, Larry, though I do not believe that was your intent."

Larry's strategy had backfired. Instead of compliance on Joel's part, Larry had managed to escalate the conflict, and potentially to jeopardize the career of a fine programmer. Discouraged and frustrated, Larry played his last card.

"Look, Joel, there is no reason to take out our differences on one of our employees. We both know that Pete is capable of doing a fine job if he is properly motivated. His lack of motivation stems from your decision to cut corners with regard to the testing process, and your refusal to allow your programmers to innovate. I am certain that Sandra Newman would not approve. If you won't voluntarily reverse those decisions, then I will have no choice but to talk with her."

Joel listened to Larry's ultimatum with a smile on his face. Eventually, he revealed the reason behind his apparent complacency.

"I have sent Sandra a memo every time I made a change in either the product development plan or in the testing procedures. In no case has she objected. Her silence indicated consent, as far as I am concerned. I don't know whether she actually agrees with me, or whether she has simply been too busy to pay attention. She is not going to second guess my decisions now, not at this late date. To do so would only make her look ridiculous."

"So," Larry thought to himself, "Joel has covered all of the bases. At least he thinks he has. What he probably doesn't realize is that his buddy, Reginald, is setting him up to fail. I am now sure of this. Joel's strategy has all the markings of a Reginald Sterling manipulation."

Joel, however, was unwilling or perhaps unable to even entertain the notion that his mentor and guide would lead him astray. Given Joel's unwillingness to even reconsider, Larry felt he had no choice but to bring the conflict and his concerns to Sandra's attention.

The opportunity for him to do so occurred a few days later. Sandra was scheduled to speak at a software convention, and asked Larry to accompany her. The company had taken a booth at the convention and, while the financial planning models would not be featured, there would be opportunities to talk with prospective customers.

Larry was not eager to attend the convention, knowing that it was the least important of the dozen or so software shows that would be held that year. He expressed his reservations to Sandra, but she would not permit him to refuse. She offered no argument, other than the simple statement, "I want you there."

Sandra and Larry had never had a conversation about either of their private lives. Thus, it seemed odd to Larry that, shortly after boarding the plane, Sandra began asking him about his private life. Larry tried to still his uneasy feeling by telling himself that Sandra was simply attempting to be friendly.

He answered her questions as briefly as possible, revealing little about the woman he had been seeing. Only later would Larry realize that his terseness had misled Sandra, allowing her to believe that he was free of any emotional commitment to another.

Before the plane had landed, Sandra had revealed a great deal about her life. She had told him of her impending divorce, and of her fear of being alone in a strange city. He did not correct her when she said as they disembarked, "So you see, Larry, we have a lot in common; two attractive, single professionals seeking to make life all that it can be."

Alone in his room, Larry thought about the conversation. By the time his bag was unpacked, he had decided that his feeling of uneasiness was irrational; that Sandra had simply needed someone in whom to confide.

Sandra said nothing more of a personal nature until dinner the next night. They had been engaged in a conversation about the relative merits and demerits of the conference when Sandra suddenly changed the subject, and asked Larry his age. When Larry responded that he was almost thirty, Sandra smiled, and looked coyly at him. Her next question almost caused Larry to drop his fork.

"Larry, are you aware that there is a trend toward older women–younger men couples? I mean, research has indicated that an older woman can bring a perspective to the relationship that is often missing in same-age relationships. The whole thing makes a lot of sense from a sociological point of view; after all, women do live longer than men."

Larry correctly heard Sandra's words as an invitation. Not knowing how to handle the situation, he attempted to pursue the intellectual discussion, feigning ignorance of her intent.

"Yes, I think it is a good thing to base relationships on true feelings, and compatibility, regardless of age. Age roles should not be allowed to limit a person's opportunities. Nor should sex roles restrict a person in business. Why, one of the best things our organization ever did was to open their executive ranks to you. Speaking of the company, there are a few things that I need to discuss with you."

But Sandra was not going to be put off quite so easily. Claiming mental fatigue, she suggested that they postpone discussion of business agendas until the next day. Then she asked Larry to take a walk with her.

Larry saw no way to refuse. Nor did he object when she took his arm as they walked. His discomfort mounting, he sought refuge in silence. He needed time; time to understand this sudden change in Sandra's behavior, and time to figure out how to respond. He felt that he was on very dangerous ground, although he was not sure why. After all, Sandra was simply flattering him.

They had been walking for about half an hour when Sandra claimed that her feet were tired, and suggested that they sit for a while. Again, Larry saw no way to do anything other than comply. When Sandra shifted her position in order to sit directly next to him, Larry again pretended not to notice. Only when Sandra put her hand on his knee did Larry respond. Standing up, he said that he had some calls to make, and wanted to return to the hotel.

Larry set the pace on the walk back, moving quickly and swinging his arms in an attempt to dissuade further physical contact. When they reached Sandra's room, Larry feigned a casual smile, and said "Goodnight." Before she could respond, he had turned and walked away.

Larry got very little sleep that night. He was disturbed by Sandra's open display of emotion, and by her lack of interest in and enthusiasm for the business.

But what worried Larry the most was the fear that Sandra would regret her actions, and respond by becoming overly formal. While he did not want her to persist in her advances, he also did not want to see barriers erected between them.

By morning, he had decided that the best strategy was to avoid all reference to the evening before, and to behave as though nothing out of the ordinary had occurred. He hoped that Sandra would perceive of his strategy as an opportunity to save face, allowing them to resume the comfortable professional relationship they had enjoyed.

But Sandra did not avail herself of the opportunity, continuing instead to behave in a coquettish manner. Whenever she caught his eye, she nodded or winked, indicating that she felt that they had established a special bond. He noticed that she took every opportunity to make physical contact, putting her hand on his shoulder, or intentionally brushing his sleeve.

Unwilling to risk a repeat of the evening before, Larry decided that he was going to have to say something to discourage Sandra. His silence and passive acceptance of her gestures simply allowed her to continue in a way that would eventually be a source of embarrassment for both of them.

Larry asked Sandra to take a walk with him before dinner. Even as he did so, he knew that his invitation would be misunderstood. But he could think of no other way.

He came straight to the point. "Sandra, I am flattered by your interest in me. But I am not interested. There is already a woman in my life. It's not that you are unattractive. You are an extremely attractive woman. But I guess you could say that I am taken. Even if I weren't, I think it would be foolish of me to get involved with my boss."

Sandra turned away from Larry, and began staring at the sidewalk. Her silence was more than Larry could endure. Wanting, needing, to know her reaction, Larry asked what she was feeling.

Sandra did not respond immediately. When she did, her speech was halting. "I feel very foolish, so foolish that I cannot bring myself to look directly at you. I pride myself on being a strong, independent, and successful woman, and yet I have been behaving like a little girl. I guess I just need to be loved right now, or at least to be told that I am lovable."

Sandra walked a few steps away from Larry before she stopped, turned, and said abruptly, "Larry, I would like to forget that all of this happened. I will never speak of it again, and ask that you do the same. I promise that you will never again have an opportunity to see me as anything other than confident and competent. All of this never occurred. Do you hear me? It never occurred!"

With that, Sandra walked quickly back to the hotel, leaving Larry standing where he was. The episode had shaken him. Through no fault of his own, his relationship with his superior had been compromised, weakened.

Sandra did not appear in the dining room that night. Nor did Larry see her later that evening. When he did see her in the exhibit area the next morning, she was focused entirely on business. All traces of softness and of vulnerability were gone. Her facial muscles were taut. Even her walk had changed. As she traversed the exhibit hall floor, she marched rather than walked.

Larry chose to leave her alone, and to postpone addressing the issues of testing and product development until they had returned to the office. What Larry did not appreciate was that Sandra's newfound determination would translate into a closer attention to the details of both his and Joel's operation. While the process would be uncomfortable, the outcome was to be beneficial.

The development of the retail package was taken away from Joel. Pete, the frustrated senior programmer, was put in charge of its development. The product development schedule was modified to allow the programmers time to implement their ideas. Thorough testing was mandated.

Larry was criticized for what Sandra regarded as a tendency to make premature promises to potential customers. She insisted that Larry reformulate his marketing plan, and submit it for review before taking any further action.

Both Joel and Larry were told in no uncertain terms that further conflict would not be tolerated. Larry's efforts to defend himself fell on deaf ears. Sandra held both men equally responsible for their inability to agree.

Feeling like a chastised child, Larry's only solace lay in the fact that the fracas had resulted in the retention of the senior programmer, the shrinking of Joel's empire, and the reintroduction of a thorough testing program. Given renewed confidence that the division would ultimately produce a high quality product, and hoping to mend the relationship with Sandra through a display of expertise, Larry approached his new marketing plan with vigor.

Exposure to other vendors at the convention had confirmed Larry's belief that the company needed to project a consistent image across product lines. Software Systems, Inc. needed to be synonymous with quality in the customer's mind. The company needed an identity, an identity that would be promoted by every member of the organization.

Larry devoted evenings and weekends to his search for the right slogan. Eventually, he settled upon the motto, "The Computer Company that Cares."

Larry's intent was to project an image of caring, and of expertise, or professionalism. His sales force would be trained in the art of building both the power of trust and expertise. As much attention would be devoted to training in interpersonal relationships as to training in financial and strategic planning. Divisional sales personnel would behave as both knowledgeable advisors and trusted friends.

His plan went beyond the confines of his division. Projection of a consistent company image required, in Larry's opinion, that the same behavioral standards apply to all the sales functions in the entire company.

He would attempt to introduce "team selling" and "cross selling." It seemed ridiculous to Larry that there were separate divisional sales forces, each focused on a single product line, and ignorant of the other lines. He would recommend that the company reorganize, or at least modify its incentive systems to encourage a greater degree of mutual support across divisions.

His marketing plan revised, Larry attempted to make an appointment with Sandra. He was told that her schedule was full. Repeated attempts met with failure. He was told to put his marketing plan on her desk. Sandra was clearly avoiding Larry.

Larry tolerated Sandra's evasiveness for several weeks before deciding to take a more aggressive stance. Arriving at the office early one morning, he positioned himself directly outside of her office. Sandra's secretary arrived first, and tried her best to get Larry to leave the office. He refused to budge. Eventually, Sandra arrived.

She was very aloof, telling Larry that she was extremely busy, and asking why she had not yet received his revised marketing plan. In response to Larry's statement that he wanted to discuss it with her in person, she repeated that her schedule was too full, and that she would prefer to review the plan alone.

With that, Sandra entered her office, and shut the door. Having vowed that he would not be put off again, Larry opened the door and entered the room. He found Sandra with arms crossed and head bowed. Miss Efficiency was nowhere to be seen.

Larry sat down and looked directly at Sandra. Eventually, she raised her eyes. The sparkle was gone. So were the anger and the determination. Pain and fatigue had taken their place. Larry felt a surge of sympathy for her, and wanted to respond as a friend.

Eventually, Sandra spoke. "I'm sorry, Larry. I have been trying to avoid you. Actually, I have been trying to avoid myself, or at least my feelings. I guess I have been behaving like some kind of robot that has gone out of control."

Larry smiled and said, "Yes, that is a fair description. Though, you certainly have managed to turn around the division in the process."

By now, Sandra was smiling. "As they say, every cloud has a silver lining. I have been abusing myself terribly in the process, however. I really need a vacation, and some time to sort out my thoughts and feelings."

"Then take one. But only after you approve my marketing plan. The production side of the house is rolling. The marketing side awaits only your signature."

"No, Larry. There is something that you don't know that will affect all the decisions we make in terms of marketing. Books International has suggested a merger. Actually, they want to buy out Software Systems. The Executive Committee is seriously considering their proposal. We either do that or go into the book publishing business ourselves. The retail distribution system is similar. So is the target market. At any rate, we are interested in availing ourselves of their existing sales and distribution network."

Larry reacted to Sandra's news with a combination of excitement and dread. He was excited about the opportunity to gain instant access to a massive distribution system. He feared both he and his plan would get lost in the larger company. But he expressed neither reaction, allowing Sandra to continue.

"So you see, Larry, both my vacation and the launching of your marketing plan must await the merger decision. I would suggest, however, that during the next few days, you devote your energies to considering ways in which you would modify or expand your plan in the event of a merger. This could represent a real opportunity for you, Larry. That is, if your plan has merit. You see, the director of marketing in Books International is nearing retirement."

Larry asked Sandra whether others in the company were aware of the proposed merger. She responded that, at least to her knowledge, no one below the vice-president level had been told of the proposal.

Sensing that the meeting was over, and anxious to return to his own office to contemplate the significance of what he had just heard, Larry rose to leave. Sandra asked him to sit down again.

"Larry, you must keep this confidential. I dread to think of the politicking that would ensue if this became common knowledge. I have chosen to share it with you for two reasons. The first is obvious;

it has a direct impact on your marketing plan. The second is personal."

Sandra paused for a moment, obviously finding it difficult to say what was on her mind. Sensing her discomfort, Larry told her that it was not necessary for her to say anything; that he could tell from the change in her behavior that they were once again friends. But Sandra needed to say more.

"I appreciate that my behavior during the convention put you in a very awkward position. Initially, I felt both rejected and embarrassed. Wanting to punish you, I avoided you. Well, I've had a chance to reflect both on my own behavior, and on your reaction. You handled a difficult situation beautifully, Larry. I feel that I can trust you, and I want to be friends."

By the time Larry left Sandra's office, he was convinced that their relationship had not only been mended, but actually enhanced. He sensed that the episode at the conference would never be mentioned again. It was no longer a taboo subject; it was simply irrelevant.

Three weeks later, the decision was made to merge with Books International. The new entity was to be called Textware, Inc. By the time of the announcement, Larry was ready with a revised marketing plan. In addition to his earlier strategies, Larry had conceived of a way to use not only the marketing and distribution resources of the book company, but its authors and subject experts as well.

Textbooks would accompany every piece of software or video released by Textware. The book would convince the buyer that there was truly an "expert in the machine." The "expert in the machine" would become their marketing slogan. The company would differentiate itself from its competitors by the quality and accuracy of the subject matter. Book sales would invite software sales, and vice versa.

Sandra enthusiastically endorsed Larry's plan, complimenting him both on his creativity and the rigor with which he had approached the financial analysis. She suggested that in the weeks to follow he become more of an expert in the area of marketing through direct mail.

"While you are doing that, I'll be vacationing. If I don't take a break now, I won't get one for months. The next three weeks will be relatively quiet. Everybody will be too busy working out the financial ramifications of the merger to worry too much about politics, power and positions. After that, watch out, Larry. It's going to get crazy around here."

Larry decided that it was an apt time for a discussion with Bill. He wanted to not only review the events of the past several months, but also to begin to understand the power dynamics of mergers. Having lived through two mergers himself, Bill would be able to tell Larry what to expect. They agreed to get together for dinner that night.

Believing that he understood the power dynamics involved in the episodes of the past several months, Larry did a self-assessment before meeting Bill.

Reflecting on the *Arsenal* Strategy, Larry realized that he had consciously used that strategy when he took the senior programmer to dinner to find out what was going on in Joel's unit.

"I suppose I was getting in a position to use corporate blackmail if necessary, in order to get Joel to do things my way. I accumulated a lot of information that could have been damaging to Joel. In the end, it helped."

Larry had to spend a lot more time contemplating the extent to which he had used the *Look-What-I've-Done* Strategy for building expert power. He had devoted a lot of time to doing a market analysis, the analysis that had convinced him that there was a greater market for the personal financial planner than for the corporate strategic planner.

"If having the facts makes you an expert, then I enhanced my expert power base. The problem is that I did not succeed in convincing everyone of my point of view. I guess I would have to give myself a fair score in that area, since I did convince the company to invest resources in pursuit of the retail market.

"The same holds true with regard to the revised marketing plan. Sandra was very impressed, and I'm sure she regards me as more of an expert because of the plan. In sharing it with her, I was really saying, 'Look what I've done.' Let's hope the strategy works as well with the book company executives."

In considering the *Fraternity* Strategy for building the power of friendship, Larry reflected on the change in his relationship with Sandra. "We're certainly closer friends than we were before, but I think that is more a result of her behavior than of mine. On the other hand, she probably would never have felt comfortable with me again had I abused her trust. I was honest with her, and I was consistent, and in a way, caring. Yes, I helped save the friendship."

Larry then reflected on steps he had taken to use the *Public Relations* Strategy to enhance the power of his presence.

"I don't know whether anyone has noticed, but I've been paying a lot more attention to the words I use, the tone of my voice, and my expressions. I guess all those presentations I have had to make, and the conferences I have had to attend, to say nothing of my meeting with prospective customers, have made me more sensitive to the need to communicate effectively. People used to say that I spoke too fast, and did not pause often enough. Well, if I do say so myself, I have improved in that department."

Larry then reflected on his use of the *Networking* Strategy to gain indirect power.

"My internal network is no better than it was. In fact, it might have deteriorated a little. I mean, take Foresight as an example. Our friendship has been sorely strained by the events of the past few months.

"On the other hand, the network of contacts I have built outside of the company is getting to be impressive. Unless I am mistaken, I have managed to earn the respect of a number of high ranking executives in a variety of potential customer organizations. Many of them sit on the boards of other companies. I think I have begun to establish a nice base for eventual product referral."

Pleased with his performance in the power-getting area, Larry turned to an assessment of the kinds of power and influence strategies he had used.

"I relied heavily on *coercive power* in an attempt to direct Joel to reinstitute testing procedures, and to modify the approach he was taking with the senior programmer.

"That didn't work. It took Sandra to mandate the changes, and to take the retail job away from Joel. In effect, I ended up indirectly using Sandra's *formal power* to direct Joel. I regret that Joel and I do not enjoy a better relationship but, all things considered, I think I did the right thing. Joel is now Sandra's problem. He has no choice but to accede to her wishes; and her wishes just happen to coincide with mine.

"I tried to use my *expert power* to enlist Sandra to support the shift from the commercial product to the retail product. Well, that certainly didn't work. I should have remembered what Bill said about commitment. Sandra acquiesced. She agreed to present my idea to others, but she lacked conviction. Of course she did. She had not been sufficiently involved in the process. I overused enlisting and underused involvement in her case.

"The enlisting strategy worked somewhat better when I made my presentation to Softner. At least I got a compromise; he agreed to develop a retail line. I think the strategy worked in that case because I used not only my expert power, the power of the facts I had accumulated, but also the *indirect power* of the prospective customers. Making that video was a stroke of genius. It brought the customer into the room, and made my point for me.

"And how did I get customers to agree to devote their time and energy to a discussion of the product in the first place? I paid them; that's how. I used *reward power* to *negotiate a trade.* Dollars in exchange for time.

"I used negotiation with the senior programmer, too. I guess Bill would call that a contest. I asked him to stay for three months. If, at the end of that time, I had not succeeded in getting Joel to change his ways, then I agreed to help the programmer find another job. The strategy worked better than I had hoped. Now that programmer is a director, and he is doing a great job."

Larry patted himself on the back for having made use of a variety of power bases and influence styles. "Flexible, that's me, flexible. Bill is going to be proud."

Finally, Larry congratulated himself on his success in not falling prey to the manipulations of others. And he confessed that he had resorted to one small manipulation, as he got Joel to volunteer information regarding production costs; information that Larry eventually used to support his argument for shifting the product line.

Bill agreed with Larry's assessment. His comments during dinner were focused on clarifying why certain strategies worked or didn't work, as opposed to challenging Larry's assessment.

Bill told Larry that, prior to electing an influence strategy, it was important to consider five factors:

- the nature of your *goals,* and those of the other
- the *controls* that are available
- the *urgency,* or time constraints
- the *balance of power* between you and the other
- the *commitment* that is required

Handing Larry a chart that he had prepared, Bill went on to describe the items on the chart, first discussing the conditions that rendered *involvement* appropriate.

Selecting a Power Strategy

CONDITIONS	STRATEGIES			
	INVOLVING OTHERS	NEGOTIATING WITH OTHERS	DIRECTING OTHERS	ENLISTING OTHERS
GOALS	Your goals are interdependent; to reach yours is to contribute to the ability of others to reach theirs and vice versa.	Your goals are independent; not related.	Your goals are counterdependent; if you succeed, chances are the other will fail.	You can't reach your goal without the others' help, but their goals are not dependent upon you.
CONTROLS	You rely on the on-going commitment and judgment of the other person.	"Rules" covering fair play and foul play exist and are understood by all parties to the contract.	You have ways to find out about "sabotage" before you're badly hurt; constant or frequent surveillance is possible.	The worst thing the other person can do is turn you down—they would not gain by hurting you in the other ways.
URGENCY (TIME)	Time is available for exploration and problem solving. Delay would not hurt either of you.	Delay would hurt the other more than you; you can tolerate a deadlock better than the other; or, delay would hurt both of you.	Delay would be detrimental to you.	Delay would hurt you more than the other person.
BALANCE OF POWER	Both parties have information or expertise the other party needs; or, both parties trust and respect each other.	Both parties can help (reward) or hurt (punish) each other.	You can reward or punish the other person more than (s)he can reward or punish you.	The other person likes you, respects you, and is not in a position to be hurt by you.
COMMITMENT REQUIRED	Long-term commitment of the others to your goals is sought.	Commitment to a contract or agreement is more important than commitment to goals.	Long-term commitment of the other person is not important; opposition or antagonism is acceptable (the other person can be "replaced").	Permission or acquiescence is more important than commitment; opposition or antagonism is not acceptable.

He pointed out that involving works best when goals are interdependent; when success for one party means success for the other. Goal interdependence, he explained, gives everyone a reason to collaborate; to work together for the common good.

With regard to controls, Bill explained that involvement is the indicated strategy when the only available controls over the performance of the other are the commitment and motivation of the other.

"The major advantage of the involvment strategy is that it generates commitment," Bill said. "People are committed only to that which they have helped to create. *If you need long-term commitment, then, involvement should be your strategy of choice.*

"But, a word of caution. *Don't get involved with people whom you do not trust or whose expertise you do not value.* Managers frequently make this mistake. Because they have been taught to believe that participative management, or involvement, is the 'right' way to do things, they pretend to involve their subordinates when, in reality, they have a fixed outcome in mind. The subordinates are set up to discover what the supervisor regards as the 'right answer.' This is highly manipulative, and the source of much employee discontent.

Involvement should be used only when the manager is actually willing to be influenced by the subordinate's point of view. Or, stated differently, involvement is an appropriate strategy when there is a balance of power with regard to trust and expertise."

Bill pointed out that the downside of relying on the involvement strategy was the time required to collaborate. "Involvement takes time; time you may not have. You did not try to involve Sandra in building the argument for a shift in product strategy because you did not feel you had the time to problem-solve with her. The strategy backfired, because you did not get the commitment you needed. In this case, your need for commitment outweighed issues related to urgency. It would have been more appropriate to problem-solve with Sandra, accepting a flexible outcome, and allowing her to influence events.

"Occasionally, it is important to remain open to a variety of responses from the other while, at the same time, relying on formal power. Such a situation exists with Joel. You and he do not enjoy a relationship characterized by mutual trust and respect. That precludes use of involvement. *Direction* is probably not indicated, since its constant use would only inspire greater antagonism and resentment.

"I would suggest that *negotiation* may be the indicated strategy with Joel. *Negotiation works well when your goals are independent or not related.* While you appreciate that marketing and production are interdependent, Joel apparently does not. Nor does he perceive that your goals are counterdependent. And you are both in a position to reward or to punish each other. The peer review system introduces a balance of power. Use it to negotiate trades and compromises. At least, in that way, you will get commitment to a contract or a deal, even though you do not have his commitment to you as a person.

"Enlistment is an effective strategy when you want, for various reasons, to rely on informal power, and when permission to proceed is more important than active commitment. That is often the case when you are dependent on the other for your goal attainment, and that dependency is not returned. Another situation that makes enlistment a useful strategy is when time constraints are such that delay would hurt you more than the other person.

"The only caution I offer here is that to enlist is to make yourself vulnerable. When people make themselves vulnerable by revealing something about themselves, then they actually grant you power over them. In exposing a need, the person seeking something risks ridicule or refusal. In making desires known, a person risks rejection. Rejection hurts.

"Consider the episode with Sandra. In sharing her feelings with you, she made herself vulnerable. You then were forced to reject her advances. That hurt, creating at least a temporary barrier between the two of you. Schiller explained the dynamic beautifully when he said, 'You saw his weakness and he will never forgive you.'

"Sandra, however, did forgive you. And you deserve credit for that. You were in a tough situation. Insisting that she see you was the best thing that you could have done. You needed to reaffirm the fact that she could trust you to maintain a confidence, and that you still respected her.

"Romance can create havoc within organizations. The problem goes a lot deeper than the inappropriateness of trading sexual favors, or demanding sexual favors, for promotions and the like. When two people who have been romantically involved split up, there are usually feelings of anger and rejection. At best, the rejected party wants to avoid the rejector. At worst, there is a desire for vengeance. Neither contributes to productivity nor to a comfortable working relationship.

"Because enlistment requires that we make ourselves vulnerable, it is a viable strategy only when the worst thing that the other person can do is to turn you down; when they have nothing to gain by hurting you, or by blocking your efforts.

"That, by the way, is the reason the enlistment strategy didn't work with Foresight. You were unable to enlist his support because he stood to gain by maintaining the firm's commitment to the commercial planning model.

"You really had no way to get Foresight to support you. For you to get your way meant that he would lose, at least in his perception. And you could not afford to waste time.

"Direction should be your strategy of choice only when your goals are counterdependent, putting you in an adversarial situation, or when your sense of urgency is such that you need immediate compliance.

"Because direction tends to stimulate resentment, however, it is important that you are able to introduce a good set of controls, enabling you to find out about sabotage before you are badly hurt. Managers who rely excessively on the directive tactic must exercise surveillance. Productivity typically grinds to a halt when surveillance ceases. In effect, when the directive cat is away, the mice play.

"It is people who rely excessively on direction who have given power such a bad name. It is not power per se which is the problem, but the constant demand for fixed outcomes, backed by threats of coercion.

"Productivity can also grind to a halt when power plays proliferate, and when winning becomes more important than productivity. That, unfortunately, often occurs during mergers, as too little attention is paid to the human aspect of mergers.

"Turf protection becomes the name of the game, Larry. Executives in both companies, but particularly those in the company being acquired, feel threatened. Suddenly, they believe that they must prove that they are indispensable.

"Then there is the scramble for resources. Games are played to build empires by capturing the greatest share of the new resource pool.

"All of this is aggravated by the tension that people feel due to sudden role confusion. Job descriptions are suddenly irrelevant. Policies and procedures are thrown into question, as two different systems must be blended.

"Often, leadership shifts, and with it norms as to what constitutes leadership effectiveness. Participative managers are replaced by persons who employ directive tactics, or vice versa. Definitions of appropriate and inappropriate behaviors are confounded. People lose their bearings, and as a result, begin to feel extremely insecure.

"In short, Larry, it's a mess, particularly if the psychological realities are not considered during the early merger discussions. In my experience, these realities are rarely given sufficient consideration. A preoccupation with the balance sheet seems to divert attention from the management of the human fears that are engendered in a merger situation."

Their evening was drawing to a close. In the time that remained, Bill could do little other than to caution Larry to remain very aware and alert during the months to come.

"Watch out for manipulations, Larry. Learn to accept ambiguity as a fact of life. Look out for the opportunities that change can create. Above all, remember that you will now have to renew your efforts to build a power base. The executives in the book company have no reason to be impressed by Larry Michaelson. You are going to have to earn their respect, and their trust, and you will have to do so quickly, before final decisions are made about the allocation of managerial talent.

"As a member of the organization that is being acquired, you start one step down on the ladder. In general, when there is a perceived redundancy of talent, the one to go is the individual from the acquired company."

Taking his power strategy selection chart and his notes, Larry left the restaurant. Bill's parting comments had left Larry feeling that he was about to face the real test of his ability to manage organizational power dynamics. The events that were to transpire over the coming months were to represent an even greater test than Larry had anticipated. He would find it necessary to frequently consult the notes he had taken that evening.

LARRY'S NOTES

Choosing an Influence Strategy

INVOLVEMENT: goals interdependent
need commitment
trust and respect exists
time to problem-solve

NEGOTIATION: goals independent
need agreement
balance of formal power exists
time is on my side

DIRECTION: goals counterdependent
antagonism okay
have power to coerce
situation is urgent

ENLISTMENT: I need the other
permission is desired
trust and respect exists
no time to involve

CAUTION: Do not involve others whom you do not trust or whose expertise you do not value. To do so is to manipulate. (Managers do this to subordinates far too often.)

To enlist is to make yourself vulnerable; to risk rejection.

When people are rejected, they tend to feel hostile.

Mergers Trigger

- Power plays
- Insecurity
- Attempts to protect turf
- Scramble for resources
- Ambiguity and confusion

To be part of the acquired company is to start one down; need to reestablish power bases; need to remain alert to power plays and manipulations.

9

Mergers and Manipulations

SEVERAL DAYS LATER, the employees of both Software Systems, Inc. and Books International were informed of the merger. Speeches by the chief executive officers of both companies were designed to stimulate enthusiasm for the marriage, and the birth of Textware, Inc. After six years with Software Systems, Larry found himself part of another entity. His feelings were a blend of melancholy and excitement.

Sandra Newman had predicted that several weeks would elapse before the announcement would lead to a proliferation of power plays and politics. She was wrong. The games began within a week.

The event that triggered the onset of the fray was the sudden departure of Harold Softner, chief operating officer of Software Systems, Inc. The public announcement stated that Softner had chosen to take early retirement in order to pursue personal interests. No one was fooled. Softner's dislike of conflict and corporate power plays was widely known. Many assumed that Softner knew that the merger was going to trigger conflicts, and thus chose to bail out in order to avoid the melee.

Others assumed that Softner had been forced out by Star, the chief executive officer of Books International, in an effort to make room for one of his own people. Those who embraced the latter assumption also anticipated that the acquiring company would pursue this strategy all the way down the line, replacing Software Systems executives with executives from the book company.

The jockeying for position began right at the top. Ralph Willit, vice-president of the Software Division, perceived that he might have a shot at the position of chief operating officer. He began currying favor with Star, chief executive of the book company, and denying any allegiance to Topper, chief executive of Software Systems.

Willit wrote a letter to Star, and offered to develop and personally conduct an orientation of the software side of the business for book executives. He hoped to use the vehicle to establish a relationship with the chief executive.

Determined not to be outdone, Tyler Watch, vice-president of the Video Division, elaborated upon the strategy. He offered not only an orientation, but a lavish dinner and cocktail party as well.

Gladhand, the vice-president of Software Systems Administration, also got into the act. Pulling all of his people off of their existing projects, he put them to work documenting the success stories of the last five years. The product, bound in leather, was hand delivered to Star, with a carefully written note stating, "I look forward to serving the parent corporation with the same high quality effort with which I have consistently served Software Systems."

These attempts at individual aggrandizement did not, in and of themselves, create difficulty. The trouble really started when the executives began to attempt to win at one another's expense. Gladhand started the rumor that Star intended to render Peter Topper, the chief executive of Software Systems, so powerless that he would resign. Tyler Watch was smart enough not to act on the rumor. Ralph Willit, unfortunately, was not so astute. Perceiving an opportunity to prove his allegiance to his new employer, Willit let it be known that he welcomed the change in leadership, and regarded Topper as only marginally effective in the role of chief executive.

Willit misunderstood the political arena. Star had a great deal of respect for Topper and had always intended to put him in the role of chief operating officer. Topper himself felt that his loss of formal power was more than compensated for by the financial rewards that he realized as a result of the sale of his stock. And he looked forward to functioning again as an operating officer. Engineering had always been his first love, and the change in position would provide him with more opportunities to put his functional expertise to work.

**MERGER MANEUVERS
KEY PLAYERS**

Star: CEO, Book Company

Topper: CEO, Software Systems

Blind: Strategic Planning, Book Company

Foresight: Strategic Planning, Software Systems

Fraid: VP Administration, Book Company

Gladhand: VP Administration, Software Systems

Other Software VPs and Directors

Willit: VP, Software

Watch: VP, Video

Newman: VP, Special Projects

Sterling: Director, Software

Abramson: Director, Special Projects

Michaelson: Director, Special Projects

Other Book Company VPs and Directors

Simpleton: VP, Marketing

Press: VP, Operations

Draft: VP, Editorial/Acquisition

Wallace: Director, Sales (Simpleton's future son-in-law)

Topper and Star were both incensed by Willit's obvious manipulation, and together decided that his just dessert was to be removed from the position of vice-president of Software Systems, and offered a lower paying job in the book company. As they predicted, Willit resigned.

The sudden vacancy at the vice-presidential level triggered jockeying for position among the directors. Within hours, any vestige of cooperation disappeared. Each thought he was an appropriate contender for the job of vice-president of the Software Division.

Reginald Sterling fought the hardest and the dirtiest battle. Not content to simply make himself look good by making his competitors look bad, Reginald used his incredible political nose to ferret out some little known and yet politically powerful facts about Books International executives.

He learned that Jack Simpleton, vice-president of marketing (books), was within a year of retirement and was vigorously grooming the director of sales to assume his position. What was less widely known was that the director of sales was engaged to Simpleton's daughter. Wanting his daughter to have the honor of being married to a highly paid executive, Simpleton was prepared to fight hard to avoid the possibility that there might be another, more capable successor to his throne.

Reginald, who made it a practice to use his connection with Joel to keep track of Larry, was aware that Larry had developed a comprehensive marketing plan. Given Larry's natural abilities, he could pose a real threat to Simpleton's future son-in-law.

An oblique reference to the situation was all that was required to convince Simpleton to have dinner with Reginald. Reginald's proposition was straightforward. He suggested a trade of favors. Simpleton would use his clout to convince Star that Reginald deserved the job of vice-president of Software Systems. In return, once appointed, Reginald would create a new position, naming Simpleton's future son-in-law the director of software sales.

Filling this role would give the young man exposure to the software side of the business. Meanwhile, both Reginald and Simpleton would work together to get Larry named director of book sales. Once in that position, Simpleton could easily arrange things so that

"When I agreed to the merger, Fairchild, I never contemplated this!"

Drawing by Ed Fisher; © 1972
The New Yorker Magazine, Inc.

Larry would fail. When Simpleton was ready to give up his post, there would be only one natural successor: someone who knew both books and software, and someone who knew sales. Simpleton's future son-in-law would emerge as the most suitable candidate.

Simpleton agreed to the arrangement, making it unnecessary for Reginald to use his concealed weapon. In order to protect himself from the possibility that Simpleton might resist, Reginald had stocked his arsenal. He had found out that one of the sales reps had been falsifying both his call reports and his expense accounts. Simpleton had been aware of the fraud for months and yet, for reasons unknown, had chosen not to reveal it.

Reginald's strategy worked. Within a few weeks of his conversation with Simpleton, he was named vice-president of the Software Division. Once appointed, Reginald began to expand his empire. His first target was the Special Projects Division. Annoyed with Joel for even thinking of competing with him, Reginald vowed to once again have his former lackey under his thumb. But first he had to take care of Sandra Newman.

Unfortunately, it was not difficult for him to do so. The book company was very traditional in its thinking, and bureaucratic in its operations. The notion of having a Special Projects Division offended its sense of order. Preferring to organize by function, Star, now the chief executive of Textware, Inc., decided that the subsequent development of the personal and corporate financial planning products would be supervised by the Software Division.

Meanwhile Larry forced himself to stay out of the fray. While others played games, he devoted his energies to the refinement of his marketing plan. He firmly believed that his best shot at securing a significant position in Textware was dependent on developing an impressive marketing plan and presentation.

In order to do so, he needed to understand the present marketing and sales strategies being pursued by the book company's executives. As a result of his quest for information, he had the opportunity to meet with most of the key players in the marketing area.

Unable to get an audience with Simpleton, the vice-president of marketing, Larry settled for a meeting with Gregory Wallace, the director of sales. Gregory was very willing to discuss the strengths of his sales force and his marketing strategy.

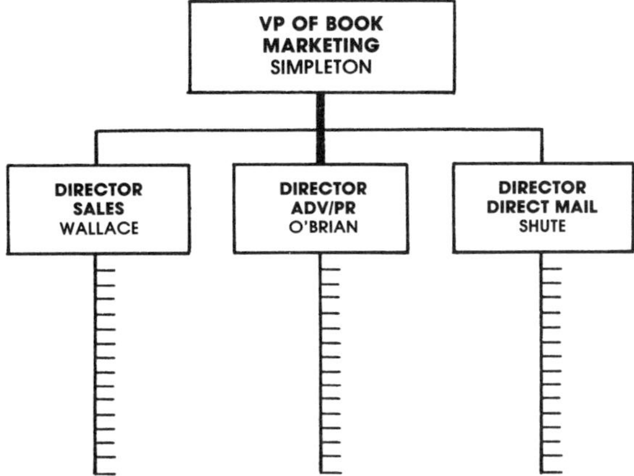

Larry was disappointed to find that what Gregory referred to as his marketing strategy amounted to nothing more than establishing quotas regarding the number of book stores each representative was expected to call on during a given week. The objective was to encourage the advantageous positioning of the books, and to discourage returns.

Meetings with several of the sales representatives convinced Larry that the sales force in general was both unsophisticated, and unfamiliar with the contents of the books they were selling. When he brought up the issue with Gregory, the reason for their lack of interest became obvious.

"They are paid to make calls, not to read books. Why, we put out seventy-five titles a year. If I asked that my people read seventy-five books, we would never sell anything!"

The otherwise effusive Gregory Wallace became noticeably silent when Larry inquired about the corporate sales effort. "Oh, we have a special staff for that. Mind you, it isn't large, but it is adequate. And we use a lot of subcontractors."

He was either unable or unwilling to provide additional information regarding the corporate marketing effort. Larry suspected that Gregory's boss, Simpleton, handled the corporate work himself. Attempts to confirm this were futile. Larry could not get an appointment with Gregory's boss. Simpleton persisted in providing one excuse after another.

It became clear to Larry that the success of the book company could not be attributed to the efforts of the sales representatives. Further inquiry revealed that the bulk of the company's sales stemmed from its direct mail operation. Unlike Gregory Wallace, the director of direct mail was competent. A man in his late fifties, he did not aspire to progress in the company. But he was a devoted, reliable employee who loved what he did.

Larry was not impressed by the Advertising and Public Relations Department. Led by a woman who seemed uniquely uncreative and unenthusiastic, the function did little other than follow a set of pre-established procedures. Regardless of their topic, authors were booked on the same television and radio shows. Advertisements were always two-color, and of the same style, regardless of the content or market potential of the book being promoted.

Larry's meeting with the director of distribution shed no further light on the marketing function. The department did little more than take orders. The director, while rigorous in his attention to detail, was not at all creative. Maintaining faultless inventory records constituted his only talent.

Having met the directors of the marketing areas, Larry decided that he did not have to meet with Simpleton in order to identify the strengths and weaknesses of the function. Clearly, the book company had a sales function, not a marketing function. The people he had met thought in terms of quotas, calls, and items put in the mail. They did not adopt a more global view, or manifest curiosity about trends in reader habits or interests.

Larry naively believed that the book company's lack of a true marketing function represented an opportunity for him. He expected Simpleton and the others to enthusiastically embrace his ideas about how to enhance the function. Preoccupied with visions of success, Larry ignored Bill's advice that he make an effort to remain highly aware of the power plays that would proliferate once the merger was announced.

Even Reginald's promotion to vice-president had not disturbed Larry a great deal. In spite of Reginald's manipulative style, he was a solid performer. And he had not been promoted for some time. Further, Larry did not anticipate that Reginald's promotion would affect him. Special Projects, after all, did not report to the vice-president of the Systems Division.

His queries completed, and his marketing plan revised, Larry met with Sandra to review his conclusions, and to develop a strategy. He shared with Sandra his impressions of the inadequacies of the present marketing function, both in the book company and within Software Systems. He reiterated his belief that a consistent corporate theme was required. The notion of promoting the "expert in the machine" still appealed, as did the concept of enhancing the credibility of the expert through the simultaneous release of software and a book written by the expert. Finally, Larry was more convinced than ever that Textware, Inc. needed to integrate its sales and marketing efforts, and that a reorganization or change in incentive systems would be required to effect such an integration.

Impressed with Larry's plan, Sandra suggested that they attempt to gain the endorsement of Peter Topper, former chief executive of Software Systems and current chief operating officer of Textware, Inc. While marketing had never been Topper's specialty, Sandra believed that the initial endorsement of the plan had to come from a very senior level. Since she did not feel they could get to Star, Topper was the natural choice.

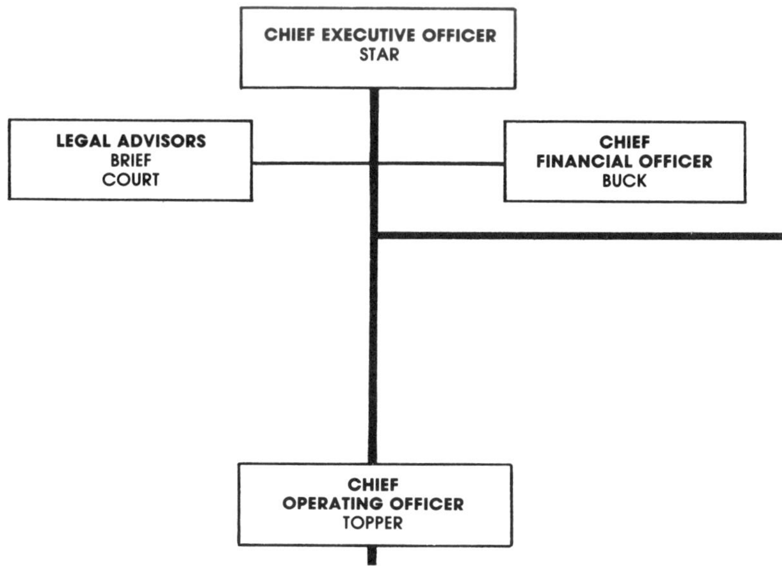

"There's going to be resistance to the idea, Larry, particularly since it was not generated by a Books International executive. The book company officials regard their company as a marketing organization; it is their perception that they purchased a technical organization. Organizational pride being what it is, I suspect that the book company will feel that we are overstepping our bounds and even denigrating their expertise by attempting to tell them something that they presumably already know. This has to be handled delicately."

"But why Topper? Don't you think that getting his endorsement of the plan will heighten the resistance? After all, he is from the software side of Textware. It might be easier to get the plan implemented by sneaking it in through the back door, a piece at a time. In that way, we would not be ruffling any feathers, or threatening anybody's turf," Larry said.

"If we can convince Topper, then there is a good chance that we can get to Star. Star is anxious to keep Topper happy. If Topper were to resign, several of our best technicians would probably leave with him. Star is undoubtedly aware of that. At least, we have to assume that he is. I think the next step is to get you an audience with Topper."

As she made the suggestion, Sandra was not aware that she would have an opportunity to meet with Topper before the day was over. The meeting, however, would not be initiated by her, and it would mark the beginning of the end in terms of her ability to exercise formal power within the organization.

Topper came straight to the point. "Sandra, as you know, Mr. Star and I have been devoting a great deal of time and energy to the organization of Textware, Inc. Merging two entities with different products and different cultures is never easy. In the end, it comes down to making some pretty difficult decisions about individuals. I cannot say that I have agreed with all of the decisions that have been made. I have had to compromise in some areas. I'm afraid that one such compromise involves your unit, the Special Projects Divison."

Sandra's heart was in her stomach. She was certain that the next words out of Topper's mouth would be to tell her that the decision had been made to let her go.

It was with a sharp sense of relief, then, that she heard Topper say, "Our decision is in no way a reflection on your ability. On the contrary, I have been very pleased with your performance. Unfortunately, there is no room in the new organization for a group that is as experimental as yours. We have decided that the financial planning

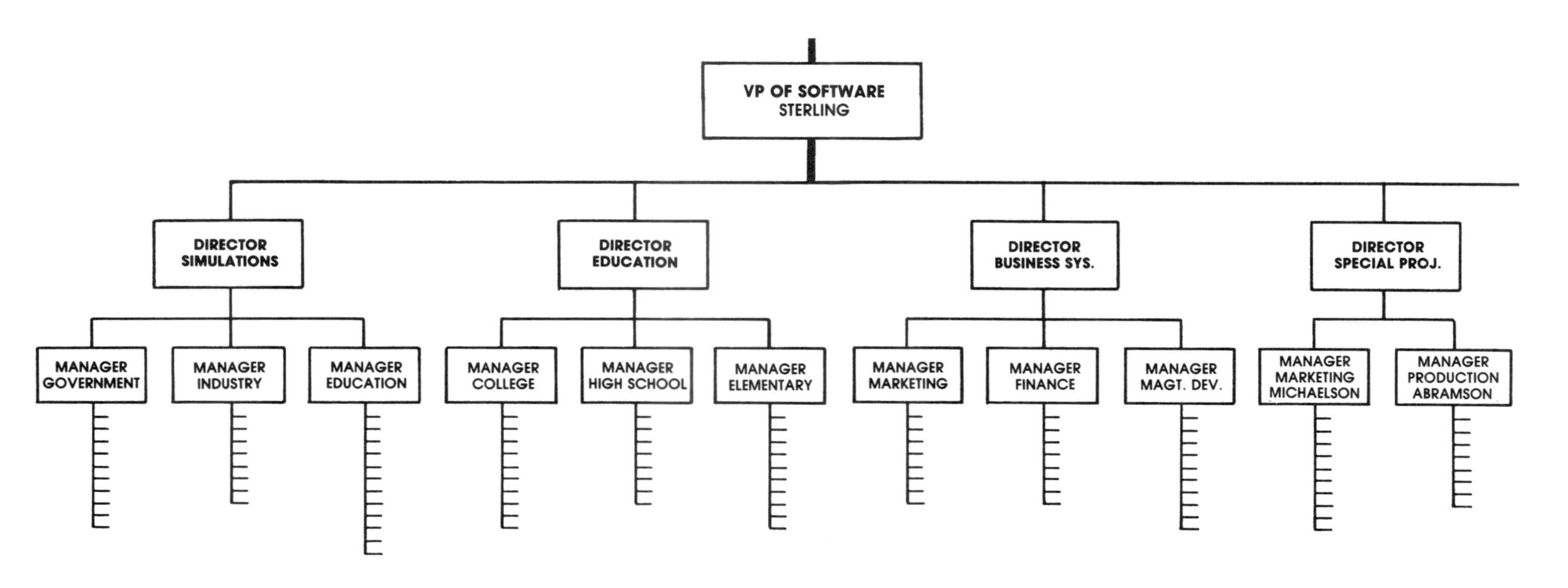

VP OF SOFTWARE
STERLING
DIRECTOR SIMULATIONS
DIRECTOR EDUCATION
DIRECTOR BUSINESS SYS.
DIRECTOR SPECIAL PROJ.
MANAGER GOVERNMENT
MANAGER INDUSTRY
MANAGER EDUCATION
MANAGER COLLEGE
MANAGER HIGH SCHOOL
MANAGER ELEMENTARY
MANAGER MARKETING
MANAGER FINANCE
MANAGER MAGT. DEV.
MANAGER MARKETING MICHAELSON
MANAGER PRODUCTION ABRAMSON

models will be incorporated into the software division, and that the development will be managed by Reginald Sterling. As of Monday, all Special Projects personnel, with the exception of yourself, will be reporting to Reginald Sterling.

"You pose us with a real dilemma. On the one hand, we value your managerial talent, and your ability to evaluate software. On the other hand, there are no immediate openings at the vice-presidential level. We do anticipate that an opening will occur within the next year or so. In the interim, we want to continue to access your evaluation skills, and your awareness of competitive products. In short, we propose that you function as a software consultant, and competitive analyst, reporting to the vice-president of Strategic Planning."

Sandra was silent for a few moments. While she hadn't been fired, she no longer felt like a valued member of the management team. Knowing that she would have to give a great deal of thought to the proposition before she could make a decision, she decided to seek additional information.

"So, I would be reporting to George Foresight. What would my compensation package look like?"

"No, you will not be reporting to Foresight. I must, by the way, request that you regard what I am about to tell you as confidential, at least until tomorrow noon. I have not had an opportunity to speak directly with all of the individuals involved in the matter.

"The assets of the book company are ten times that of Software Systems, Inc. It is only appropriate that the man who has overseen the growth of those assets should continue to function as the vice-president of Strategic Planning. Michael Blind will continue in that position. Foresight will report to him, specializing as he always has as the chief planner regarding software products. You, too, would report to Blind. Hoping that you will accept our offer, I have arranged for you to meet Blind later this afternoon. I am confident that you will find him to be a most affable individual."

"If you don't mind my asking, what of Peter Buck? Will he be reporting to Blind as well?"

Topper smiled, and nodded his head ever so slightly, indicating that he found Sandra's question to be astute. "No, Buck will be reporting directly to Star, and will function as the chief financial officer. The chief financial officer of the book company will be asked to take early retirement. Buck is one of the best financial analysts

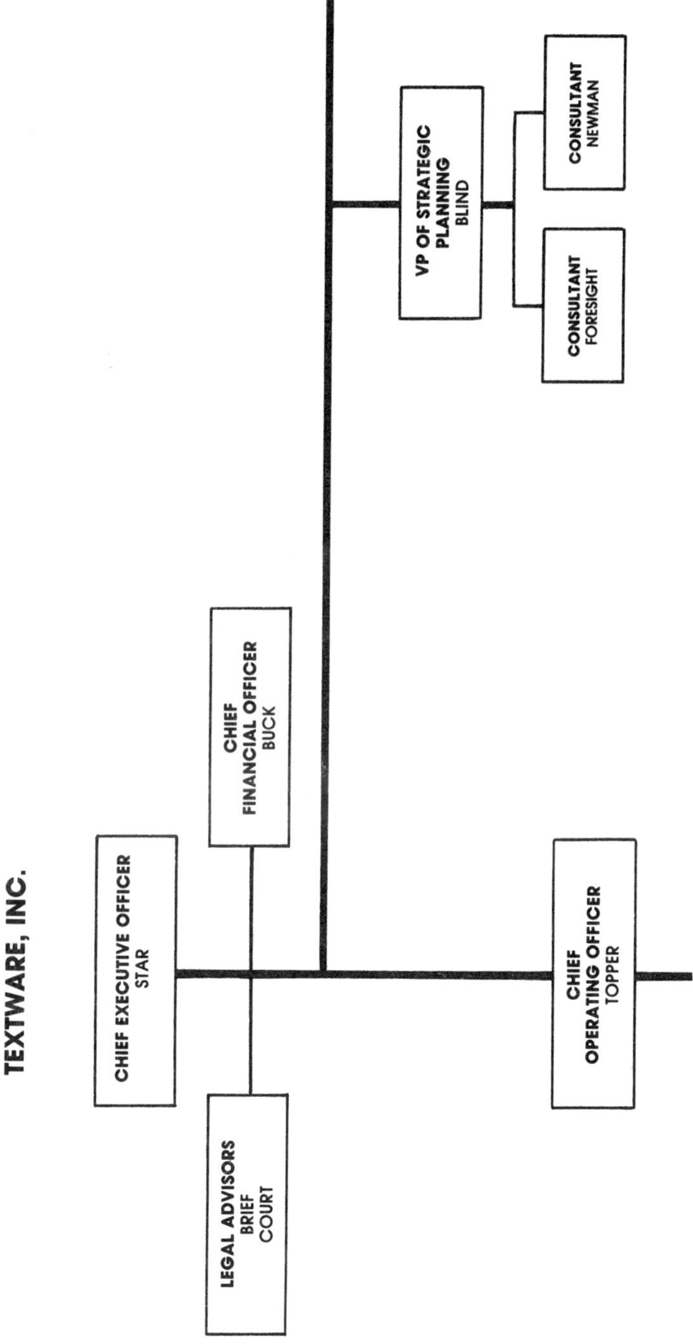
TEXTWARE, INC.
CHIEF EXECUTIVE OFFICER
STAR
LEGAL ADVISORS
BRIEF
COURT
CHIEF FINANCIAL OFFICER
BUCK
CHIEF OPERATING OFFICER
TOPPER
VP OF STRATEGIC PLANNING
BLIND
CONSULTANT
NEWMAN
CONSULTANT
FORESIGHT

around. His soon-to-be-retired counterpart is, at best, an accountant. That was one of the few easy decisions we had to make."

Sandra did not like Peter Buck, finding him to be not only uncreative, but cold, aloof, and closed-minded as well. Her instincts told her that Foresight had been sacrificed in order to allow Buck to continue to hold the position of chief financial officer. Realizing that she and Larry had won the battle, only to lose the war, she felt despondent. It took all of the energy she had to introduce the subject of Larry and his marketing plan.

Her timing was perfect. Realizing that the news he had just given Sandra had been devastating, he was only too willing to do something to compensate. And he remembered that Softner had spoken highly of Larry. Topper agreed to listen to Larry's plan the next day.

By the time Sandra reached her own office, she had made one decision. Regardless of her promise of confidentiality, she would share everything with Larry. Only if he had the benefit of full information could he adequately plan the approach he would take with Topper.

Sandra began by telling Larry the good news. He was elated, and ready and eager to present to Topper. He complimented Sandra on her ability to make things happen, suggesting that she was intuitively good at managing organization power dynamics.

"Well, Larry. I wish that were the case. I thought that I better act quickly, while I still have some clout around here. As of Monday, I will be simply a staff person, if I decide to remain with the company at all."

Sandra then proceeded to tell Larry about the disposition of the Special Projects Division, and of the decision to have Foresight report to Blind. With rancor in her voice, she shared the news that Buck would be named chief financial officer of Textware, Inc. Larry drew the same conclusion that Sandra had drawn; Foresight had been the sacrificial lamb in that particular power play.

"Topper has to be very upset. Foresight is a favorite of his. That had to be a very tough decision for him to make. It will be even tougher for Foresight to hear about it. I wish Foresight and I were better friends at this point. He's really going to need a friend.

"And Larry, you may also need a friend. I admit, you have a nice opportunity tomorrow to impress Topper. But as of Monday, unless something changes in the interim, you will be reporting to Reginald. You can't tell me that doesn't upset you."

"You bet it upsets me, but I am not going to let that happen. What I haven't told you is that I have decided that I need to be in an organization that will permit me to implement my marketing ideas. I have been patient long enough. If the new organization is unwilling or unable to give me a real chance in the marketing area, then I would be better off elsewhere."

Hearing Larry speak so confidently made Sandra reflect on her own dreams and abilities. Thoughts which had remained fuzzy all morning suddenly became clear to her. "My position is similar, Larry. I am not going to sell myself short. I am going to take them up on their offer for now, but as of Monday, my résumé will be in circulation."

Believing that both he and Sandra were survivors, and would in the end prevail, Larry spent the evening thinking about Foresight. Together, they had created a strategy that had culminated in the creation of the Special Projects Division. Now, on the eve of the demise of the division, Larry wanted to talk to his old friend. On more than one occasion, he reached for the telephone, planning to alert his friend to the events that were about to transpire, and to offer his support.

But he resisted the temptation. Sandra had broken a confidence in talking with Larry. To alert Foresight would be to jeopardize Sandra. He could not bring himself to do that. Instead, he spent his time contemplating ways in which he might be of assistance to Foresight.

Larry awoke the next morning with an idea. In a few hours, he would attempt to get Topper to endorse his plan. A key part of that plan was the coupling of books and software, or the presentation of the "expert" through both text and software. The commercial strategic planning model was still regarded as an important product introduction. Foresight was the author of that model. Why not commission Foresight to write the book to accompany the software?

The more Larry thought about the idea, the more it excited him. Foresight would now lose control of the use of the model; that was obvious. To commission him as author of the definitive text would at least prevent Buck and Sterling from taking credit for the original idea. And it would provide Foresight with a role other than Blind's subordinate.

Finally, the appointed hour for the presentation arrived. Topper was clearly impressed, and even canceled an afternoon appointment in order to prolong his discussion with Larry. By four-thirty that afternoon, Topper had agreed not only to endorse the plan, but to do whatever he could to carve out a position that would enable Larry to work on the implementation of his ideas. And he had reacted enthusiastically to the idea of asking Foresight to author the text on strategic planning.

That night, Larry called Foresight and suggested that they get together. The evening represented a reunion of two soldiers who had temporarily lost sight of one another in the heat of battle. Now that the firing had ceased, they were happy to rediscover that, while both had been wounded, neither had been killed. Feeling a renewed sense of mutual support, they derived enough energy from the relationship to return once again to the strategy table.

They compared notes and shared perceptions of the new players on the game board. Through Foresight, Larry learned that Simpleton, the vice-president of marketing, was little more than an overpaid peddlar. Foresight suggested that Larry reconsider accepting the offer.

"The kind of marketing you are talking about is strategic, not tactical. Perhaps a better place for you is the Strategic Planning Department. Let me make some inquiries. I'll talk to Blind within the next week or so.

"Blind is good; not as good as I am, but good. His claim to fame lies in the area of cost reduction, not overall strategy. But then, that's what the book company has needed, given the relatively low growth rate of the industry. The software business is a different story. Strategic thinking is essential. It's a fast growth industry, with new competitors emerging every day. It is no easy matter to find a market niche, and to then use that niche to gain market share. Blind is not the right man for the job."

Larry empathized with Foresight, suggesting that it must be very painful to contemplate having to report to someone who had been promoted past his level of competency. Foresight, however, corrected Larry.

"No, Blind is not incompetent. He is simply competent in a different area than I am. Of course, it is a blow to my ego to lose the title of vice-president of strategic planning. My first reaction when Topper told me of the decision was to resign then and there. However, I do know that Blind is a decent manager, and he is willing to admit that he does not know everything there is to know about planning. I believe that he will give me a lot of room. In reality, my responsibilities won't change much.

"And I am very excited about the prospect of authoring a book. What I'm losing in title, I'll be gaining in credibility. You have done me a big favor, Larry."

By the time the evening ended, Foresight and Larry felt that they were once again in control of their destinies. With both Foresight and Topper on his side, Larry was convinced that he would never have to endure reporting to Reginald.

His belief that he was safe was confirmed the next day when Topper called Larry and said that, as a result of a meeting of all the vice-presidents, the decision had been made to name Larry the director of book sales. Further, he was told that he would be reporting to Simpleton. The present director of sales would become the director of software sales.

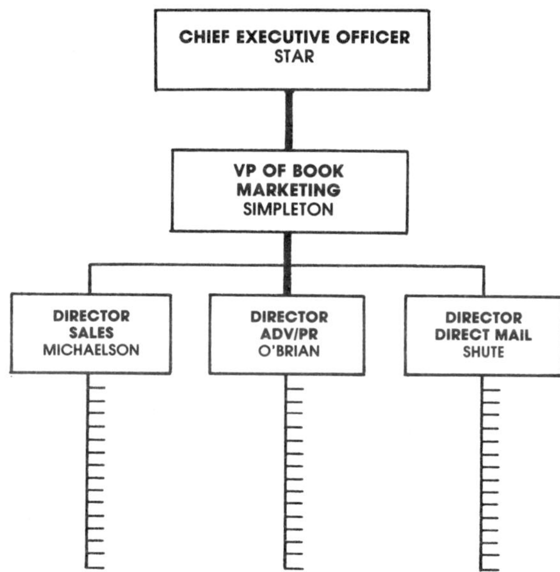

"That will give both of you exposure to the other side of the business. While you won't have direct control of software sales, I'm sure you and Wallace can collaborate. Everyone is excited about the notion of coupling books and software. Foresight's text will provide a test case."

In spite of the fact that he had gotten almost everything he wanted, Larry had an uneasy feeling. Unable to verbalize that feeling, he thanked Topper for all he had done, and decided to ask Bill if they could meet for a drink after work.

Bill was amazed to learn of the events that had transpired since he and Larry last talked, and pleased that Larry had apparently been able to steer clear of power plays and manipulations.

   "You did a superb job of first building and then using *expert power* as you developed and then presented the marketing plan.

"And, you used Sandra's power to get to Topper who, in turn, convinced Star and the other vice-presidents to give you a shot at marketing. That represented a masterful use of the *indirect power* of others.

"Having gained Topper's trust and respect, you then used that leverage to enlist Topper's aid in helping Foresight. In the process, you rebuilt the power of trust which you and Foresight had formerly enjoyed. He has a lot to thank you for. Chances are, you protected his reputation as originator of the financial planning model. As Darwin pointed out, 'In science, the credit goes to the man who convinces the world, not to the man to whom the idea first occurs.'

"The only criticism I have is that you failed to build enough indirect power to establish a sufficient network to get to Simpleton. As a result, you are in the unfortunate position of having to report to duty to a commander whom you have never met."

Larry corrected Bill, explaining that he still had a few days in which to decide whether to take the job as director of sales, or to attempt to convince Blind to carve out a position for him in strategic planning.

"It still seems odd to me, Larry, that Simpleton has agreed to make you his director of sales, when only a week or so ago he made it impossible for you to see him. That tells me he either discounts the importance of the position, or that he has been given no other option by the powers that be."

Larry pointed out that he had an appointment with Simpleton the next day.

"Yes, but the decision has already been made, hasn't it? I mean, as far as they are concerned?"

Larry had to agree that that was both true, and peculiar.

"The other thing that puzzles me, given the history, is that Reginald did not use his new status as vice-president to block you from leaving the Special Projects Division. I would have thought that he would have used all the power at his disposal to get you under his thumb."

"I would have thought so, too. Apparently he was in agreement with the idea. At least Topper said the vice-presidents had no trouble reaching consensus."

"That all strikes me as strange. I believe there is a reason for your uneasiness. You may be part of a manipulation, but, then again, you may not. Perhaps we are being a bit paranoid. Maybe Reginald is so delighted with his newfound power base that he has decided you are no longer a worthy adversary."

"Yes, and Simpleton is only a year away from retirement, and may not really care who functions as director of sales. He may be one of those persons who has already retired, psychologically speaking."

"Yes, that would explain things. That fact also convinces me that the position of director of sales has a lot to offer, Larry. Why, it is conceivable that you could become the next vice-president of marketing. That would be quite an accomplishment for someone who is just this side of thirty.

"It appears that you have learned the true key to success. Rely on expertise, supported by trust. *If you know what you are doing, and if others trust as well as respect you, then you have no need to manipulate or to engage in political warfare.*

"Of course, that is not as easy to do as it sounds. *While reliance on expert power inspires commitment to your approach, you've got to work hard to continue to give the other reasons to respect your opinion.* The more you reveal to others, the less clear it becomes that you are the expert and they, the novices. As others learn from you and become equally expert, the importance of the power of trust and friendship increases. As I said, you seem to have mastered the art of both types of informal power."

Denying the doubts they both felt, Bill and Larry toasted the new director of book sales of Textware, Inc. While they had admitted both to themselves and to each other that the decision was being made without sufficient data, they were equally aware that Larry had not only survived the merger, but had actually gotten closer to realizing his dream. Wanting to minimize the dangers, they allowed themselves to do so.

Larry was to learn in the months to come that he still had a lot to learn, and that it was sometimes impossible to avoid getting caught up in organizational power plays.

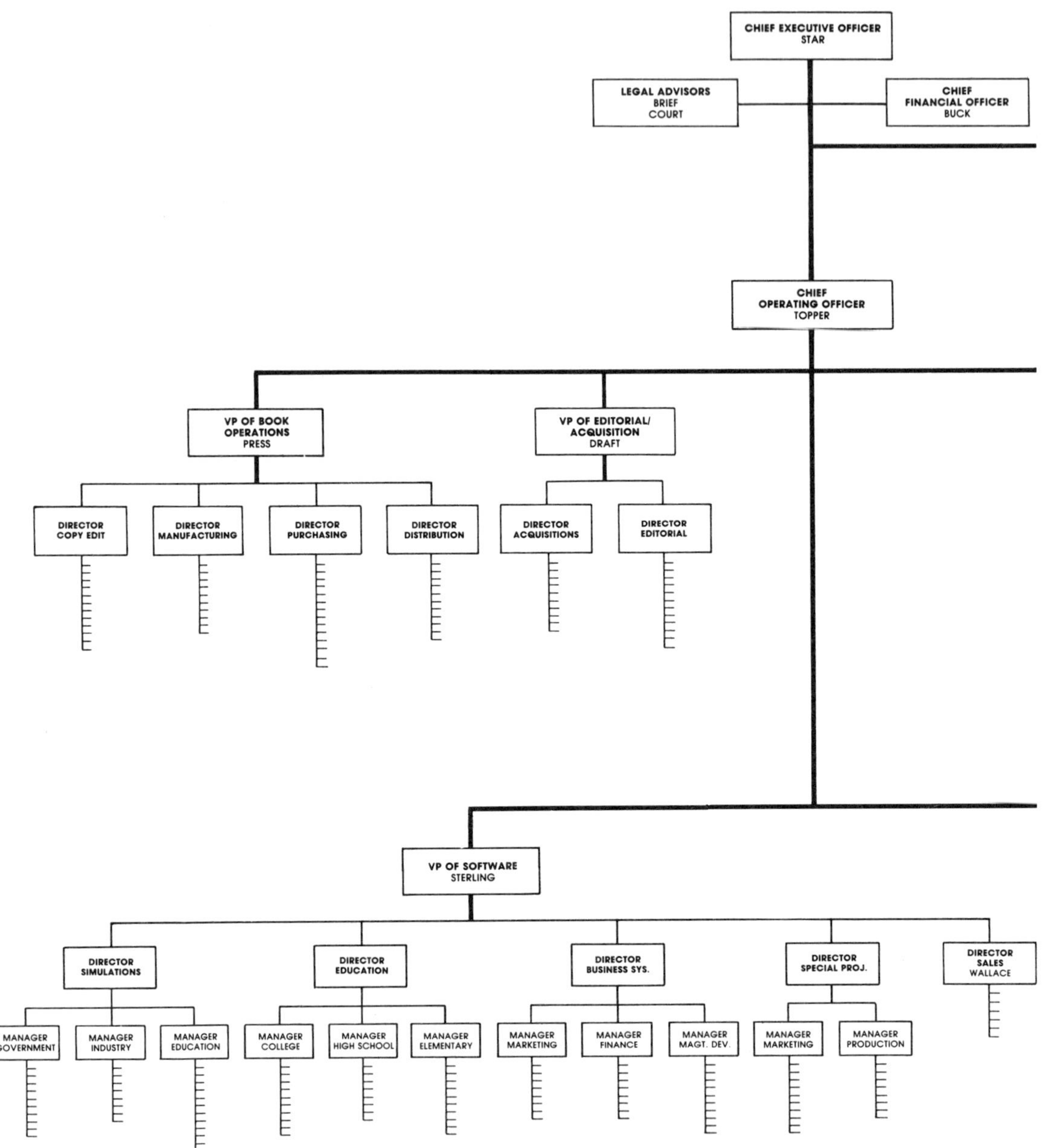
TEXTWARE, INC.
CHIEF EXECUTIVE OFFICER
STAR
LEGAL ADVISORS
BRIEF
COURT
CHIEF
FINANCIAL OFFICER
BUCK
CHIEF
OPERATING OFFICER
TOPPER
VP OF BOOK
OPERATIONS
PRESS
VP OF EDITORIAL/
ACQUISITION
DRAFT
DIRECTOR
COPY EDIT
DIRECTOR
MANUFACTURING
DIRECTOR
PURCHASING
DIRECTOR
DISTRIBUTION
DIRECTOR
ACQUISITIONS
DIRECTOR
EDITORIAL
VP OF SOFTWARE
STERLING
DIRECTOR
SIMULATIONS
DIRECTOR
EDUCATION
DIRECTOR
BUSINESS SYS.
DIRECTOR
SPECIAL PROJ.
DIRECTOR
SALES
WALLACE
MANAGER
GOVERNMENT
MANAGER
INDUSTRY
MANAGER
EDUCATION
MANAGER
COLLEGE
MANAGER
HIGH SCHOOL
MANAGER
ELEMENTARY
MANAGER
MARKETING
MANAGER
FINANCE
MANAGER
MAGT. DEV.
MANAGER
MARKETING
MANAGER
PRODUCTION

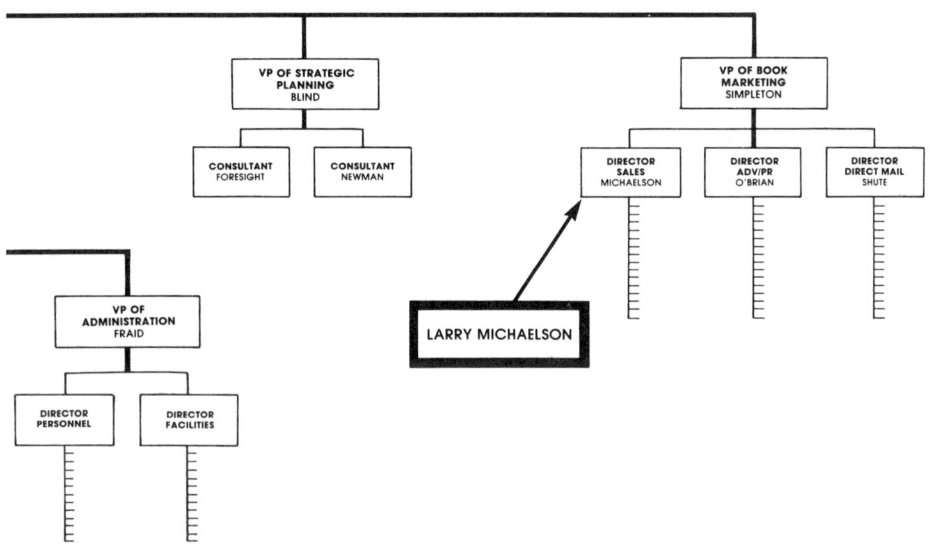

VP OF STRATEGIC PLANNING
BLIND
CONSULTANT
FORESIGHT
CONSULTANT
NEWMAN
VP OF BOOK MARKETING
SIMPLETON
DIRECTOR SALES
MICHAELSON
DIRECTOR ADV/PR
O'BRIAN
DIRECTOR DIRECT MAIL
SHUTE
LARRY MICHAELSON
VP OF ADMINISTRATION
FRAID
DIRECTOR PERSONNEL
DIRECTOR FACILITIES

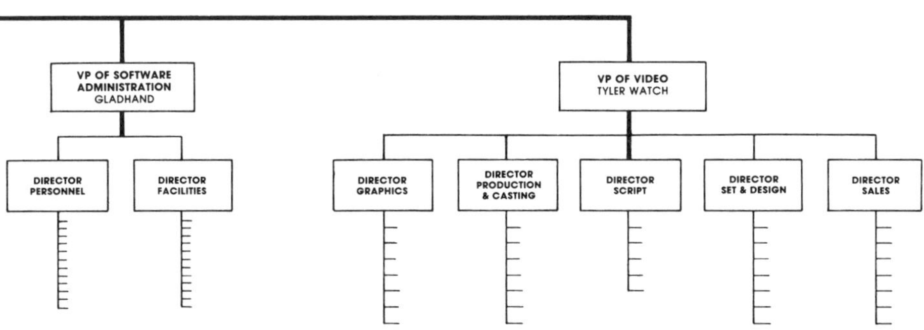

VP OF SOFTWARE ADMINISTRATION
GLADHAND
DIRECTOR PERSONNEL
DIRECTOR FACILITIES
VP OF VIDEO
TYLER WATCH
DIRECTOR GRAPHICS
DIRECTOR PRODUCTION & CASTING
DIRECTOR SCRIPT
DIRECTOR SET & DESIGN
DIRECTOR SALES

LARRY'S NOTES

The key to success is reliance on solid expertise and trust. Know what you're doing, and you don't have to rely on deceit. Inspire trust in others, and they will support you. There is then no need to manipulate or to engage in warfare.

The power of expertise diminishes as the other learns and becomes equally expert. Therefore, it is important to generate trust as well as respect in a relationship.

10

...And More Power Plays

LARRY MET WITH Simpleton the next day. The two men found that they had a natural aversion to one another. The inauthentic politeness that both demonstrated did little to ease the tension. Larry sensed that he was in the presence of an adversary.

His feelings of uneasiness were not stilled by Simpleton's praise of the marketing plan. Nor did he trust what appeared to be a total endorsement of its implementation.

"Follow your dream, my boy. Get Gertie O'Brien, the director of advertising, working on the new corporate logo and slogan. I think that the notion of the 'expert in the machine' is brilliant. Gertie will cooperate as long as you tell her what you want done and how you want it done.

"Of course, we can't just arbitrarily impose the new logo and theme on the corporation. Both Star and Topper will have to approve. The other vice-presidents should have an opportunity to vote as well. At any rate, we can get Gertie started on the development of the graphic art.

"With regard to the sales force, I agree wholeheartedly that they could stand a little training in interpersonal relationships. Go to it, boy, with my blessings."

Larry asked Simpleton whether he was free to begin integrating the sales efforts across the corporation, as he had proposed. In response, Simpleton told Larry to slow down, and take one step at a time.

"Do not be hasty, Larry. Just work your magic with the book sales force, and the rest will take care of itself."

Larry was struck by Simpleton's use of the phrase, "work your magic." That was a pet phrase of Reginald Sterling. Could that be a coincidence? Or had Reginald and Simpleton been talking?

Larry decided to introduce Reginald into the conversation and watch Simpleton's reaction.

"I think that if we ever do decide to bring all of the sales personnel in Textware, Inc. into one division, certain executives will resist. I am thinking particularly of Reginald Sterling."

Simpleton's response was brief and unrevealing. "You may be right. I don't believe it is an issue at this point in time."

Larry tried one more time. "No, but it will be soon. I don't think it will be possible to promote a consistent corporate image and theme unless we integrate the sales departments. I would hope we could begin to take steps to ready people like Reginald for such a move. Would you be willing to do that?"

"My boy, you are worrying about events that may never happen. Just work with your present staff, and leave Reginald to me."

So, he knew him then; knew him well enough to refer to him as Reginald. Larry pushed. "So, you know Reginald, then. I guess you've heard that he and I have had some difficulties in the past."

"I know nothing of the sort and, frankly, am not interested in knowing. I want performance from you, not politics. Enough. Let's get to work. Let me show you your office."

Larry's instincts told him that Simpleton and Reginald had collaborated. But he could not determine what it was they hoped to accomplish. Further inquiry seemed impossible, however. Simpleton had already left his office, leaving Larry with no choice but to follow him.

Gregory Wallace, the former director of sales, had not yet vacated Larry's new office. When they arrived, they found Gregory wringing his hands, putting knick knacks in a box, and issuing orders to the two women in the room. Surmising that Gregory was enthusiastic about his new position in Software, Larry greeted him without reservation. Gregory's response surprised him.

"So, Larry, there was more behind your interest in sales than met the eye. I had no idea you were going to try to take over. Actually, perhaps I am getting the better end of the deal, although it was not a deal in which I wanted to participate."

Putting his arm around Gregory's shoulders, Simpleton offered reassurances. "Now, Gregory, we've been all through this. It was with great reluctance that I allowed the software side of the house to take you from me. Believe me, it is in your best interest in the long run."

Dropping his voice, Simpleton added, "I have your best interests in mind, Gregory. A year from now, you will understand that this move was wise. In the meantime, trust me. After all, we are almost family."

Larry had overheard enough of Simpleton's comment to understand that there was some kind of unique bond between Simpleton and Gregory. That being the case, the transfer made even less sense. Larry vowed to learn as much as he could about that relationship before he inadvertently tripped a hidden mine.

Wanting to give Gregory time to finish clearing out of the office, Simpleton took Larry on a tour of the department, introducing him to a number of people. In spite of the cordial greetings he received, Larry felt unwelcome. There had been few personnel changes in the department over the last several years. Everyone knew everyone else well, and had learned to respect individual boundaries and to tolerate differences.

Then the merger occurred, creating the same fears in the hearts of Books International employees as it had in the hearts of the Software Systems' employees. Now one of their own had been moved out of the safe confines of the family in order to make room for an alien.

The alien's reputation had preceded him. Discussions among the sales reps had not been complimentary. "Software Systems' superstar has deigned to join our humble family. Whoopee! If he thinks he's going to come in here and change everything, as we hear he did in prior positions, then he better think again. We like things the way they are."

Larry did not yet understand the culture of the book company; nor did he appreciate that his innovative, entrepreneurial style was incompatible with an organization that had grown comfortable with bureaucracy, the status quo, and the management of the routine. Larry had been a maverick in Software Systems. As a catalyst of change, he would be viewed by Books International people as a misfit.

Larry became more aware of the problem as he attempted to meet with his new staff. As he had done in prior positions, he began by calling a meeting of the entire sales function. During the meeting, he attempted to position himself as the boss who would "play boss" only when the situation demanded. Stating that he preferred to manage through involvement rather than direction, Larry encouraged the group to share their ideas openly with him. His words of encouragement fell on deaf ears, however. The barrier of politeness remained. No one was willing to risk stating his or her views openly.

The staff meeting was followed by a series of individual meetings with the sales personnel. In these more intimate meetings, the same behavior persisted. Time after time, Larry heard the "party line." No one ventured a real opinion, or openly challenged either the status quo or Larry himself.

Larry began to realize that it was going to be extremely difficult to build the power of trust and expertise with his new staff. He was beginning one down; they felt they already had reason to mistrust him. And they were very aware that he knew little or nothing about the book business.

Unable to learn about the department through conversation, Larry turned to the call reports filed by the sales reps. He hoped the reports would give him a sense of the problems and opportunities facing the department. He needed to determine the ratio of calls to sales, and to pinpoint patterns in the data. Did one salesperson have a consistently better track record? Did there appear to be a certain group of accounts which consistently defied efforts to close the sale? Which were the "easiest" accounts to handle? Within these accounts, what was the ratio of book sales to book returns?

Larry's study of the reports revealed a glaring inconsistency and presented Larry with a serious management problem. As Larry would learn in the months to come, the inconsistency was to trigger a series of events that would further alienate him from his new staff, and actually threaten his job.

Roger Fulton, a sales representative in his late fifties who had been with the company for more than thirty years, had been reporting a call volume that was far in excess of the average. Further, given the size of his region, and the distance between cities in that region, it seemed almost physically impossible for him to have actually made those calls. The sales figures, or the ratio of calls to sales, cast further doubt on the accuracy of the call report. The man was reporting an excess of calls, and a dearth of actual sales. His expense reports, however, were consistent with the call reports.

Larry decided to begin his sales training effort with Roger Fulton. Roger, he reasoned, had the energy of two men. Yet something was lacking in his ability to close a sale. Larry assumed Roger would appreciate an effort designed to enhance his sales effectiveness.

Larry called and invited Roger to have lunch. He chose lunch over a more formal meeting, hoping to minimize the status differentials that existed, and to begin to build a relationship with the man. He hoped that the establishment of a relationship with one of the salesmen would earn him the reputation of being a friendly and open person, thereby making it easier to break down the barriers that existed with the others.

But the strategy that had once worked so well backfired this time. As lunch progressed, Roger became increasingly tense and defensive. He could not seem to hear that Larry simply wanted to help him. Regardless of what Larry said, Roger continued to respond, "Look, I'm doing all that I can, more than I can. I have some tough accounts in my region, that's all. It's amazing that I manage to close as many sales as I do. My return rate is low, after all. This is a tough business. I should know. I've been at it for more than thirty years."

Larry tried another tactic. Perhaps Roger would relax if they talked for awhile about his life outside the company. Larry asked about Roger's family, and expressed concern that they might resent all of the time Roger spent on the road.

Roger, however, would say no more than, "No, they understand that a man has to make a living." He seemed even less comfortable talking about his personal life than he had been discussing his sales performance.

A month passed. Larry again reviewed Roger's call reports and noticed a significant change. Roger's response to their luncheon conversation had been to cut back on the number of calls he made. Larry despaired that all he had succeeded in doing was demotivating Roger.

Larry called Roger into his office and asked about the change. Again, Roger's response was defensive. "Well, my call volume was lower, but so were my expense reports. I figured that was the real reason for the lunch. You thought my expenses were out of line. As you can see, they are back in line."

Larry had never said that he was concerned about Roger's

expenses. That Roger had made that assumption triggered Larry's suspicions. Larry asked to see Roger's complete personnel file. Comments made by various supervisors over the years did not match the profile of a potential cheat. "Roger is hard working and dedicated." "A fine salesman, Roger really cares about his customers." "Roger is part of the backbone of this organization. He is a solid, reliable worker."

Gregory had not made any notes in Roger's file. The numbers he had used to rate Roger on the standard performance review form revealed little. Hoping to allay his suspicions, Larry called Gregory. Gregory had very little to say, claiming that Simpleton had always taken a special interest in Roger, as well as in the other long-term employees and that, as a result, he had had very little direct dealings with Roger.

Larry then called Simpleton. Not wanting to waste his superior's time with a personnel problem, Larry came right to the point. "I have reason to believe that Roger is falsifying his expense reports. Gregory was unable to tell me anything. I wonder if you have any information that might help me manage the situation."

Simpleton's response surprised Larry, given Gregory's claim that Simpleton had preferred to supervise Roger directly. "I couldn't tell you much about Roger. However, if you suspect Roger, then you better run it down. We will tolerate a lot around here, but we will not sit still for that kind of behavior. Falsification of expense accounts in this company is not a misdemeanor; it is a crime punishable by termination."

His mandate clear, Larry decided that he would not confront Roger until he was more certain that a wrongdoing had occurred. But it would take time to gather facts; time he did not have given the other demands on him. He had a function to launch, after all, and could not afford to devote all of his energies to a single employee. He decided that, during the months to come, he would make an effort to visit each of Roger's accounts, assessing the depth and nature of the relationship he had managed to establish, and getting an indication of the frequency of his visits. Only with that kind of firsthand information could he either dismiss or confirm his suspicions.

Still seeking to identify the problems and opportunities facing the Sales Department, Larry launched a customer relations audit. Visiting several key accounts in person, and accessing the perceptions of others through a questionnaire, Larry determined that the majority of customers were satisfied with the way the company handled orders and returns. The distribution system was working nicely.

The customers were not happy with the approach taken by many of the sales reps, however. They claimed that the representatives did not understand either the product or their needs. In response, Larry introduced an intensive workshop on customer relations, mandating that all sales personnel attend.

Understanding that a training program per se would do little to change behavior unless the changes were reinforced, Larry decided that the performance evaluation and compensation systems required modification. The existing systems rewarded activities, not results, and failed to encourage a sufficient consideration of the customer.

But Larry did not feel that it was politically wise for him abruptly to introduce new systems. Remembering how his relationship with Gladhand had suffered as a result of such a maneuver, Larry felt that he had to gain the commitment of Alan Fraid, the vice-president of administration for the book company.

Unfortunately, Fraid was a staunch defender of the bureaucracy, and of the culture that it supported. Fraid was comfortable in a highly structured, predictable environment. He made no distinction between managers and parents, believing that employees were like children, requiring stability and discipline.

The personnel systems that he had put into place reflected his value system. The performance review evaluated employees on the basis of traits which all good children were supposed to display. The penalty for marginal performance was chastisement. The reward for superlative performance was negligible. Employees who put in their hours and appeared busy, and did not make waves, were almost guaranteed lifetime employment.

Larry suggested to Fraid that new systems be introduced to encourage the sales representatives to take responsibility for their own actions, and to stimulate a greater level of concern for the customer. Fraid's response was evasive, though cordial.

It seemed that the norm of avoiding conflict through false politeness pervaded the company. That was beginning to drive Larry crazy. "It's impossible to fight when the opponent will not even declare himself," thought Larry.

Larry decided to approach Simpleton, hoping that the vice-president of marketing would be able to convince Fraid to at least consider modifying the systems. Simpleton complimented Larry on his idea, but refused to take any direct action. "That's Fraid's department, Larry. And it appears that it will remain Fraid's department. I suggest you find a way to get along with the man."

What had Simpleton meant when he said, "And it appears that it will remain his department"? Was Gladhand about to be fired? Larry hoped that was not the case. After a stormy beginning, Larry and Gladhand had finally managed to create a workable relationship. Gladhand had become increasingly comfortable with Larry's organizational innovations as those innovations brought visibility to Gladhand and his function.

Thoughts of Gladhand triggered an idea. Larry thought that perhaps Gladhand could be of help now. Gladhand was regarded as an expert in personnel systems, Larry reasoned. Perhaps he could help convince Fraid, Topper, or Simpleton of the need to modify the systems in the book company.

Gladhand responded immediately to Larry's request for an appointment. Larry, after all, had infiltrated what Gladhand now perceived to be the enemy camp. The decisions made to date had convinced Gladhand that, in the end, either he or Fraid would go. At this point, the contest was a draw. But Gladhand knew that Fraid had the advantage of belonging to the acquiring company. If it was the intent of the book company to impose its culture on the Software organization, then Gladhand would lose. His only hope was to convince Star he had an expertise that Textware could not afford to lose.

Larry did not know that Gladhand's efforts to gain credibility with Star had met with only limited success. Nor did he know that, during his discussions with Star, Gladhand had attempted to take full credit for innovations introduced by Larry.

Pleased that Gladhand was supportive, Larry gave no thought to the possibility that he was about to be a pawn in a game designed to defend Gladhand's turf. Instead, Larry told him of the difficulties he was having getting the authorization to introduce new personnel systems in the sales area. Gladhand empathized with him, and asserted that he thought it was important that Larry keep fighting. Perceiving his opportunity, Gladhand offered to help.

"I can get to Star, Larry. And I can put in a good word for you at the next Executive Committee meeting. If you will provide me with the details of the systems you propose, I will make sure they get a hearing."

Larry did as Gladhand suggested, and gave him a complete description of the personnel policies and procedures that prevailed in Books International. He also armed Gladhand with a tight argument in favor of modifying those procedures. Gladhand had managed to get all that he needed from Larry.

Confident that he had done everything possible to pave the way for the introduction of new evaluation procedures and compensation systems, Larry turned his attention to the corporate logo and theme, and to the experiment around the coupling of books and software.

It had been several weeks since he had asked Gertie, the director of advertising, to put her graphics people to work on the logo. Given Simpleton's promise that he would instruct Gertie to cooperate, Larry was surprised to learn that his request had been given such a low priority that literally nothing had been done.

Larry shared his displeasure with Gertie, and reminded her that Simpleton felt that work on the logo deserved high priority. Gertie, however, had gotten a very different impression from Simpleton.

"I'll tell you exactly what he said to me, Larry. He said, 'Gertie, I know you have a lot to do, but we want to keep our new team member happy. He has some notion about a new logo and theme. I'm not saying it's a bad idea; it may have a lot of merit. Try to work it in, OK? Of course, it should not take precedence over the other things that you are doing.'"

Larry immediately appreciated that he had made a strategic error. He had tried to use indirectly Simpleton's formal power to direct Gertie to work on the logo. His directive had been vague. Had Gertie been committed to the idea, she would have found the resources to do the job. But she could not be committed; Larry had never taken the time to involve her. He began immediately to attempt to rectify the situation.

Gertie responded quickly. In spite of her suspicions about Larry, the idea of being able to influence the future of the company by helping to promote a consistent theme and image appealed to her.

Her distrust of Larry began to wane when she took the risk of suggesting a substantial change in the logo. She had anticipated that Larry would react defensively, and be unwilling to modify something in which he had invested so much time and energy. But Larry was delighted with her suggestion, immediately perceiving the benefits of her approach. The logo and related theme became their joint project, reflecting the opinions and perceptions of both.

The more they worked together, the warmer and more open their relationship became. Gertie began to look forward to having coffee with Larry in the morning. She learned to respect Larry's devotion to his work and to admire his political courage.

While Gertie did not have an extensive formal power base, she did have an informal relationship with almost everyone in Books International. Armed with her contacts, and Larry's network of supporters throughout the software side of the organization, they proceeded to implement their strategy for gaining acceptance of the new logo and theme.

The strategy entailed the development of commitment at the grass roots level of the organization. Larry and Gertie planned to treat the employees of both organizations as though they were consumers. They intended to bring them together in groups, and ask them to assume the perspective of a customer as they reacted to the theme and logo.

The strategy provided several benefits. First, it would generate employee commitment to that which they had helped to create. Second, in asking employees to think like consumers, Larry hoped to instill in them a greater degree of sensitivity to the marketplace. Third, by mixing people from the book company and Software Systems, Larry and Gertie would be encouraging everyone to view themselves as part of a single organization.

Believing that no one could possibly object to their strategy, Larry and Gertie began sending out invitational memos. The first batch of memos drew an enthusiastic response from the invitees. Encouraged, Larry and Gertie sent out a second round of invitations. This time, the response was extremely poor, as the majority of persons invited declined the invitation.

Larry inquired, and discovered that several of the vice-presidents had heard about the meetings and had issued explicit instructions, barring attendance. Larry's contacts informed him that Reginald Sterling had been vociferous in his statement that no one from the Software Division would attend. His stated reason was that no one in the division could spare the time.

Gertie learned that Fraid had been the ring leader of the resistance within the book company. Given his preference for adherence to functional lines, he objected to ad hoc groups that crossed those boundaries. Further, he felt that people from marketing had no business attempting to alleviate the psychological barriers that continued to separate book people from software people and vice versa. That, he felt, was an organization development problem; and, therefore, something that should fall within his province.

Given the extent of the resistance, Larry decided that Simpleton would have to intervene, and convince his peers that the discussion groups were a good idea. If, as Larry suspected, Simpleton and Reginald were acquainted, then perhaps Simpleton could even use his power to convince Sterling to cooperate. Simpleton, however, was unwilling to assist.

"I agree that Textware employees need to understand the customer's point of view. I'm not sure that involving them in the development of a logo and theme is going to do much to instill that point of view. As for your meetings, well that represents a real opportunity cost in terms of lost man hours. No one really has the time to spare, including yourself, Larry. Say, what progress have you made with regard to Roger? Were your suspicions founded or not? That is the kind of issue that requires immediate attention."

Larry assured Simpleton that he had not lost sight of the issue, and was visiting Roger's accounts as time permitted. He reminded Simpleton that he was simultaneously working to meet the other objectives which they had mutually agreed were important. He told him that the sales training efforts were going well; and, he reminded him of the problem he was having getting systems modified in order to reinforce the training on the job. He briefed Simpleton on the customer audit, and statistical analyses that he was doing in order to pinpoint marketing problems and opportunities. Finally, he referred again to his efforts to introduce a common theme and logo across the company and to the blocks that were being set up by the vice-presidents.

Simpleton had simply nodded, revealing nothing. Was he pleased or displeased with Larry's efforts? Larry could not tell. Would he ever take a stand and support Larry with the other vice-presidents? Thus far, Larry had seen no signs of real support. Was Simpleton a friend or a foe? Again, Larry felt incapable of making a clear determination.

Tiring of Simpleton's ambivalence, and trusting that Gladhand could and would approach Star, Larry requested a second meeting.

He hoped that Gladhand could help him convince Reginald and the others to allow the ad hoc teams to continue to meet.

Gladhand was less enthusiastic this time around. When Larry inquired as to the outcome of his attempts to talk with Star about the new performance evaluation and compensation system, Gladhand said only that Star was considering it. Unconvinced, Larry probed for more information.

Gladhand clearly did not like being probed. "Look, Larry, I am not a mind reader. He told me he would give the matter serious consideration. I've done all I can do."

Larry had no choice but to accept Gladhand's statement. He went on to describe to Gladhand his efforts regarding the corporate logo and theme, and the objectives he hoped to achieve through the ad hoc discussion groups. When he mentioned Fraid and the barriers Fraid was erecting, Gladhand visibly winced, but said nothing.

Larry took a chance. "Gladhand, I gather from the expression on your face that Fraid represents a threat to you. He also represents a threat to me; not to my position, but to my ability to achieve my objectives. I suggest we join forces and develop a strategy to minimize the threat he poses."

Gladhand did not react well to Larry's suggestion "How could a director be of political help to a vice-president? No, Larry. Like I said, I have done all I can for you, and I cannot imagine that you can do anything for me."

Leaving Gladhand's office, Larry decided that he had erred in relying on Gladhand to present his case to Star. Gladhand apparently did not have the clout that Larry had assumed he had. Further, it was clear that he was running scared, and was therefore not to be trusted.

Larry decided to go directly to Topper. That, he reasoned, did not constitute a bypassing of Simpleton. Simpleton did not report to Topper; he reported directly to Star. Topper, however, would know what was going on, and had the power to go to Star.

Curious as to how Larry was faring in his new position, Topper agreed to see Larry. As he listened to Larry's recitation of the events that had transpired, Topper became increasingly irritated. Misunderstanding the source of Topper's reaction, Larry launched into an apology.

"I guess I should not be burdening you with this. To be honest with you, I came to you because I have exhausted all other possibilities. Every time I turn around, there is another political hurdle to jump. The politics and the power plays are making it almost impossible for me to accomplish my objectives. I almost feel that I have been set up to fail."

"Larry, under normal circumstances, I would agree that coming to me with these problems is inappropriate. People need to learn to manage their boss, as well as their peers and their subordinates. But, from what you have said, you have done everything in your power to gain the cooperation of Simpleton, Fraid, and Sterling. And the circumstances are not normal. I would suggest that more than half of the organization's energies are currently being diverted into politics and games, and away from productive pursuits. That concerns me a great deal. I intend to do something about it."

Larry realized that he had taken a great risk in revealing as much as he had to Topper. It was conceivable that Topper would direct Reginald to cooperate, and insist that Star reprimand the other recalcitrant vice-presidents. If they became aware that Larry's complaints had triggered the reprimand, they would try even harder to block his efforts through more subtle, devious means.

Larry was more frustrated than he had been since his days as a trainee. He felt that he could not make anything happen. Work on the logo and corporate theme was on hold. Larry had not been able to make any progress with regard to the revamping of the performance review and compensation systems. Efforts to further massage the sales statistics were fruitless; he had done all that could be done. Attempts to assist Foresight in the preparation of the book did not provide a sufficient distraction. Foresight was progressing nicely, and felt no need for Larry's assistance at that point.

The only area to which Larry could devote his attention was the as yet unresolved problem with Roger Fulton and his suspect expense accounts. Fearing the worst, Larry did not look forward to the task.

Careful to avoid running into Roger, Larry made appointments with all of Roger's accounts. His stated agenda was to complete a market audit. His actual agenda, of course, was to determine whether Roger's call reports, and therefore his expense reports, were accurate.

The first few appointments convinced Larry that gathering the information he required was not going to be as easy as he had anticipated. Once the accounts determined that Larry was Roger's boss, they became far less willing to discuss either Roger's approach or the timing and frequency of his visits. Larry did not sense that their reluctance to talk stemmed from the desire to protect Roger, but rather from a wish to avoid involvement in a boss-subordinate conflict.

Unwilling to deny that he was Roger's boss, Larry decided to hire a consultant. Presumably, the customers would feel freer to talk with an uninvolved third party.

While the consultant did succeed in gathering the data Larry needed, he had to posture himself as Roger's replacement-in-training in order to do so. By the time Larry learned of the consultant's deception, it was too late to do anything about it. Had the results cleared Roger, it would have been difficult to explain Roger's subsequent continuation on the accounts. As it was, the data confirmed Larry's suspicions. Roger's call reports, and his expense accounts, were fraudulent.

Larry had never before had to fire anyone who had given such long years of service. In the past, he had been able to deal with marginal performers through transfer to more suitable positions, or through a combination of feedback and development programs. But, in this case, there were no options. Roger was guilty not of marginal performance, but of what Simpleton had labeled a crime against the company. A reprimand would not suffice. Roger had to be fired.

For once, Larry regretted that he had the formal power to hire and fire. Unable to tolerate being in the presence of a man he was about to destroy, Larry let the axe fall quickly, spending only a few minutes with Roger.

"Roger, I have conclusive proof that you have been submitting falsified call reports and that you have been padding your expense accounts. I'm afraid that, as a result, I have no choice but to fire you. You are to clear out your desk immediately. I expect you to be off the premises by noon."

Roger simply stared at Larry, his face without expression. Then, without uttering a word, he stood up and slowly walked to the door. His normally erect shoulders were slumped. His head was bowed. He looked like a broken man.

Larry was completely unnerved by the experience. He would have preferred that Roger get angry, denying the accusation, and slamming the door in protest. But Roger had not fought back.

Putting his head down on the desk, Larry shut his eyes. He wanted to cry, but could not. His head ached; his back hurt; he felt nauseous. He might have remained in that position for hours had his secretary not buzzed him on the intercom to announce that one of

"Go find out what's happening unbeknownst to me."

Drawing by Stevenson; © 1983
The New Yorker Magazine, Inc.

their key accounts was on the phone, irate that an order had been incorrectly filled.

It took Larry a full hour to quiet the customer, and to then rectify the situation that had caused the problem in the first place. He had welcomed the distraction, and the respite it provided from the anguish caused by his own thoughts and the lingering image of Roger as he departed.

Overwhelmed by fatigue, Larry went home early. In making the decision to do so, he did not consider the impact the dismissal would have on the other employees. As he was to discover the next morning, the impact was devastating.

Before he was even able to hang up his coat, Larry was approached by three of the senior members of the salesforce. They demanded a meeting. Given the historic reluctance of his subordinates to express their opinions, Larry knew that a crisis of major proportions was occurring.

The most senior of the three began. "We feel it is our duty to speak up about the way you treated Roger. You have destroyed the life of a man who has given more than thirty years to this company. Not only that, but you gave no consideration to the fact that he has been a solid and reliable performer for most of those thirty years. We believe that the action you took was arbitrary, unfair, and inhuman. If that is the way this department is going to be run, then we want out. Yes, all of us, and we are going to do our best to convince others that they ought to leave, too. You are an unfeeling, insensitive, cruel man."

Larry listened to every word, too shocked to even consider defending himself. When the spokesman had finished, a terrible silence prevailed in the room. Finally unable to tolerate the silence or to look Larry in the eye, the spokesman began to walk out of the room. The motion jarred Larry into responding.

"Wait. Please wait. I have something to say. I think it is important for all of you to understand the entire situation. Given my desire to protect Roger's reputation, I had not planned to speak this openly. However, it appears that you need to know the full story.

"For months, Roger has been padding his expense accounts. And I don't mean just a little. I mean a lot. Hundreds of dollars a month. There's no excuse for that."

"That's where you're wrong. If anybody ever had an excuse for doing such a thing, then Roger did. Roger's daughter is dying of leukemia. He would have killed if need be in order to buy her the best care available. She's expected to live only another few months. You didn't care enough to even try to find out why Roger needed the money. We knew what Roger was doing. Even Simpleton knew what Roger was doing. We also knew that, in time, Roger would not only stop padding his accounts, but would actually underreport expenses until he had paid the company back."

"Wait a minute. You say that Simpleton has been aware of this all along? I mean, aware of the leukemia, and of the padded expense accounts?"

"He never said as much, but we know he pretended not to notice. The guy's got a heart. That's more than we can say about you."

Larry was sorely tempted to defend himself by telling his people that Simpleton had not only told him to pursue the matter, but had stated in no uncertain terms that, if his suspicions were founded, then Roger was to be terminated. But he thought better of it, wanting time to reflect on all he had heard before undercutting Simpleton in the eyes of his subordinates.

It was very difficult for Larry to allow his people to continue to believe that he was uncaring, arbitrary and cruel. Yet that was exactly what he felt he had to do. A far greater injustice was occurring; that was now very clear. Suddenly, all the pieces had fallen into place. Larry could not redeem himself in the eyes of his subordinates until he had dealt with Simpleton.

Larry was so angry that he feared he might resort to physical violence. Nor could he stand to delay the confrontation. His anger was too great; it required expression.

Marching past Simpleton's startled secretary, Larry opened the boss' office door and entered. Blinded by anger, Larry was driven to act, regardless of the consequences.

"Mr. Simpleton, I am furious at you; so furious that I cannot be silenced by threats, or lulled into complacency by polite, evasive assurances. You have been setting me up to fail. What's worse, you put me in the position of destroying another human being. You have lied to me, and you have undermined me. I want, no, I demand, a complete explanation. I am not leaving this office until I understand everything that is going on around here, and until we have figured out a way to put Roger's life back together."

Simpleton's composure and evasive response infuriated Larry.

"I understand that you are upset, Larry. You have every reason to be upset. It is very painful to have to fire a person, particularly a person who has historically been a loyal and devoted employee. Because I understand, I will not hold this outburst against you. I will even overlook the accusations you are making. You are behaving like a child, Larry, and not like a mature manager."

"I am *not* behaving like a child, Simpleton. And you will not throw me off the track by making me the bad guy. I am not here to discuss my maturity or lack of maturity. I am here to discuss the vicious and underhanded games that you are playing. If you will not come clean with me, then I am going directly to Star."

Simpleton continued to maintain his composure as he said, "Larry, it is not smart to threaten a superior. I suggest you shut your mouth before you provoke me."

"I am not going to shut my mouth. You have lost your power over me, Simpleton. Right at the moment, I don't care if you fire me. You can't hurt me, Simpleton. You can't hurt me any longer."

Still, Simpleton maintained his composure. "Do not be so sure of that, young man. Do not be so sure of that."

"You knew all along that Roger was padding his expense accounts, and you knew why. You were willing to turn your back, to pretend that you didn't know about the behavior, trusting that Roger would pay it back. If he hadn't, I doubt very much that you would have ended his career. It is not that you are such a humane individual. You simply would not have wanted to risk losing the misplaced trust of the other employees.

"The firing was unnecessary. Roger could have been reprimanded, and forced to refund the money over time. Or he could have been given early retirement. Anything but what happened. You made Roger the sacrificial lamb. You used him in order to undermine me. What I want to know is *why* you want to destroy me!"

"My, my, Larry. You are getting paranoid. I am getting very worried about you, my boy."

"You should be worried, but not about me. I plan to take good care of myself. Part of taking care of myself is getting to the bottom of this."

"There is nothing to get to the bottom of, Larry. Look, if it will make you feel better, if it will stop this ranting and raving, then we will reinstate Roger. Of course, some punitive action will be required, and he will have to be watched very closely. I'll go even one step further. I will call Roger myself and make amends. I don't want you to worry about it. You need a vacation, Larry. Take the rest of the week off. Get yourself together. We'll start with a clean slate next week. As I said, we'll forget this ever happened. I must say, though, you came awfully close to provoking me. Now, Larry, I have work to do."

But Larry was not ready to be dismissed. Feeling that he had absolutely nothing to lose, he continued. "I don't trust you to call Roger. I am going to do that myself. And I am going to make it very clear to both him and the other members of the sales force that, in dismissing Roger, I was simply following your orders."

"Larry, I am losing patience with you. No one would believe that I would issue such an order. Nor would they believe that such a headstrong person as yourself would unquestionably follow such an order. From what Sterling tells me, you have never been a willing follower. Even as a trainee, you were a troublemaker. No, Larry, your strategy will not work."

Larry had finally rattled Simpleton enough to make him reveal his connection with Reginald. The nature of the game was becoming increasingly clear. Larry persisted.

"So, you do know Reginald Sterling. I should have figured as much. The whole thing is beginning to make sense to me. At least I understand what has been going on, though I do not know why. You never had any intention of allowing me to succeed. That's why you have not gone to bat for me with Fraid. And Reginald's refusal to support the ad hoc groups is all part of the master plan."

"If you could hear yourself, you would know how bizzare you sound. Larry, take a vacation. If you don't, and if you keep talking this way, I'll have serious reservations about your ability to function in your job. The only one who is destroying you, Larry, is yourself. You are your own worst enemy. Now, get out of my office. I do not want to see you around here until next Monday. Good day."

Feeling drained and empty, Larry walked slowly back to his own office. Asking his secretary to get Roger on the telephone, he waited. After a few minutes, his secretary announced that Roger was at home, but had refused to come to the phone. Larry asked to speak with Roger's wife. She also refused.

Larry placed several more calls that afternoon, and each time Roger refused to talk with him. Eventually, Larry left the office and drove over to Roger's home.

Larry asked Roger to return to his job. He told him that the company valued him highly, and that he, Larry, wanted to work with him to find a way to repay the excess expenses without, at the same time, making it necessary to compromise his daughter's care.

Roger did not respond until Larry asked him a direct question. "I can forgive your error in judgment, Roger. Can you forgive me for treating you the way I did?"

"You have a job to do, and you did it. There is nothing to forgive. You cannot be expected to bend the rules. I, on the other hand, must do whatever is necessary to make my daughter's last months as comfortable as possible."

Roger seemed more willing to talk than he had in the past. Larry urged him to do so by asking about his daughter, and expressing his sorrow over her condition. By the time Larry left, Roger had agreed to return to work, and they had begun to establish an open relationship.

On the way home, Larry decided that he needed to take a few days off in order to rekindle his energies and prepare for the battle that he knew would ensue.

Returning to work somewhat refreshed, Larry was immediately faced with a request from Star that Larry come to his office. Anticipating the worst, Larry assumed that Simpleton had won and that he, Larry, was about to be fired.

Star's secretary took Larry into the president's office, offered him coffee, and told him to make himself comfortable. "Mr. Star had to step away from his office for just a few minutes. He'll be back shortly." With that, she left, closing the door behind her.

This was the first time Larry had been in the president's private office. A warm and comfortable office, it was cluttered with photographs and books. The desk, however, was uncluttered. Larry could not help but notice that his marketing plan, formulated almost seven months earlier, lay open in the middle of the desk. Next to it was one of the company's performance appraisal forms. It, too, lay open. Larry wondered whether the documents were related. To his knowledge, no appraisal form had been completed on him in over a year. Puzzled, it was all he could do to resist standing up and reading the name on the form.

He was glad that he had resisted the temptation, for even as the thought passed through his mind, the door opened and Star walked into the room. Star wasted no time before coming to the point.

"Larry, I have spent the better part of the last two days thinking about you. First, Topper approached me, urged me to reread your marketing plan, and described all the difficulties you were having implementing the plan.

"One of the sources of your difficulties presented himself to me within hours of my conversation with Topper. Simpleton submitted a performance review on you with the recommendation that you be dismissed. He has made the claim that your behavior is irresponsible, that you have antagonized the entire sales force, and that you are incapable of taking direction. Those are pretty serious accusations."

Larry sensed that Star was not finished and so forced himself to remain silent. Within a few moments, Star continued.

"Well, Topper had spoken so highly of you that the performance review did not make any sense. In an effort to understand the inconsistency, I requested a meeting with your former manager, Sandra Newman. She was effusive in her praise of both your managerial skills and your sense of the marketplace. The more I listened, the more convinced I became that Simpleton was trying to get you out of the way.

"There have been too many casualties as a result of this merger, and I will not see you be the next. Actually, your situation might not have come to my attention had I not recently issued a memo stating that all promotions, demotions, transfers, and dismissals occurring at the director level and up were to be cleared with me. I know of no other way to contain the power plays that seem to be afflicting us these days.

"The long and the short of it, Larry, is that I am going to take a chance on you. As you probably know, Simpleton is due to retire in five months. Well, I've decided to escalate the timing a little. In spite of your youth, your relative inexperience in the book business, and the fact that your corporate experience spans only seven and a half years, I'm going to give you a shot at implementing your marketing plan. As of Monday morning, you will be the acting vice-president of marketing in the Books Division. Because of my own interest in marketing and because I want to monitor your progress myself, you will be reporting directly to me."

Larry was speechless; he had entered the room believing that his career with Textware was about to end. He would leave the room with a mandate to pursue his first love, and with the power to really make things happen.

With so many thoughts racing through his mind, Larry found it difficult to utter a coherent sentence. Finally, he was able to mutter,

"Thank you, sir. I appreciate your confidence in me, and promise that I won't let you down."

But Star had not yet finished. "Yes, I do have confidence in you, Larry, but I have a few concerns that I want to share with you. I know that you are intellectually curious and analytically astute, that you are comfortable with innovation, and that you are courageous. All of these traits are important to success in the marketing role.

"Equally important is the ability to get people within the company excited about the marketing function. In effect, everyone should perceive of himself or herself as being 'in marketing.' I am concerned that you will try to move too quickly, forcing your point of view on others. Remember, the book company is used to moving slowly.

"I will monitor your performance for one year. At the end of that period, if you have been effective, I will consider making you the permanent vice-president of marketing, and expand your function to include the marketing of both books and software."

His head reeling with the excitement of success, Larry called Bill, and invited him to dinner. Before he hung up, he warned Bill that he had lived through a political nightmare and survived, but that he wanted to learn all he could about manipulation and how to avoid it. In preparation for their dinner, Larry devoted the rest of the afternoon to contemplating the events of the past several months, and to doing a self-assessment of the power and influence strategies that he had used and misused. He was eager to talk when dinner began.

"About the only thing that I did right was to get myself promoted to acting vice-president. In doing so, I really enhanced my *reward, coercive,* and *position* powers.

"I did not work hard enough to build friendships within the book company. I think that they still perceive of me as a deviant, an alien. And the firing of Roger certainly didn't help. It is going to take awhile to convince people that I really am a very caring person.

"I did a much better job of *networking* outside the company. During the course of the customer audit, I built a lot of good relationships with our clients.

"Nor did I do enough to give people within the book company reasons to respect me. Most still do not think that I know much about the book business. While I did my homework, I did not create enough opportunities to show them what I can do. The only exception is

Gertie O'Brien. I think she really respects my expertise, at least in the marketing area.

"And Gertie is highly motivated with regard to the logo and theme. She is going to be a real asset. I suppose that is because I involved her, and stimulated her commitment.

"With regard to my use of the various power bases and influence strategies, the only thing I did exceptionally well was to use my expertise to enlist Star. My marketing plan apparently impressed him enough to convince him to take a chance on me, and to allow me to implement my plans.

"I guess I would have to credit myself for enlisting Topper. I used his power with Star to get Star's attention. Had I not done that, Simpleton would probably have succeeded in getting me fired.

"While it was appropriate to rely on Topper, my reliance on Gladhand and on Simpleton was extremely unfortunate. In enlisting their aid, I made myself vulnerable. That was dumb. I should have listened to my gut feeling that neither could be trusted.

"Nor did my attempt to enlist Fraid succeed. Perhaps I should have involved him in the problem, though I doubt anything would have worked. He is so stuck in his ways. Perhaps if I had done a better job of establishing a network within the book company, I might have been able to convince others to persuade Fraid.

"But my greatest error was to allow myself to be victimized by the power plays and manipulations of others. Simpleton set me up to fail. Gladhand attempted to protect his turf at my expense. Reginald was effective in his effort to block the continuation of my discussion groups.

"I was even guilty of manipulating others. I mean, I did not set forth my true agenda when I interviewed Roger's accounts. That certainly could have backfired."

At this point Bill intervened.

"It sounds as though you have spent the last six months going from one manipulative nightmare to another. I think that it is high time you learned more about manipulation. Hopefully, a little knowledge will go a long way toward keeping you out of unnecessarily risky situations in the future.

"*To manipulate is to pursue a hidden agenda; to pretend to want one thing while the actual goal remains unstated.* Manipulators use a variety of approaches. Some rely on informal power and others on formal power. Some hide their true agenda, but reveal their power base. Still others will subject you to the double whammy, hiding both their actual agenda and concealing or lying about their power base. Putting this all together, we find that there are four classic types of manipulations.

"The kind of manipulation we most often hear about is seduction. Most of us think of seduction as a sexual activity. In corporate life, the payoff is nonsexual, but the dynamic is the same. *Seduction involves the use of informal power (the power of friendship, expertise or presence) combined with the pursuit of a hidden agenda.* 'Do as I ask because you like me, trust me, or respect me and in the process, you will end up doing for me that which I will not declare as my true agenda.'

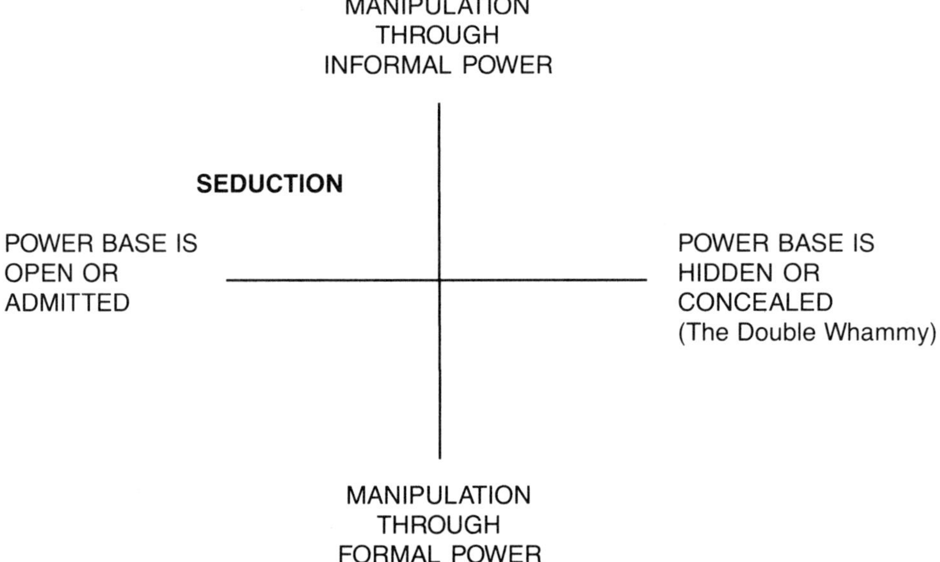

"You provided me with two good examples of seduction. I would imagine that Gregory thinks you seduced him. You used the power of your shared interest in marketing (friendship power, the power of shared goals) to convince him to tell you all about the sales department (your apparent motive) when, in reality, you were scheming to take his job away from him."

"I was not, Bill. That is absolutely untrue!"

"I know that, but I bet that Gregory doesn't. Let me give you another example. You established, or attempted to establish, discussion groups to get people's reaction to the new logo. In effect, you were using your informal power to cajole people into accepting the logo you and Gertie had developed."

"Yes. You've got me there. However, in my defense, I do have to say that we were at least somewhat willing to listen to suggestions."

"For argument's sake, we'll assume you were open to suggestions. Still, you were manipulative. You had two agendas that you did not reveal. You were trying to develop a total company spirit, and you were trying to make people more aware of their impact on the customer. You did not reveal either objective.

"You also provided me with an example of manipulation through entrapment. *Entrapment occurs when the individual uses his or her formal power to pursue a hidden agenda. The power base is open or admitted; the agenda is concealed.*

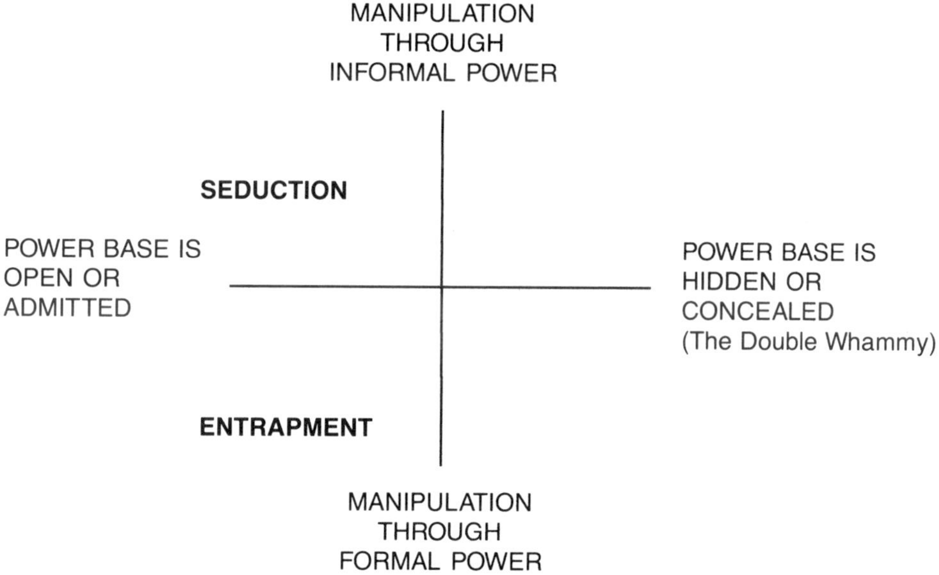

"Simpleton used his formal power, his position power, to tell you to terminate Roger if your suspicions were confirmed. His stated agenda was to discourage the padding of expense accounts. As it turns out, his actual agenda was to create a rift between you and your staff so that he could substantiate the claim that you were a bad manager.

"By way of summary, then, we have considered two manipulations that combine the *open* or admitted use of a power base combined with a hidden agenda: seduction (with its reliance on informal power) and entrapment (with its reliance on formal power).

"The other two types of manipulations involve an even greater use of deception. *Disclaimer as a tactic involves both a concealed or falsified informal power base and a hidden agenda.*"

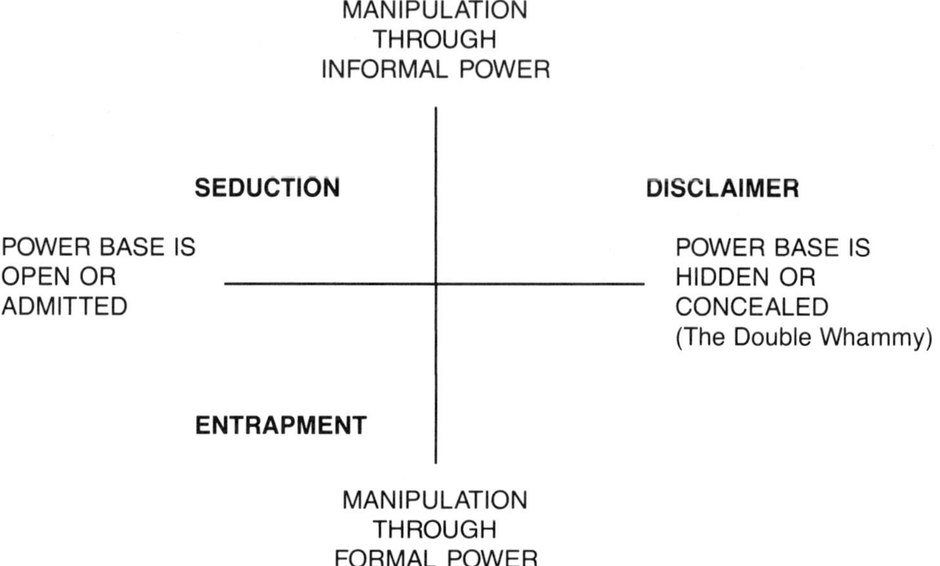

"I think I get the point," said Larry. "I remember a time when Gladhand used disclaimer with me. He denied that he had the time to help me search for qualified candidates. His apparent objective was to pursue existing priorities. His actual agenda was to make it more difficult for me to succeed. He wanted revenge; you see, I had disrupted his tidy trainee program by getting promoted earlier than his schedule generally allowed."

"You, yourself, were guilty of a disclaimer during your efforts to confirm or disconfirm your suspicions about Roger. When you went to see his accounts, you pretended that you were interested only in doing a market audit (false agenda) and that the information would be used only to enhance client relations (false use of the power of shared goals).

"*The fourth manipulation, camouflage, resembles disclaimer and involves the denial or falsification of the formal power base and the simultaneous pursuit of a hidden agenda.*

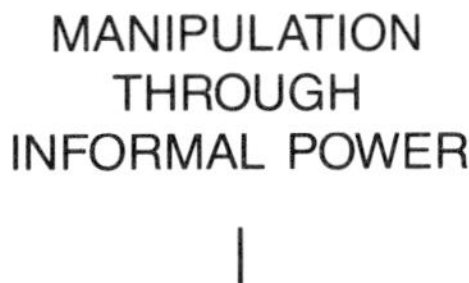

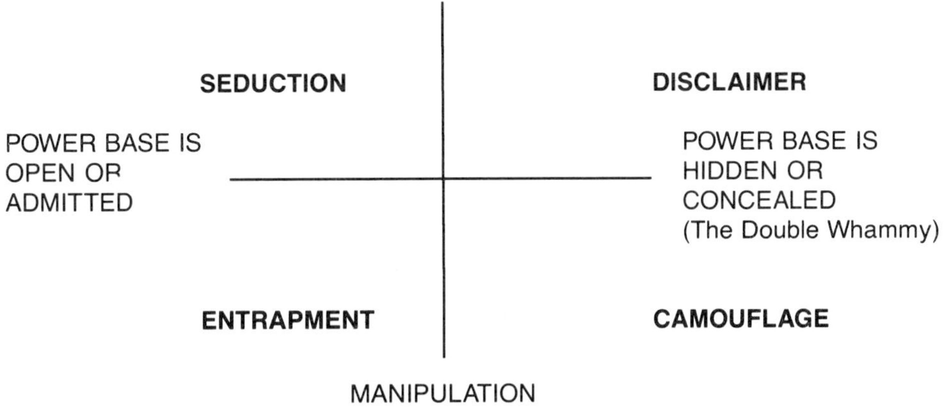

"You were the victim of camouflage. Gladhand led you to believe that he could and would get to Star to plead your case for revised compensation and performance evaluation systems. His apparent objective was to assist you. His actual objective, as you have only recently learned, was to gain a competitive edge over Fraid by taking credit for your ideas.

"Simpleton used every form of manipulation in his attempts to get you, Larry. He never had any intention of supporting you, or of enabling you to reach your objectives. On the contrary, his actual agenda was to set you up to fail. How do you feel about him at this point?"

"Furious would be too soft a word. I regard Simpleton as one of the most devious, unreliable, untrustworthy people I have ever met. I will never trust him again."

"Nor should you. As Lawrence Stine wrote, 'Trust that man in nothing who has not a conscience in everything.' Your reaction to Simpleton illustrates the reason that manipulation is a strategy to be avoided. *When people discover that they have been manipulated, they feel hostile, defensive, and cautious. They are unlikely to respect or to trust the manipulator in the future.* Ethics aside, the manipulator takes a tremendous risk as he or she increases the likelihood of a hostile backlash, and diminishes possibilities for building and using expert power and the power of trust in the future.

"On top of that, manipulations generally backfire. Consider Simpleton; he is out as a result of his manipulations."

"So is Gladhand, Bill. He, too, was offered early retirement. Alan Fraid is now the vice-president of administration, responsible for both books and software."

"Both Simpleton and Gladhand provide examples of the fact that manipulators typically get caught."

"Well, for awhile it looked like the manipulators were going to take me down with them. I am pretty fortunate to have survived one manipulation after another."

"Yes, you are very fortunate indeed. Part of the reason you prevailed is that you handled yourself well; for the most part, that is. You did the only thing that can be done when someone is trying to manipulate you. You confronted the manipulator in a direct, straight-forward fashion. In doing so, you let the individual, in this case Simpleton, know that his strategy wasn't working. While you never got him to reveal his true agenda, you did provoke him into taking an action that eventually backfired."

"Let's hope that Sterling proves to be his own worst enemy. That guy is a master at manipulation. He has been at it for years, and has never gotten caught," said Larry.

"I do not suggest that you wait for fate to take its course. Confront him, Larry. It is possible that he continues to believe that you are unaware of what he is attempting to do and will thus continue in his deception. Call it, Larry. You have nothing to lose and everything to gain.

"If you are to imbue the organization with a marketplace perspective, then you are going to need the support of everyone in the company, Larry. Your new position is going to require that you be extraordinarily adept at managing organization power dynamics. Your job will be that much more difficult given the conflicts and tensions that still exist because of the merger. And you are going to be forced to work with two rather distinct organization cultures. Yes, Larry, you face a greater challenge than you have ever faced before."

As he left Bill, Larry felt prepared to meet the challenge. The copious notes he had taken made him feel more secure. He vowed to avoid being victimized again, and anticipated with pleasure the first day on the job as acting vice-president of book marketing.

LARRY'S NOTES

Manipulators attempt to conceal their objectives from their targets of influence; they pursue a hidden agenda.

Seduction: Hidden agenda combined with open use of informal power . . . e.g., failure to state openly objectives of logo discussions . . . remember to make other objectives clear when reinstituting the groups.

Entrapment: The hidden agenda combined with the open use of formal power . . . . e.g., Simpleton setting me up to get Roger.

Disclaimer: A double whammy . . . . pursuing a hidden agenda while denying or falsifying the informal power base . . . . e.g., my telling accounts that I was doing a marketing audit.

Camouflage: Another double whammy . . . . pursuing a hidden agenda while denying or falsifying the formal power base . . . e.g., Simpleton telling me that I have his full support.

Manipulation is a dangerous tactic, and should be avoided if at all possible . . . . destroys trust . . . makes it difficult or impossible to build and use expert power or the power of trust . . . creates suspicion and hostility.

The thing to do when you think you are being manipulated is to confront the manipulator in a straightforward, direct fashion.

TEXTWARE, INC.

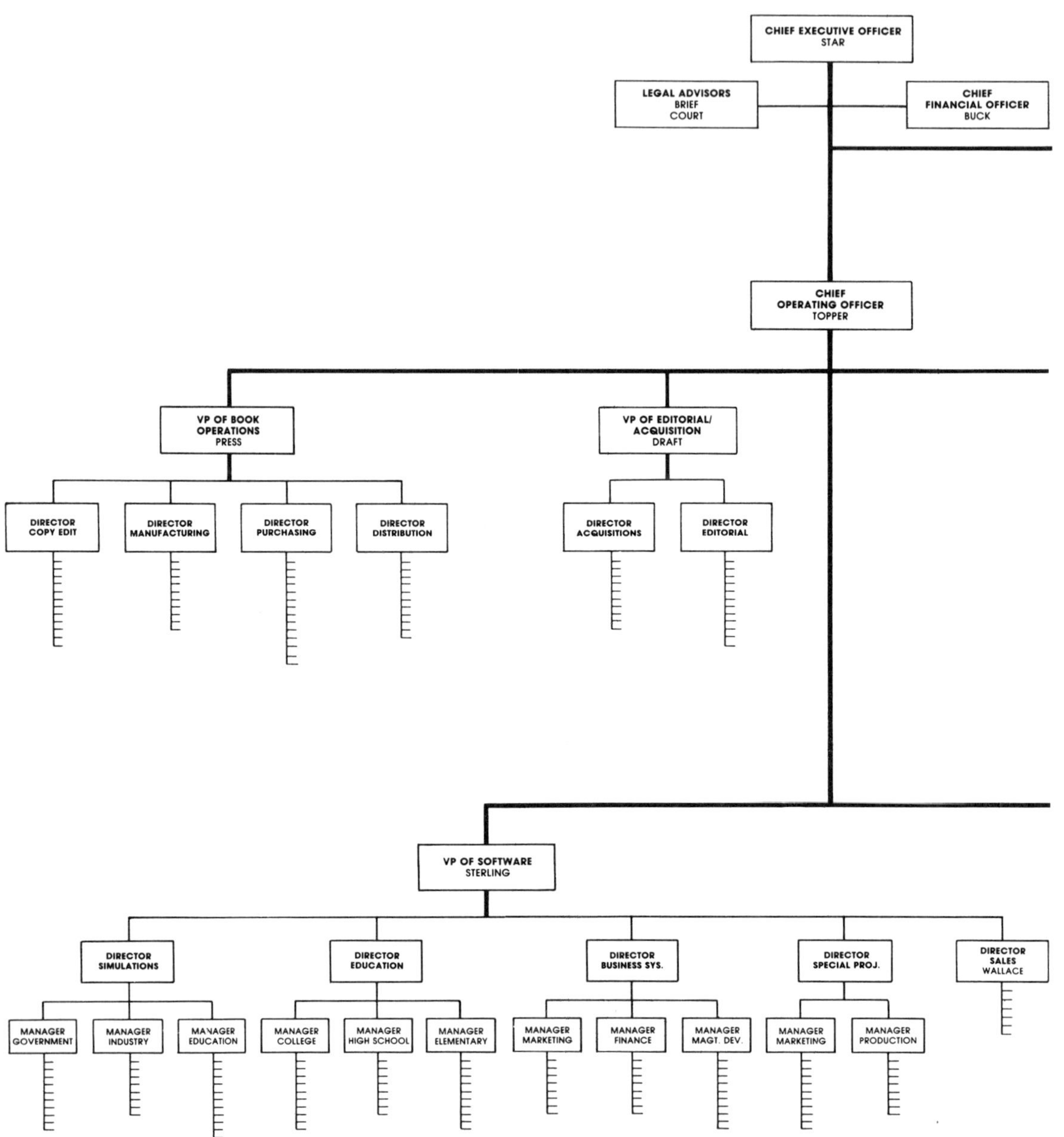

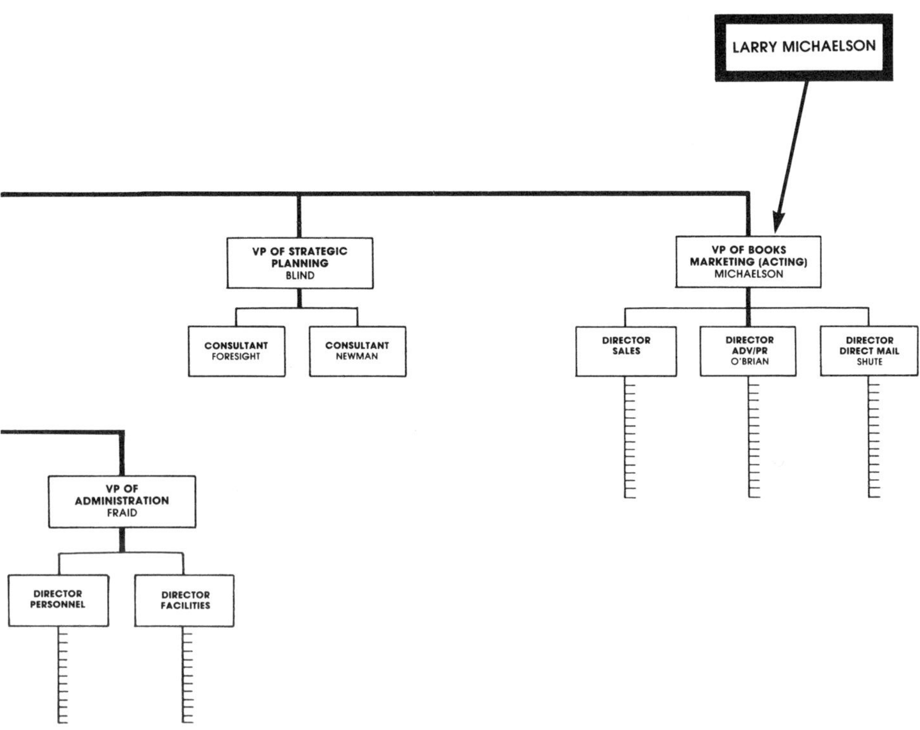

LARRY MICHAELSON
VP OF STRATEGIC PLANNING
BLIND
CONSULTANT
FORESIGHT
CONSULTANT
NEWMAN
VP OF ADMINISTRATION
FRAID
DIRECTOR
PERSONNEL
DIRECTOR
FACILITIES
VP OF BOOKS MARKETING (ACTING)
MICHAELSON
DIRECTOR
SALES
DIRECTOR
ADV/PR
O'BRIAN
DIRECTOR
DIRECT MAIL
SHUTE

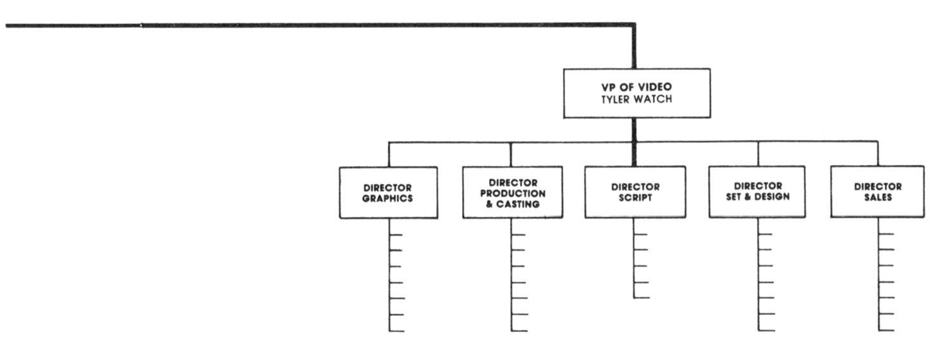

VP OF VIDEO
TYLER WATCH
DIRECTOR
GRAPHICS
DIRECTOR
PRODUCTION
& CASTING
DIRECTOR
SCRIPT
DIRECTOR
SET & DESIGN
DIRECTOR
SALES

11

Villains
and Virtuosos

Larry's first project as an acting vice-president was to reconsider the marketing plan he had developed so many months before. He determined that it required little modification. His overall objectives remained the same:

- to get employees of both the software and book areas thinking more in terms of the customer
- to implement the notion of book-coupled software
- to enhance the professionalism of the sales force, enabling them to act more like consultants and less like peddlars
- to introduce a consistent and dynamic corporate theme and logo, featuring the "expert in the machine"
- to sell books

Reflecting on his last objective, to sell books, Larry realized that what he regarded as his least challenging objective constituted, in fact, the core of his formal responsibility. While Star had applauded his overall marketing plan, and urged him to proceed on all fronts, he did not have the formal power to do so. The software sales force continued to be managed by Gregory Wallace, who reported to Reginald Sterling. The video sales force reported to Tyler Watch. Larry had direct authority over only the book sales force.

Nor, Larry realized, did he have the authority or the formal power to mandate the acceptance across the organization of a consistent logo and corporate theme. On the contrary, promotion of the slogan "the expert in the machine" emphasized software, not books. Yet he continued to believe in the idea, convinced that books could sell software, and vice versa.

The more he thought, the more sober he became. "So that's what Bill meant about my having to use everything I know about power dynamics. In order to accomplish my objectives, I am going to have to find a way to persuade others. Even Reginald. I will simply have to find a way to gain his cooperation, if not his commitment. There is no option.

"The same thing holds true within the book company. My success is dependent on the performance of the vice-presidents of both the Editorial Division and the Operations Division. I have almost no relationship with either John Draft, vice-president of editorial, or with Victor Press, vice-president of operations. And it's not likely that Fraid will help me deal with them. If anything, he mistrusts me. Our styles are so very different."

It is fortunate that Larry devoted the time to reflecting on his objectives and relationships. The afternoon of his first day on the job, Star and Topper called a special meeting of the Executive Committee. Their purpose was to introduce Larry, their new member. As acting vice-president, he had both the right and the responsibility to participate on the committee.

Membership on the Executive Committee brought with it a lot of power. While both Star and Topper reserved the right to ignore or veto the decisions made by the group, they tended to rely heavily on it as decisions were made which impacted upon the overall organization.

As Star made the announcement about Larry's promotion, Larry watched the faces of each member of the assembled group. Tyler Watch smiled, and nodded at Larry, expressing with his gestures both approval and encouragement. Reginald moved his chair away from the table, and looked up at the ceiling. His gesture clearly conveyed the message, "I do not approve of this decision, and will do my best to ignore it, and you." Buck conveyed a similar message as he persisted in making notes while the announcement was being made. Fraid at least looked in Larry's direction. His expression was noncommittal, revealing neither hostility nor acceptance.

John Draft and Victor Press accepted the news with apparent

neutrality. Larry did not yet know them or the politics of the book company well enough to appreciate that neither had had a great deal of respect for Simpleton. Draft had found Simpleton uniquely uncreative and uninteresting as a person. Press had been consistently frustrated by Simpleton's inability to predict the market reaction to their books. Early sales did not seem to correspond to the volume of the first printing, forcing Press to hold a number of poor sellers in inventory, and to rush to reprint books that Simpleton had predicted would be low volume sellers. Both Draft and Press accepted Larry, believing that he had to be better than the man he replaced.

With the introduction over, Star asked if any of the vice-presidents had issues to raise with the group. Since the meeting had been called specifically to introduce Larry, and was not one of their "regular" sessions, no one had anything to bring to the table.

Initially, Larry kept quiet. He was uncertain as to whether he had the right, or the position power, to raise an issue at this early stage in his career as a vice-president, or as an acting vice-president, to be more precise.

But Larry's courage prevailed. Deciding to avail himself of the opportunity to openly request the cooperation of the other vice-presidents, he requested the floor.

"Most of you are unfamiliar with the marketing plan that I hope to implement. It is my understanding that the plan has the endorsement of both you, Mr. Star, and you, Mr. Topper."

At this point, Larry paused, allowing both executives to indicate that, indeed, Larry's plan met with their approval. Their endorsement was not as clear as Larry would have liked, however.

Star responded, "Larry has some very interesting and innovative ideas. I believe that, as an organization, we should encourage innovative thinking. I expect all of you to at least consider the merits of Larry's approach. His first job, of course, is to sell books."

Topper's response was only slightly more supportive. "It is Larry's hope that, at some point in the future, books will help sell software, and vice versa. The experiment around the simultaneous release of a financial planning text and software is, in my opinion, a very exciting venture. As a group, we should do everything we can to realize in the marketplace the benefits of the merger."

Appreciating the limitations of their endorsement, Larry took matters into his own hands. "Part of realizing the benefits of the merger in the marketplace is coming up with a consistent logo and theme. Only if we do so will our consumers have a clear image of us, regardless of whether they have purchased our books or our software. I feel that promotion of the commercial planning model text and software presents a good opportunity to launch a new logo and theme, and therefore, a new image.

"I also believe that by involving our employees in the development of that theme, we will make them more aware of the marketplace. I have a strong bias that everyone in the company should view themselves as part of the marketing function. For this reason, I would like to reintroduce the discussion groups, and ask that each of you support them by allowing your people to attend."

No one responded directly to Larry's request. After a moment of silence, Star adjourned the meeting. Reflecting afterward, Larry thought that raising the issue of the logo and theme, and of the discussion groups, had been an effective strategy. Reginald and Fraid had both had an opportunity to register their complaints publicly. That they had failed to do so weakened the legitimacy of a subsequent resistance.

Within the week, Larry and Gertie reintroduced the discussion groups. Prior to doing so, however, Larry approach Fraid and enlisted his aid in designing the meeting process and agenda. Impressed by Larry's new status, Fraid agreed to assist, hoping to at least share in the credit for helping to diminish the psychological barriers that existed within the organization.

Attendance at the discussion groups was superb, stimulated by employee interest in the issue, as well as the desire to court favor with the newest vice-president.

Remembering his conversations with Bill about manipulation, Larry opened every one of the discussion groups with a clear statement of his three agendas. "It is my hope to get your reaction to our proposed logo and theme; to inspire you to think of the customer more often; and, to encourage the emergence of a team spirit that encompasses both the book company and the software and video organizations."

The results of the discussion groups were very positive, both with regard to the logo and theme, and the breaking down of barriers between "book people" and "software people." By the time all units had had a chance to comment on the logo and theme, an idea had emerged that seemed to represent the thinking of every part of the organization.

The entire organization would strive to promote the image of the "friendly expert." Every book and piece of software that was to be released by the organization would be checked and rechecked for content accuracy. All authors and editors would be told that, while stylistic differences were important, all text must be "friendly," or easy and fun to read. Heavy academic treatises would no longer bear the hallmark of the company. Similarly, all software would be "user friendly." Finally, the company would not release books or software that were faddish or amusing without being enlightening. The logo featuring a smiling face adorned with an academic's mortar board would connote both expertise and friendliness.

With the commitment and support of the "grass roots" of the organization, Larry took the new logo and theme to the Executive Committee, seeking its endorsement and the authorization to proceed. Anticipating Fraid's support, and acceptance by Draft and Press, and hoping for Watch's commitment, Larry did not believe that he could now be derailed by the Buck and Sterling coalition.

They did make every effort to do so, however. It was obvious that their rebuttal had been well planned and rehearsed.

"We hold our authors responsible for technical errors, asking that they indemnify us in their contracts. We cannot then turn around and make a public claim to be the experts in every field in which we publish. Further, the term user-friendly and the concept it represents is sorely overused; it is the theme song of almost every software producer. It lacks originality."

Larry's initial response was to use all of the market research data at his disposal to combat their arguments. In return, Buck and Reginald took turns, using the power of thought and verbal eloquence to confuse the committee.

The debate raged for several hours. Eventually, Star interrupted, stating that it was obviously not possible to reach consensus that day, and asking each member of the committee to think through the issues, preparing to meet again in another two weeks.

Larry left the meeting discouraged, believing that, once again, political allegiances had prevailed over judgment and expertise. Only after several days had passed was Larry able to even entertain the notion that Reginald and Buck may have made good points. He realized that his reluctance to consider their arguments seriously stemmed from Reginald's past manipulations.

"Bill's right," he thought out loud. "It is very difficult for Reginald to influence me on the basis of trust, or even expertise. It is almost as though I leave him no option but to either use his formal power over me, or attempt to manipulate me. For both our sakes, I must approach him, sharing my reasons for being unable to hear him, and expressing the desire to develop a more productive relationship in the future."

Reginald granted Larry an audience, and listened politely while Larry described the events of the past that made it so difficult for him to work with Reginald in the present. Reginald neither denied nor confirmed his participation in prior manipulations.

Feeling relieved that he had at least expressed his resentment, Larry continued, stating that he thought Reginald had made some good points about the logo and theme, and that he was willing to listen to any suggestions that Reginald might care to make.

Reginald declined the offer, claiming that time did not permit him to dwell on marketing slogans. Responding to the contempt in Reginald's words and tone of voice, Larry believed he had made no progress whatsoever in terms of building a more productive relationship with Reginald.

He did allow himself to consider Reginald's argument against the "friendly expert," however. After a great deal of thought, he had to admit that the term "expert" was troublesome, and the term "friendly" was overused.

Brainstorming sessions with Gertie and others generated the revised slogan, "the approachable professional." That seemed to capture the theme they hoped to promote, while responding to Reginald's concerns.

Not wanting the employees to think that he had arbitrarily disregarded the work of the discussion groups, Larry distributed a memo, explaining the reason for the modification and requesting reactions. For the most part, the employees felt that the new slogan represented an improvement.

Larry anticipated another fight, another debate, another attempt by Reginald to block him. He was pleasantly surprised to find that, while Reginald did not offer enthusiastic support, neither did he offer a counterargument. It seemed as though a temporary peace had been declared.

Nor did he understand the reason for Fraid's vociferous support. Fraid rarely said anything in Executive Committee meetings. It was unlike him to render a clear opinion about anything, at least in that forum. His mode was to play it safe, assessing the way the political winds were blowing before casting his own vote.

Several days after the meeting in question, Larry found an opportunity to thank Fraid for his support, and to inquire as to the reason for it. Fraid's answer fascinated Larry, teaching him another lesson in power dynamics.

"I've been watching you closely ever since you were named acting vice-president. What you may not know is there is a pecking order at the vice-presidential level. Until you arrived, I was on the bottom. To be more precise, Gladhand and I shared the bottom rung of the ladder. Administration does not carry as much clout as the operating areas.

"Anyway, I remained on the bottom rung, even after I was given responsibility for corporate-wide administration. Then you entered the group and the dynamics changed. You see, as an acting VP, you are on probation. That puts you on the bottom rung along with me, or maybe even a rung below me. My period of probation ended when I defeated Gladhand.

"I guess I empathized with your position as low man on the totem pole. Then I saw Sterling and Buck attempting to undermine you. I basically do not like those guys, and I thought you needed a friend in court. I mean, we folks on the bottom have to stick together if we are going to make anything happen."

Larry commented on how much he appreciated the support, and how glad he was that they had overcome their earlier problems. Wanting to enhance the relationship with Larry, Fraid was eager to explain his earlier behavior.

"I felt like you were invading my turf. And I was running scared at that time. You were probably not aware of it, but for awhile there, I was afraid of Gladhand. There's only room for one VP of administration, after all. And it appeared that you and Gladhand were friends, or at least that you had an understanding. At any rate, I feel a lot more secure now, and I no longer believe that you are attempting to invade my turf. I mean, you involved me in the design of the discussion groups. I enjoyed the process, and gained a lot of respect for the way you think."

Delighted to have found an ally, and anxious to proceed with the full implementation of his marketing plan, Larry decided it was an opportune time to readdress the issue of modifying the compensation and performance review systems.

"I don't mean to criticize your systems, but the existing procedures, and the items on the evaluation form, really do not reward results. I think it is very important, particularly in the sales area, to encourage both a market orientation and a results orientation. One way to do that is to change the way sales personnel are compensated. I would like to introduce a commission structure into the department."

Fraid argued for awhile, explaining to Larry that there was no precedent in the company for a commission structure. Eventually Larry was able to convince him to collaborate around the experimental introduction of an incentive-based system.

Pushing his luck, Larry went on to suggest that Fraid consider modifying the entire system in order to encourage a greater degree of cooperation across functions. He shared with him the successes he had had in introducing a bonus system that was dependent on the results of the entire unit. He pointed out that, as functional lines began to blur, people started collaborating instead of competing.

"That forced the production people to collaborate with the salespeople, and vice versa. It encouraged the writers to work more collaboratively with the programmers. Why, that single change was responsible, I believe, for more than doubling the productivity of the unit."

Larry had gone too far, failing to take into account that Fraid was a slow and methodical individual who was uncomfortable with ambiguity and, consequently, with change. His response to Larry's request was clearly defensive.

"The systems we have in place are working, Larry. There has never been a conflict between Production and Marketing, or between Editorial and Operations. Unlike you folks from software, we already know how to work as a team. My energies would be better spent in trying to put workable systems into the software and video side of the organization. It appears that your innovations over there are causing more problems than they are solving."

Fearing that Fraid would rescind his offer to help with the introduction of a commission system for the sales force, Larry dropped the argument. He reminded himself of the need to be patient given the bureaucratic culture of Books International.

His patience wore thin, however, when he ran into a problem first with the Editorial Division, and then with Operations. Both problems stemmed from the tight adherence to functional lines of authority that Fraid insisted be maintained. They were aggravated by the personalities of the vice-presidents in charge of the two functions.

John Draft, the vice-president of the Editorial Division, was a highly intuitive, creative, unorganized individual who had once aspired to be an author. After years of semi-starvation, he had relinquished his dream, taking a job as an editor with the book company. His tendency to overedit the books assigned to him had gotten him into trouble early in his career. The authors objected to the liberties he took with their work, and his supervisors complained about his inability to stick to schedules, attributing the problem to his tendency to rewrite as opposed to edit books.

Eventually John was moved out of the product development area and into the acquisition area. His responsibilities were no longer to edit books, but to find authors. Again, his frustrated ambition to become an author got in his way. Like a parent who tries to live through his child, John began to base his acceptance or rejection of a potential author on the extent to which the author mirrored his own style and interests.

Not knowing what to do with their talented and yet troublesome employee, the company had moved John out of personnel development books, and into the educational book area. The problem persisted. Still hoping to salvage an employee with potential, the company had then assigned John to the business management books area. John had almost no interest in this area. As a result, his tendency to rewrite and to choose authors in his own image diminished, and his performance improved.

Ten years later, John was named vice-president of the Editorial Division. Now, unfettered by a position description which denied him access to the authors and topics which he most loved, his old bad habits re-emerged. Once again, he began to attempt to live out his dream of being a writer through excessive attention to the work of those whom he regarded as "pet authors."

Acquisition decisions began to reflect his preferences. Schedules began to slip as he strove for perfection and a mirroring of his own style. Authors whom he liked were given preference over authors who were in a better position to respond to the needs and desires of the reading public.

Meanwhile, Larry's sales force was becoming more and more sensitive to the market. With increasing frequency, they came to Larry with ideas for books that would respond to a market demand.

Larry took the ideas to John Draft, who listened politely and then ignored any suggestions that did not reflect his own biases. It became obvious that he was either unwilling or unable to put the marketplace above his own personal interests.

Larry was increasingly frustrated by his apparent inability to convince Draft to acquire books that his marketing sense told him would sell. A display of facts and figures as to what people were buying did not seem to help. Draft persisted in arguing that his pet subjects were always about to become popular.

Fortunately, Larry did not have a problem with Draft's editorial standards. They had always been in agreement that the best books were at once accurate, thought provoking, and easy to read.

It was during a discussion about their shared belief in simplicity and accuracy that Larry got an idea. Draft had been touting the attributes of his favorite author, Herbert Browning. "He is a master with words, and can present any subject. In fact, he is willing to write about any subject. It is the architecture of the sentence which fascinates him, not the subject."

Larry had his answer. He would call Browning himself, and convince him that he should undertake the writing of one of the books that the sales force had determined would respond to a market need.

The strategy worked beautifully. Draft could not say "no" to his favorite author. Larry had his opportunity to prove that responding to the needs and desires of the marketplace would benefit everyone: the author, Draft, Larry, and the company as a whole.

The problem he faced with the vice-president of operations was more difficult to solve. Unlike Draft, Press was a highly analytical and controlling individual. Once production schedules were set, he adhered to them with a vengeance, allowing no modification or slippage. Draft's tendency to submit manuscripts several weeks late drove Press to distraction. Caring little about the content of the books, Press could not understand why Draft could not adhere to schedules.

When conflicts arose between the two men, Press generally won. Unlike Press, Draft had a strong need to be liked, and an equally strong need for approval. The expression of anger troubled him. That gave Press power over Draft which he frequently used to pressure

Draft into submitting manuscripts for production before Draft's perfectionist editorial standards had been met. Schedule slippage was thus minimized.

As a result, books were produced and delivered on schedule. Accounts liked that, and regarded the book company as one of their most reliable vendors. However, Press' vigor diminished the organization's ability to respond to unanticipated opportunities. Press would not modify production schedules in order to get a "hot" book out the door in a timely fashion. His inflexibility stemmed not only from his personal need for organization, but also from a basic disbelief that it was possible to predict the response of the market.

The magnitude of Larry's frustration increased dramatically as the time neared for the release of Foresight's book and the related software. It was essential, from a marketing point of view, to release the two products simultaneously. Only if this occurred could one product stimulate sales of the other. Further, to release the software without the book would severely weaken the image of professionalism that Larry was struggling to promote.

Both products were scheduled for release in April. In October, one of the firm's major competitors announced that it would release its strategic planning product in February. The announcement took Textware completely by surprise. Larry's understanding of the software market convinced him that, in order to protect market share, it was essential to escalate the production schedule and beat the competitor to the market.

Reginald agreed, sharing Larry's sense of urgency. The software package would, he promised, be ready by February. Foresight, too, agreed to do his best to complete the manuscript faster than he had planned. His ability to do so, however, was dependent on Draft's willingness to free his best editors to assist Foresight, and on Press' willingness to escalate the production schedule.

Draft had never been enamored of business management books. He would probably have resisted assigning his best editors to the project had he not been convinced by Browning that good authors should be able to write with the buying public in mind. Larry had succeeded in getting Draft to incorporate a marketplace perspective into his thinking.

Press presented a bigger problem. After looking at a draft of the manuscript, and consulting his production schedule, Press announced that he was unwilling to accommodate a February release.

"There are hundreds of graphics in that book. It is a typesetting nightmare. There is no way we can produce that text by February. The best I can do for you is mid-March. And, Larry, that is final."

Larry, however, was not willing to take "no" for an answer. "Look, there has to be something we can do. Go outside; subcontract the job."

"No way, Larry. Like I said, the graphics are too tricky. I don't know of a subcontractor who could handle the job; not in that time frame, anyway."

"Then contract out some of your other work, freeing your resources to work on the strategy text."

"My resources are fully committed, Larry. I am not going to allow you to create a crisis in my area. Six weeks will not hurt the sale of the book. Six weeks, Larry; I mean, be reasonable!"

"Six weeks will make the difference between a successful product introduction and an unsuccessful one. Six weeks is an eternity in the software market."

"I am not interested in software, Larry. I manufacture books. You cannot convince me that six weeks makes any difference whatsoever when it comes to selling books."

"We are not selling books, Press. We are selling expertise, professionalism. We're putting the expert in the machine and attempting to convince the public that the expert *is* an expert because he has written a book on the subject."

"Like I said Larry, and I am getting sick of repeating myself, I make books. That's what I do. I do it well. I am going to continue to do it well. I've got more than twenty books in production right now. I will not disrupt the production of those books just because you've got this pet project."

"It is not my pet project, Press. It belongs to the entire organization. And it represents a major opportunity for this company. A simultaneous release of the software and the text is essential."

Press would not budge from his position, at least not without facts. And Larry could not manufacture facts. There was little precedent for what they were attempting to do. The idea was innovative. Supporting it required belief and a willingness to rely on hunches and intuition. Press rarely did that, preferring the analytical approach to decision making.

Believing that he had no other option, Larry went to Topper, asking him to intervene and direct Press to do whatever needed to be done in order to get the strategic planning book produced by February first. Topper refused.

"I have made it a policy to intervene as little as possible in the operations of the book company. For one thing, I am not sufficiently familiar with either their technology or the demands on their resources. For another thing, I believe it is important to allow the book company executives a great deal of autonomy. To do otherwise at this point is to aggravate the tensions that resulted from the merger. Finally, I believe that it is essential for you to build a positive working relationship with your peers. A mandate from me would only create bad feelings between you and Press. That, Larry, is to be avoided at all cost. In this case, I will not intervene. The cost is not worth the benefit."

Larry tried to explain to Topper that the cost of failing to release the text and software simultaneously was very high. Accustomed to thinking in terms of product and technology, rather than in terms of the marketplace, Topper did not agree that the situation was urgent.

"Timing matters, Larry, but it matters less than product quality. To sacrifice quality for schedule is always a mistake."

"I am not suggesting that we sacrifice quality. I am suggesting that if we fail to hit the market in February with both barrels blazing, we will have lost our competitive edge."

"I don't believe that, Larry. Quality will protect our place in the market."

Larry wanted to point out that there were any number of fine products that never sold because the market either was unaware of them, or was already wedded to a competitive product. He wanted to argue that product sales were more dependent on perception than on reality, but he stopped himself. Topper simply did not think like a marketing executive. Larry was not going to change that.

Larry considered going to Star, and asking him to intervene, first with Topper and then with Press. Unlike Topper, Star had grown up in marketing. He would, Larry believed, agree that it was important to release both products simultaneously.

Topper's comment about the importance of maintaining a solid relationship with Press stopped him from pursuing that strategy. Topper was probably right, Larry thought. Press would resent Larry if he used the power of the chief executive to force a response.

Not knowing where else to turn, Larry considered going to Reginald Sterling. Reginald, after all, had agreed that it was essential to get the software to the market before the competition did so.

Perhaps he could be convinced that it was equally urgent to release the book in February. Appreciating that it was unlikely that he could enlist Reginald's help, Larry decided that he had more to gain than to lose by trying.

Unfortunately, Reginald did not perceive of the book as an essential part of the package. It was his belief that, while sales of the software would promote sales of the book, the reverse was not true.

"People who have paid hundreds of dollars for software are very likely to be willing to spend another twenty dollars for a book. The converse is not true. Those who have invested twenty dollars for a book cannot be expected to automatically want to invest twenty times that amount in software. In short, Larry, helping you get the book out the door will not do anything for me. I really don't care about the release of the book. When it comes out, or even whether it comes out, is of absolutely no concern to me. Nor do I believe it should be of concern to the organization. It is certainly not going to be a best seller, Larry."

"I do not expect that it is going to be a best seller. I am convinced that the book will stimulate software sales, however. In fact, it was my intent to have my sales force promote not only the book, but the software as well. I simply assumed that your marketing staff would promote the sale of the book to their corporate accounts."

"That, Larry, has never been my intent. I will not have them distracted from their focus on software by asking that they act as book peddlers."

"Offering the book will enhance both the credibility of the software, and the credibility of the salesperson, Reginald."

"I do not agree."

"Do you agree that in our advertising campaign, we should promote both the book and the software?"

"Again, I do not agree with you. Gregory has already purchased space in the major computer magazines. We do not plan to make reference to the book. Books are not advertised in computer magazines, Larry. You take care of the book business, and leave the software to me."

Larry was on the verge of losing his temper. Struggling to maintain an even tone, Larry reminded Reginald of the Executive Committee's decision to promote a common theme and logo.

"Reginald, I would like to remind you of the decision to emphasize the theme of the 'approachable professional' in all book and software promotions."

"I have every intention of promoting that theme, Larry. I do not need to get into the book business in order to do so, however. As I said before, you worry about books, and I'll concentrate on software. By the way, I do not appreciate your constant attempts to meddle in my affairs. Stick to books, Larry."

Distraught, Larry went in search of Sandra Newman. She knew the players, and shared Larry's belief in the viability of book-coupled software. Larry hoped she could help him devise a strategy to convince both Press and Reginald to cooperate.

Sandra did more than suggest a strategy. She was able to provide Larry with hard information on which to base an extremely convincing argument.

"Larry, Macrosoft has just announced that they are going into the book publishing business. The trade press stated that the reason for their decision is a study which revealed a high correlation between people who purchase professional books and people who purchase software. But that is just the tip of the iceberg; the study apparently covers marketing and distribution methods, as well as the criteria people use as they select books and software. If I'm not mistaken, the data will provide you with all the ammunition you need to make both Press and Sterling tow the line."

Larry asked Sandra if she had any idea as to how to obtain the complete study. The look on her face, and her momentary silence, told Larry that he had presented her with a real dilemma.

"Larry, there is something that I haven't told you. And I must ask that you keep it in confidence. Foresight and I have decided to leave Textware and to open a consulting practice. We are sick and tired of what we both regard as unempowered positions. The only thing we can use to make anything happen around here is the power of our expertise. Given the fact that organizations tend to be political creatures, the power of expertise is not enough.

"We are forced to function as consultants who lack even the power of the mystique of the outsider. I am convinced that outsiders are able to exert a special form of leverage simply because they are outsiders. They are assumed to be brighter than or more special than any insider, regardless of what the insider knows.

"The reason it is so important that you regard all of this as confidential is that we hope to keep Textware as a client. Our ability to do that will be in part dependent on the way we manage our exit. We are hoping to buy a little time; to line up some other accounts before we take the plunge."

"That makes sense. I am excited for you, and saddened for myself. I haven't seen much of you or of our budding author of late, but I have always taken great comfort from the fact that you were here and available if I needed you."

"I'm not going to the moon, Larry. As a matter of fact, I will probably be of more help to you in my role as consultant than I could be as an employee of this organization. The Macrosoft study is a case in point. You see, part of the reason I am watching them so closely is that it appears that they may become a large client of ours. In fact, my connections in that company are already good enough for me to access the entire study. The dilemma I face is that, in releasing the study to me, they would be trusting me to maintain the confidence of the data. Textware, after all, is a competitor of Macrosoft."

Larry assured Sandra that he did not want her to compromise either her position or her ethics, stating that he would find another way to solve his problem. But Sandra was not comfortable with that, and continued to dwell on how she might be of help without, at the same time, putting herself in a position of conflict of interest. Eventually she arrived at a solution.

"Larry, I am going to request the full study, but I will not share it with you in its entirety. You tell me what you need to know, and I will do my best to give you the answers. I am comfortable doing that. For one thing, I still work for Textware. In addition, Macrosoft does not have a financial or strategic planning product. The firms are not direct competitors in that area."

Sandra was thus able to provide Larry with all the ammunition he needed to convince the Executive Committee that the simultaneous release of text and software was essential. Star approved the hiring of additional resources, if necessary, to make the deadline.

Nor was Press antagonized by Larry's victory. Wisely, Larry had prewired Press, letting him know in advance that he had not given up the fight and that he planned to present a convincing case at the next Executive Committee meeting. Impressed with hard data, Press had finally agreed to modify schedules and reallocate resources.

Larry had not elected to inform Reginald. Past experience had convinced him that Reginald would only use the information to build a counterargument. Time was of the essence. While Larry was confident that he would finally prevail, he could not afford to allow Reginald to stage a filibuster that would postpone a decision.

Surprised by Larry's tactic, and disarmed by the strength of Larry's data base, Reginald was forced to concede that the marketing of the book and of the software should proceed in tandem.

Larry left the meeting pleased that he had won his point, but frustrated that it had taken so much energy to remove what he regarded as unnecessary obstacles. Only days later was he to learn that he had accomplished a great deal more than simply removing the barriers erected by Press and Sterling. As Larry was to learn from Star the next day, he had impressed both Topper and Star with the soundness of his arguments.

"Larry, I have been pleased with your performance over the last eight months. You have become quite an expert in the book business. And you have established productive relationships with my other executives, which I know was not an easy thing to do. Finally, you have created a sales force that is not only highly motivated, but more customer or market sensitive than I thought possible. You are to be congratulated."

Believing that Star had finished, Larry thanked him for the praise and recognition and stood, ready to leave. Star stopped him.

"Wait, Larry. I have more to say. During the last Executive Committee meeting, it became obvious to me that politics were getting in your way. In spite of what must have been an extremely frustrating situation, you did not come running, asking me to intervene on your behalf. A lesser person would have tried that.

"You succeeded in overcoming political barriers. However, in order to do so, you had to invest a lot of unnecessary time and energy. I am now convinced that the marketing function needs to be integrated. We lose precious time due to the separation of software and book marketing. As of this moment, all of our sales and marketing people will report directly to you. While this will not please Sterling, it is in the company's best interest. Of that, I am convinced. By the way, you are no longer an acting vice-president. You are now the vice-president of Textware Marketing. As before, you report directly to me. You have earned your stripes, Larry. Now, go for it."

Elated, Larry called Bill and asked him to join him for a special dinner. It had been almost ten years since they began their discussions about power and influence strategies. The efforts had culminated in Larry's promotion. The event deserved a celebration.

Believing that he was ready to graduate from the school of power dynamics, it surprised Larry when Bill began a rather formal assessment of the strategies he had pursued. Noticing Larry's surprise, Bill reminded him, "As Thomas Huxley so sagely observed, 'If a little knowledge is dangerous, where is the man who has so much as to be out of danger.'

"At any rate, I compliment you on having enhanced your power to reward and to coerce, and the power of your position. This most recent promotion of yours enhances all three forms of leverage.

"Your success with the Executive Committee and, I suspect, the single most important reason for your promotion, was your application of the Look-What-I've-Done Strategy to support the argument that the simultaneous release of the book and the software was important. Gathering information, and thereby making yourself an expert, is a tactic that offers a lot of upside gain, with little downside risk.

"I find particularly interesting your use of the Fraternity Strategy to establish friendship power with Fraid. He finally stopped fighting with you and began cooperating with you because you pointed out to him that you had shared goals, and could help each other succeed.

"A very interesting part of the strategy was your use of your shared disadvantage. That prompted Fraid to declare publicly his support of you at the Executive Committee meeting. In effect, he was saying, 'We are both in the same tough spot. It is the weak guys against the strong guys.' You deserve credit for allowing Fraid to see that you shared the unenviable position of being the low men on the totem pole. That is an interesting way to use the fraternity strategy. Quoting Homer, 'There is strength in the union even of very sorry men.'

"Your efforts to gain Press' friendship were not as successful. Apparently, he is less interested in friendship than in figures. Feelings are less important than facts. But we will talk more about that in a few minutes. I think, had you been more aware of and responsive to his personality and style, you could have saved yourself a lot of valuable time.

"On the other hand, the Fraternity Strategy worked nicely with Draft. You showed him that you had something in common; namely, a belief in simplicity of writing style. From there, you went on to establish a relationship characterized by mutual understanding.

"I think you also deserve points for attempting to clear the air with Reginald. In confronting him, you indicated that you wanted to establish a better relationship. You also tried to point out to him that your goals were interdependent. Unfortunately, the strategy didn't work, but, as I said, you had to give it a try.

"You have always performed well in the area of enhancing the power of your presence. You continue to dress well and to speak well. In effect, you project the image of an executive. I applaud you particularly for your efforts to build a corporate and product image. In effect, you are attempting to enhance the presence power of the organization in the marketplace. From what you've told me, your approach is sound.

"I was not very impressed with your networking efforts. You spent a lot of time attempting to deal directly with your antagonists. As I hear it, you did not devote much energy to courting others in the organization who might have helped you persuade Fraid, Draft, or Press. You did, however, get to know Browning who, in turn, convinced Draft to commission a book that was responsive to the demands of the marketplace.

"With regard to your use of power bases and influence strategies, it appears that you have learned to take into account personality variations as you select your strategy. It seems that you took the time, and had the wisdom, to figure out that Press, Draft, and Fraid were motivated by very different things, and could be threatened or frustrated by different situations."

"Are they ever different! Fraid is a very analytical type; you know, passive and methodical. He hates conflict, avoids taking a stand, and would probably die before he would express a strong emotion. Draft is passive, like Fraid, but relies less on facts, and more on feelings. Then there is Press. He's a doer, almost relentless in his pursuit of an objective. And he's a logical, linear sort. Expressions of emotion are not typical of Press."

"And, then, there's you, Larry. You represent yet another type of individual. You assume a leadership role, as does Press, and yet you decide on the basis of feeling and intuition, as does Draft.

"At any rate, you are to be complimented on your apparent appreciation of personality differences, and on your willingness and ability to modify your style accordingly.

"You used the power of friendship and shared goals to enlist Draft. With Press, you continued to enlist, but shifted your strategy slightly, becoming an advisor on the basis of hard data. He apparently respected that. With Fraid, you used a combination of expert and friendship power to involve him in a problem-solving mode around the discussion groups and the compensation and evaluation systems. That was nicely done. In involving him, you made him feel less threatened, and less inclined to attempt to protect his turf.

"I also applaud your continued use of involvement with the employees who participated in your discussion groups. You retained their commitment when you went back to them with the revised logo and theme, asking for their reactions.

"I don't think you did as well with regard to using the Directive Strategy. You attempted to get Topper to intervene with Press. It is fortunate that he did not do so. If he had, Press would probably still be fighting you.

"Your use of the power of your position as a new member of the Executive Committee was very nice, indeed. By raising the issue of the corporate logo and theme during that first meeting, you took advantage not only of your position as a vice-president, but also of what I like to call a 'honeymoon period.' As the new man on the block, you and the others were the newlyweds. It would have been difficult for them to deny openly your requests at that point. Again, your timing was superb."

"Well, it would have been nice if the honeymoon could have lasted a little longer," replied Larry. "Reginald did a very effective job of destroying the marital bliss with his constant arguments and attacks."

"You are talking about *filibuster*. Yes, that is a very interesting form of directing. In effect, Reginald was using his position power and the right to disagree to consume meeting time, thereby rendering it impossible for the group to reach a decision.

"You are also to be congratulated on your ability to consider Reginald's suggestion. A lesser man might have discounted everything he said as being nothing other than a manipulation, or an attempt to block. You did not do that. You first tried to involve Reginald, pointing out that your goals were interdependent. When that didn't work, you moved to negotiation: 'I will sell software, if you will sell books.' Only after that failed did you use the power of the Executive Committee to direct Reginald to cooperate with you. The flexibility you displayed is admirable. So is your obvious willingness to continue to learn, in spite of your recent success."

Larry confessed, "I admit that you made some points this evening that I had not considered. I guess I still have a few things to learn."

TEXTWARE, INC.

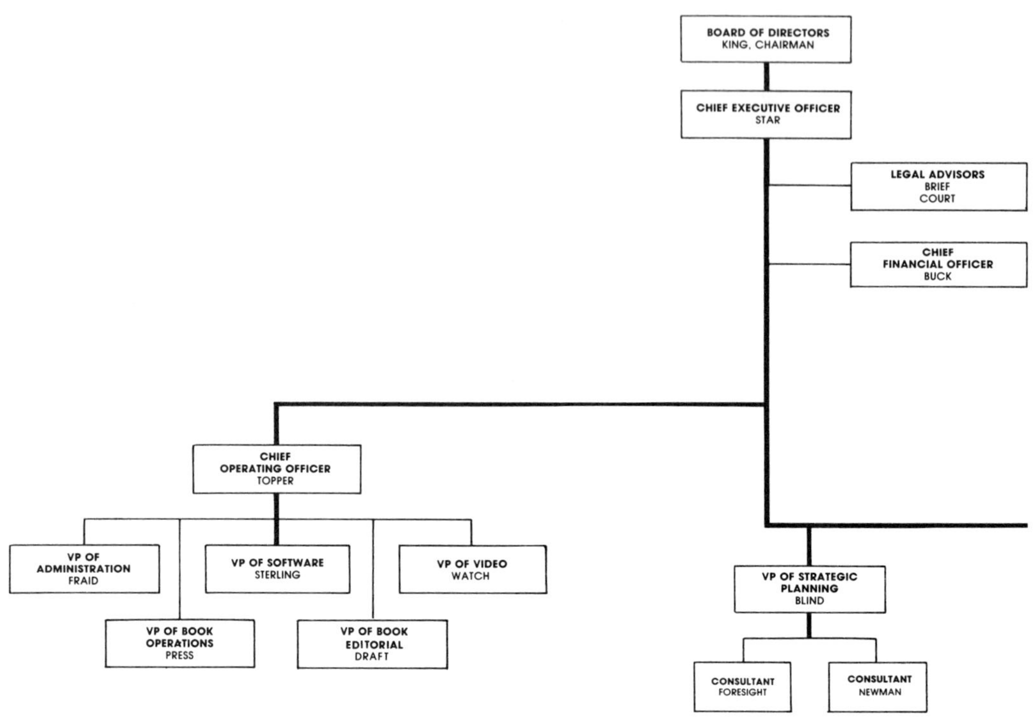

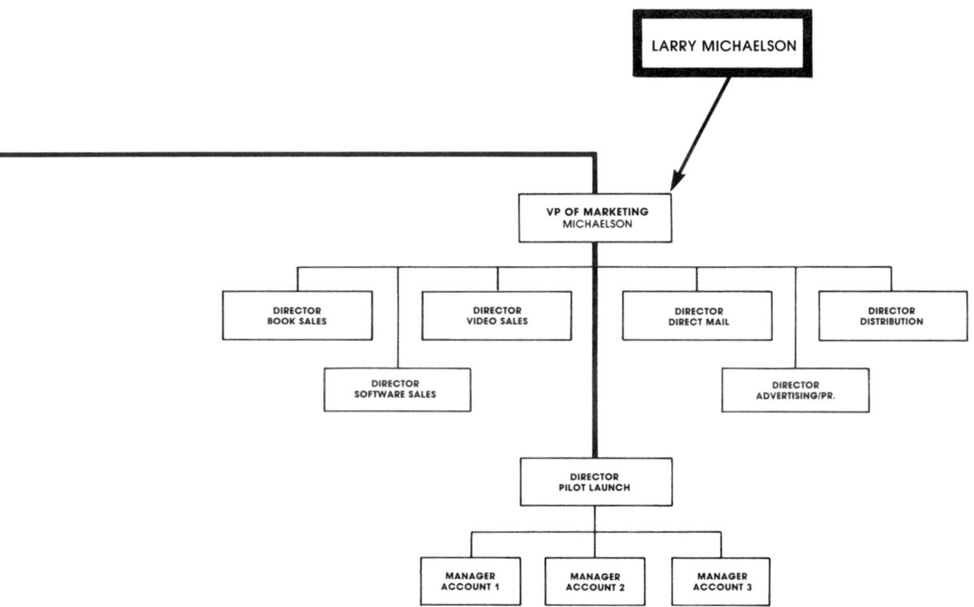

LARRY MICHAELSON
VP OF MARKETING
MICHAELSON
DIRECTOR
BOOK SALES
DIRECTOR
VIDEO SALES
DIRECTOR
DIRECT MAIL
DIRECTOR
DISTRIBUTION
DIRECTOR
SOFTWARE SALES
DIRECTOR
ADVERTISING/PR.
DIRECTOR
PILOT LAUNCH
MANAGER
ACCOUNT 1
MANAGER
ACCOUNT 2
MANAGER
ACCOUNT 3

"Benjamin Franklin once said, 'None but the well-bred man knows how to confess a fault, or acknowledge himself in an error.' I would take that further. In my opinion, none but the well-bred man understands that the learning process never ends. You are clearly a well-bred man, my friend."

LARRY'S NOTES

New relationships, triggered by role changes (e.g., promotions), enjoy a honeymoon period. You can sometimes get things done in that period that you could not otherwise accomplish as easily.

People band together to confront a common enemy....use of the we vs. they tactic....part of the fraternity strategy.

Filibuster is a *directing* tactic...blocking; using position power, or the right to disagree.

It's important to consider the personality type of the target of influence when selecting a power base and an influence strategy.

Differences between people exist along the dimensions of reliance on facts vs. reliance on feelings and intuition; taking an active stance vs. taking a more passive stance; needing to be powerful vs. needing to be liked.

It's dangerous to get your boss to do the dirty work; reliance on the indirect formal power of the boss can antagonize peers.

12

Global Visions and Turf Realignments

AS HE EMBRACED his new role, Larry was already well aware that authority is not always commensurate with responsibility. In the months that had preceded, Larry had had to make things happen in areas over which he had no direct control. Efforts to persuade and to cajole had taken time; time that he no longer had, given the imminent release of the financial planning software package and associated book.

Now that he had been granted full authority over the entire marketing function, he began to panic. The absence of direct authority had been frustrating. It had also provided an excuse. He couldn't blame himself if Reginald's salespeople failed to perform. Now, the buck stopped with Larry.

He realized that he was going to have to move quickly if the launch of the financial planning package was to succeed. Sales representatives who were used to selling books needed to learn how to market software. Conversely, the software sales force needed to learn the art of textbook sales. And they all had to become more savvy with regard to corporate sales.

Nor did Larry feel he could tolerate the "we versus they" feeling that existed between the book sales force and the software folks. Regarding their own product as more sophisticated than books, the software sales personnel tended to feel that they were "better than" their counterparts in the book business. That had to change, and change fast.

Assuming that physical proximity would make a difference, Larry decided that he had to get enough space in either the software building or the book building to bring his entire force under one roof. Doing so required that he convince another area to move. Fraid was a natural. His people continued to be split between the two locations. Fraid's function, Larry reasoned, would also benefit from working in a common location.

Anticipating little resistance, Larry was horrified to discover that few were willing to move. Fraid himself was the least of the problem. Once it was agreed that Fraid would continue to reside in the book building, and that Larry would move into the software building, Fraid was content. It was the directors, managers and supervisors who reported to them who resisted.

The episode provided Larry with a lesson in status and turf. Directors who had become accustomed to having private offices objected violently to moving into a landscaped area in which office walls were only six feet high, and did not reach the ceiling. Their rationale for resisting was that they could not conduct confidential conversations without fully enclosed offices.

Conversely, those who had grown accustomed to the more lavish (though less private) landscaped office environment resisted the move into private offices. These people claimed that they would be unable to maintain an "open door" policy in such an environment, and that their relationship with their subordinates would suffer as a result.

Larry listened, and sought to effect compromises. Nothing seemed to work. Realizing that precious time was slipping away, Larry mandated the change, and convinced Fraid to do the same. Anticipating that he would have to endure the adverse consequences of having been directive, Larry was pleasantly surprised to discover that, within a few weeks, almost everyone had become accustomed to their new turf. New status symbols rapidly emerged to replace those that had been sacrificed.

Believing that physical proximity would not, alone, stimulate the integration of his staff, Larry reorganized, introducing account teams that were made up of all functions from both software and books. Every individual then had to report to two bosses: a functional head and an account director.

The dual accountability system created a great deal of stress within the Marketing Department. Individuals who had grown up in

PEOPLE SURROUND THEMSELVES WITH SYMBOLS OF POWER

*"Shibler, what's this I hear about your office
containing a rootbound philodendron?"*

Drawing by Frascino; © 1983
The New Yorker Magazine, Inc.

the highly predictable, structured book company environment had a particularly difficult time adjusting to the new structure. Unable to cope with the stress, several of the old-timers resigned or requested early retirement. Larry accommodated their requests, believing that the motivation of the entire team would be enhanced by the voluntary removal of those who could not cope with change and ambiguity.

Star observed Larry's actions with a combination of interest and concern. While he appreciated what Larry was attempting to do, he worried that the changes were being introduced too rapidly. He did not interfere, however, until the director of direct mail, an individual who had been with the book company for twenty-five years, approached him directly.

"Michaelson is throwing a monkey wrench into everything. If I can't control my people, and I can't, then the whole system is going to fall apart. Now, instead of doing what I tell them to do without question, my people tell me that their account executive doesn't agree, or may not agree. I won't stand for it. I cannot be held responsible for the performance of people I do not control."

Star called Larry into his office, and suggested that he remember that change which is introduced in an evolutionary fashion is far more enduring than change which comes about as a result of revolution.

"You are moving too fast, Larry, particularly for the people from the book company. Slow it down. Maintain your vision, but slow it down."

Eventually, they worked out a compromise. Larry's new dual accountability system would exist side by side with the functional hierarchy. The account executive system would operate only with regard to the new product launch. Only those people who were comfortable managing the conflict inherent in the two-boss structure would be asked to participate in the new product launch. For the rest of the staff, it would be business as usual.

Larry had no choice but to use the new product introduction as a pilot, an organizational as well as marketing experiment. Appreciating the importance of the outcome, Larry concentrated most of his energies on the launch. The bulk of his energies were devoted to training his staff in the art of developing corporate client relationships. Hoping to intensify awareness of the marketplace on the part of his staff members, Larry held weekly meetings during which every participant was expected to share at least one insight that had resulted from conversations with prospective corporate buyers.

Finally, Larry worked on convincing the most talented of his employees to work on the pilot project. Gertie O'Brien posed the greatest problem. She seemed unable to function in the ambiguous structure of the pilot, and requested that she be transferred out of the pilot area. Larry fought her decision, knowing that no one else had as much expertise in the area of advertising and public relations.

But Gertie was adamant. In insisting that she be tranferred, she suggested that Larry give Gregory Wallace the job. Her argument was convincing. Gregory was very familiar with both books and software. An artist by avocation, he had a feel for the creative side of advertising.

The very mention of Gregory rekindled memories that Larry wanted to forget; memories of Simpleton, and of manipulations, and of the episode with Roger. And yet, thought Larry, Gregory was not responsible for any of that. He, like Larry, had been a pawn in the game played by Reginald and Simpleton.

The nature of the game had finally become clear to Larry. Gregory had married Simpleton's daughter. That explained why Simpleton had been so solicitous of his former director of sales. It also explained why Simpleton had wanted Larry to fail. Larry had more expertise in the marketing area than did Gregory. Only by getting Larry out of the picture could Simpleton make a case in favor of giving Gregory the job of vice-president of marketing upon Simpleton's retirement.

Gertie's recommendation and request made Larry stop and think about Gregory as an individual, apart from Simpleton, and about his performance to date. Since moving out of Reginald's area, Gregory had performed well as director of book sales. He was, in fact, one of the more capable managers outside the pilot effort. Yet Larry had never considered involving him in the new product launch, in spite of his familiarity with both software and books.

Larry had to admit to himself that his desire for vengeance had prevailed over sound judgment and his sense of fair play. His interview with Gregory confirmed that that had been true. Freed from the constraints posed by having to report to his future father-in-law, Gregory had become much more assertive, and more confident. Gertie had been right. Gregory wanted to be part of the product launch, and had a number of ideas about the advertising campaign.

The advertising function flourished under Gregory's direction. Gregory proved to be not only highly creative, but also extremely adept at negotiating with key publications for space.

Unfortunately, Gregory's negotiative ability was not enough to compensate for what Larry and Gregory discovered was a serious budget deficit. In the months that had intervened since the last budgetary cycle, competitors had increased their advertising budgets tenfold. Textware would not be able to attract sufficient attention to the financial planning package without investing an additional million dollars in the advertising campaign. An increase of this size could not be approved solely by the Executive Committee. It would require authorization by the Board of Directors.

Assuming that Star controlled the Board, Larry devoted his

energies to attempting to convince Star and Topper that the additional investment was warranted.

Star's reaction was one of shock. While he appreciated the importance of advertising, his career in publishing had not exposed him to advertising budgets of that size for a single product. Unwilling to commit himself, Star promised only to discuss the matter with Topper.

Topper had a keen appreciation of the levels of investment required to produce a software package. However, he believed that product quality spoke for itself in the marketplace. He recommended that the Executive Committee consider making no more than an additional five hundred thousand dollar investment in the advertising program.

Lacking a firm commitment from either Topper or Star, Larry was pessimistic about his ability to convince the Executive Committee. He needed an ally, a believer, at a high level. That left only Peter Buck, the chief financial officer.

Buck and Larry had had very little to do with each other during the past few years. Their earlier feud over the planning model had dissipated. Larry hoped that Buck did not harbor resentment, and that he felt secure enough in his position as chief financial officer to set politics aside, and to consider the wisdom of Larry's request on its own merits.

Buck was at least willing to grant Larry an immediate audience and to listen attentively to his full arguments. He even conceded that the issue deserved further consideration, and promised to give it a great deal of thought prior to the special session of the Executive Committee.

Not content to rely entirely on Buck's reaction, Larry decided to strengthen his argument by inviting Sandra Newman to speak at the session. Her familiarity with the competitors' advertising budgets would, he believed, add credibility to his request.

Sandra was happy to oblige, welcoming not only the opportunity to assist Larry, but also the chance to enhance her own visibility within the corporation. Another opportunity to display her expertise would make it easier to convince Textware to become a client.

The special session of the Executive Committee was an event that none of the participants would quickly forget. Sandra and Larry were extremely effective in their presentation. By the time they had finished, Topper had indicated that he was considering reversing his earlier opinion, believing the investment of one million dollars might be warranted.

Buck did not agree, having decided that the organization would be better off investing its finanical resources in the acquisition of a small computer hardware firm. Larry had not anticipated that his proposal would be judged in relation to another, completely unrelated project. Unaware that the organization was even considering such an acquisition, he was unprepared to challenge the notion. While his instincts told him that entering the portable computer market was a bad idea, it was difficult for him to refute the argument. After all, entrance into the hardware field would enable the company to offer a fully integrated package.

It came as no surprise to Larry that Reginald was vocal in his support of the acquisition of the hardware company. Watch supported neither proposal, indicating that he believed the company needed to invest more heavily in the video area. Claiming that he was not yet prepared to present his idea, Watch let it be known that, within a matter of weeks, he would ask that the Executive Committee consider entering the business of teleconferencing.

Fraid said little during the meeting, as was his habit. Neither did Draft. Press further complicated the agenda by reminding the group that within the year he would need a significant amount of capital to upgrade his production equipment.

Not wanting to bias the decision, Star had been careful not to reveal his opinion until everyone had had the opportunity to register their vote, or to abstain. While his efforts to appear impartial were admirable, he carried it too far, failing to keep the discussion focused on Larry's request.

Larry was annoyed that "his meeting" had been allowed to degenerate into a disorganized scramble for available dollars. Despairing that any resolution would be reached, Larry was pleasantly surprised when Star finally regained control of the meeting, and announced that he supported Larry, and had decided to propose to the Board that Larry's request be honored.

Larry assumed that he had won his case; that the presentation to the Board was only a ritual. If the Board entrusted Star with the running of Textware, then they would surely respect his recommendation regarding the investment. Thus, Larry was startled when, several days later, Star informed him that he had succeeded not in gaining Board approval for the expenditure, but only in getting Larry an invitation to address the Board directly.

Puzzled that Star was not making the presentation himself, Larry inquired. Star's response told Larry that the battle was far from won.

"Larry, I do not have control of the Board. In fact, I would say that Buck is more influential than I am. You see, the Board is composed of several committees. The most powerful committee is the Audit Committee, which is headed by James Wiley. Wiley, as you undoubtedly know, is the chief executive officer of Laserware. While Wiley is brilliant, he is also militaristic in his view of life and people. He and I have never gotten along. Our value systems are simply too different. In fact, at one point, he voted for my dismissal. Fortunately, the other members of the Board thought such a move was premature.

"I tell you all of this because you can expect a real fight. Wiley is convinced that Buck is a genius. He views Topper as a scientist who does not belong in the executive suite. He appears to view me as an overly soft, indecisive individual who is incapable of running a high technology corporation."

Larry thanked Star for his openness and for his honesty, appreciating that it must have been difficult for the executive to admit his vulnerability to a subordinate.

As Larry prepared for the presentation to the Board, he was highly aware that a great deal more was at stake than his advertising budget. In the one hour that was allotted to him, he would have to both build and use the power of expertise and presence. He would not get a second chance. The impression he made would affect his future. To impress the members of the Board was to add a number of highly powerful people to his network, his sphere of influence. To fail to impress them was to close doors to many future opportunities. The more he dwelled on the importance of the presentation, the more nervous he became.

In spite of the tension he was feeling, Larry's speech was faultless in its eloquence, and irrefutable in terms of its logic. Challenges presented by Buck were met head on. Questions posed by Wiley were answered with dispatch. Larry was pleased with his performance, believing he had projected the seriousness and intensity befitting a vice-president.

Star and Larry debriefed after the meeting. Star informed Larry that, while he had succeeded in securing a budget increase of three quarters of a million dollars, he had done himself a personal disservice.

"You impressed, Wiley. That much I'll give you. Your stiffness and apparent aloofness really put off a couple of other members of the Board, however. Particularly King, the chairman. King, as you probably know, was the original founder of Books International. In spite of the fact that he has a tendency to live in the past, and to glorify the way things used to be, the other members of the Board still defer to him, out of respect for who he was, if not who he is. Well, King is a strong advocate of humanitarian management. He believes that organizations owe their employees a comfortable, safe and secure work environment. In short, he likes 'nice guys.'

"You did not appear to be a 'nice guy' today, Larry. In fact, several members of the Board found you to be extremely rigid and lacking in warmth. Because they could not get a sense of you as a person, they were suspicious of your true motives. To be honest with you, Larry, I have never seen you behave that way. Were you so terrified that you could allow no humor and no casual dialogue?"

Larry assured Star that his apparent rigidity had stemmed not from fear but from determination.

"Well, loosen up, Larry. That kind of determination will end up costing you more votes than it gets you."

Larry worried about Star's comments for several days. Eventually, he allayed his concerns with the thought that he now had sufficient resources with which to make a strong impression on the market at point of product introduction. The success of the product would, he reasoned, convince the members of the Board that he was a valuable member of the firm.

With the new product launch planned, and its implementation in the hands of capable subordinates, Larry began to devote his attention to the broader marketplace, attempting to gain a sense of the emerging trends that would affect the industry. Larry viewed as his major responsibility the monitoring of the pulse of the market and the anticipation of changes in values and buying patterns. In effect, he accepted personal accountability for overall marketing strategy, delegating what he perceived to be the marketing tactics of distribution, sales, advertising, etc.

The monitoring of social and psychological changes required that Larry devote most of his time and energy to talking with people outside of the organization. In an effort to understand the needs people hoped to fulfill through software and books, Larry met with a wide range of individuals. He attempted to understand the needs of the handicapped clerical worker whose personal computer enabled her to earn a living at home. He talked with high-level professionals who relied on software to help them organize their thoughts. He met with aspiring young entrepreneurs who hoped to use software in lieu of staff.

He also talked to book buyers, striving to understand reading habits and their relationship to software purchase. And he talked to people who did not rely on books as a source of information, wanting to learn why they preferred other media.

Larry's hard-won skills in building trust and in developing the kind of relationships that encouraged openness were constantly challenged, as he had to modify his style in response to the variety of individuals with whom he spoke. He had to learn to listen without evaluating, reminding himself that people were different, and had a right to maintain those differences.

Stereotypes began to break down, and in their stead emerged an intense social curiosity. No longer perceiving of the computer and the professional book as the exclusive tools of the professional or of the intellectually elite, Larry began to envision other potential markets.

"People who buy professional, business and educational texts, and people who buy software seem to have one thing in common," he reasoned. "They all have a basic feeling of empowerment; a can-do attitude; a belief that they are capable of improving themselves, of growing, and of learning. They are open to and curious about new experiences, and are willing to admit areas of weakness, as well as areas of strength.

"Everyone basically wants to feel empowered. They want to feel good about themselves, and to do something about overcoming barriers to the realization of their potential.

"*That* is the potential market for software and related books. And *that* should constitute our corporate image: the company that helps people empower themselves," he said aloud to himself, surprising the person who occupied the airplane seat next to his.

Back at the office, Larry read everything he could find regarding emerging social and cultural trends. He learned that the drive to feel more empowered was widespread. People were rejecting medical institutions, preferring self-administered therapy and treatment. The emphasis on self-sufficiency was evident in the number of people who shunned corporate life, electing to pursue entrepreneurial interests and basic crafts. The proliferation of consciousness-raising programs provided further evidence that the public-at-large had come to believe that the "answer" lay within themselves, not in external authority figures.

Suddenly all of the pieces of the puzzle fell into place. Textware would create complete personal empowerment packages. Books and related software would be released to cover all of the areas in which a sense of mastery was essential to personal empowerment. The series would cover health and stress management. Letting his imagination wander, Larry conceived of a product designed to enable self-diagnosis of illness.

Psychological experts would be approached as well, enabling the company to develop a series on mental and emotional health. Programs would be developed to assist in the diagnosis and treatment of relationship difficulties.

The personal financial package that was already under development would fall under the same umbrella, enabling people to achieve a sense of control over their financial resources.

"The possiblities are infinite," said Larry to Star, after describing his overall concept. "I am proposing that the entire corporation focus on this concept, and this concept alone. I realize that such a conversion will require that we stop development of a number of projects in which we have sizable investments. There may be a way to sell those projects to other firms. I believe in this one, Star. I really believe in this one."

But Larry's vision did not stop there. "And, we've got to get into the hardware business. The market that I am suggesting revolves around the 'common man' and the 'common woman.' These are not the people who can afford to pay several thousand dollars for a personal computer. If we are going to become the organization that empowers the masses, then we have got to find a way to make decent hardware available to them. Perhaps we can get into the leasing business, or maybe we should investigate buying a hardware firm. Perhaps we should build our own. Maybe we will even give away machines. I don't know. I *do* know that the issue needs to be addressed."

Star was stunned. After several minutes of silence, he said, "Larry, do you realize the implications of what you are saying? You are suggesting a total shift in our business; a total redefinition of our purpose and mission."

"True, but I am *not* suggesting a change in technology, per se.

Why, we already know how to produce software and books and even video. Speaking of video, I see a real market for that also. That, too, will depend on our ability to make the hardware available to the 'common man.' If we can do that, then there is no reason why we can't develop video discs as part of the health series, for example. Imagine the impact of having a video disc that shows you the human body while the software is helping you diagnose what ails you! Again, I say, the possibilities are endless!"

Star and Larry spent months discussing the concept. Eventually, Larry grew frustrated by conversations that failed to result in action. It seemed to him that Star regarded the discussions as nothing more than a fascinating intellectual exercise. He began to understand why Wiley regarded Star as indecisive.

Larry began to expose others in the organization to his idea. His belief in the concept was so intense that he did not worry about losing credit for the idea as a result of having shared it with others. Turf protection and turf expansion did not concern him, dedicated as he had become to the concept.

He talked about the idea to anyone who would listen, not caring whether the individual was a vice-president, a director, a manager, a supervisor, or an employee. Some reacted with open enthusiasm; others appeared interested but uncomfortable. Still others seemed threatened, and suggested that Larry drop the notion and get back to work.

It occurred to Larry that the reactions of others varied depending on their perceptions of how implementation of the idea would impact upon them. Those who perceived that pursuit of the concept would protect or even expand their turf responded enthusiastically. Those who could not make the translation seemed disinterested. Resistance came only from persons who could not readily see a role for themselves in the organization that Larry was describing.

Reginald Sterling, for example, was surprisingly enthusiastic about the idea. "Naturally," thought Larry, "he wanted to buy a hardware company over a year ago. He believes that he would be the one to run the Hardware Division. Of course, it's empire expansion that excites him, not the idea itself."

Tyler Watch, from whom Larry had expected support, was highly resistant. "Of course," Larry thought, "Watch knows that the video component won't materialize for a long time, given the high price of the disc players and the inability of the 'common man,' to purchase the equipment. If, as an organization, we focus on the 'common man,' Tyler will become less important, at least in the short run."

Draft, on the other hand, was elated with the idea, and demanded to hear all of the details. That did not come as a surprise to Larry. The personal development field was Draft's favorite. Implementation of the idea would enhance his opportunities to work with topics that excited him, and with authors whom he most respected.

Press was disinterested, saying only that whatever the company did, he wanted plenty of notice about shifts in production schedule.

Fraid reacted to the idea with a blend of interest and concern. While he did not perceive that the change in direction would either enhance or detract from his power base, he was fundamentally uncomfortable with change, preferring to tolerate the limitations of the known than to explore unknown opportunities.

Buck was unwilling to react until he, in his words, had "an opportunity to explore every aspect from a financial point of view." His attitude and demeanor temporarily dampened Larry's enthusiasm.

Topper, fortunately, was supportive of the idea, agreeing that it warranted at least further exploration. "I can't comment on the notion from the point of view of the marketplace," he said, "but I must admit that the idea of attempting to develop low priced hardware appeals to me. It's been a long time since I've had an opportunity to attempt to meet such a technological challenge."

"Self-interest," thought Larry," it all amounts to self-interest. People seem to make decisions on the basis of what's good for them, not necessarily what's good for the organization as a whole. It's amazing, absolutely amazing, that corporations do as well as they do. I guess they do because the man or woman at the top is able to maintain the corporate view. And I begin to understand the importance of the Board. The Board's charter is to look after the stockholders' interests. That, presumably, requires the ability to look beyond turf issues and to disregard individual empires, bearing in mind the total corporation."

Six months passed before Larry was able to convince Star to put his idea on the official discussion agenda of the Executive Committee. Now convinced that neither Star nor Topper would fight vigorously for such a massive shift in corporate direction, Larry's objective in presenting to the Executive Committee was to get the authorization to present the concept to the Board.

His networking efforts paid off. The only strong opponent to the idea was Buck. Star remained intrigued, but indecisive. The decision was made to allow Larry to approach the Board.

Larry knew that there were two key figures on the Board. Wiley, Chairman of the Audit Committee and King, Chairman of the Board. In order to impress Wiley, he had to appear to be unemotional and analytical. Gaining King's confidence, on the other hand, required that he be open, warm, sensitive and intuitive.

While Larry knew that he faced a big challenge, he felt confident. After all, he assured himself, he was in fact both analytically astute and sensitive and intuitive. He knew how to simultaneously build expert and friendship power.

Larry was at the peak of his form the day of the presentation. Without exception, the members of the Board were impressed. In spite of the fact that the Board promised only to deliberate further about the change in strategy, Larry felt that he had been successful.

He had to be extraordinarily patient, however. Patience had never been one of Larry's strengths. The Board met only once a month, and insisted upon exploring all of the ramifications of the proposal. Buck slowed the decision process by persisting in presenting his concerns about the financial viability of shifting strategy. Six months passed before a final verdict was rendered.

The verdict was well worth the wait. The Board urged Star and Topper to proceed with a revamp of their long- and short-range strategic plan in order to reflect what they perceived to be the wisdom of the vice-president of marketing.

Further, the Chairman of the Committee on Corporate Organization recommended to Star that Larry be named "chief marketing officer." It had apparently become clear to the Board that corporate decisions had reflected financial and technological considerations to a far greater degree than they had reflected the marketplace.

In spite of the fact that Star's background was in marketing, his input into the strategic planning process did not result in a sufficient consideration of emerging market trends and cultural shifts. That was due, in part, to the fact that the pressures of the role of chief executive made it difficult for Star to find enough time to reflect on the marketplace. The problem was aggravated by Star's tendency to be indecisive.

While finding it difficult to make decisions himself, Star had no trouble enthusiastically endorsing decisions made by others in whom he had confidence. Thus it was with a sense of shared victory that he told Larry of the Board's decision to create the position of chief marketing officer.

"The Board has been very impressed with your ability to think strategically, your intellectual curiosity, your comfort with innovation, your social curiosity, your interpersonal skills and, above all, with your courage. They feel, and I totally agree, that these are essential attributes for effective performance of the role of chief marketing officer.

"Your job, Larry, essentially will be to imbue the culture of our organization with a marketplace perspective by injecting strategic marketing into the strategic planning process. If you are to do so, you must be involved throughout the planning process. In effect, you are asked to be more than a prophet of consumer preferences. You are asked to help us translate those preferences into a business definition which continues to be responsive to the consumer.

"But your job will encompass a lot more than consumer watching and planning. If the marketing perspective is to become operational, you will have to be able to influence decisions as to the products we offer, the markets we pursue, our pricing policies, the technologies we utilize, and the way we allocate our financial, physical and human resources.

"As I understand it, Larry, you have been somewhat of a maverick since the day you joined Software Systems, Inc. eleven years ago. Well, what we are now telling you is that we are giving you license to function as an extremely powerful organizational maverick. It is essential that you continue to take an independent stand, to encourage innovation, and to remind us that running a business is as much a matter of artistic judgment as it is of science.

"It is not without trepidation that we invite you into the executive suite, Larry. Mavericks, after all, make people uncomfortable; particularly empowered mavericks. Yet we set aside our discomfort, recognizing that your function is the key to success in this era of rapid technological change, cultural diversity, and consumer impatience with the unresponsive institution. The time for the chief marketing officer has come. Your time has come, Larry. Congratulations."

Larry had devoted eleven years to the realization of a dream. Now that the dream had become a reality, he experienced a blend of elation and despair. On the one hand, he felt let down, somehow disappointed. He had enjoyed the struggle; the journey had been as important as the destination itself. He would miss the fighting, the strategizing, the struggling, the challenge. On the other hand, challenges of a different kind now faced him, and he looked forward to meeting them. He experienced at once sorrow at ending an era, and excitement at beginning another.

Larry called Bill and invited him to dinner. In spite of the fact that he wanted to share the good news immediately, he forced himself to set the date for two weeks in the future. In the interim, he worked on sorting and compiling all of the notes about organization power dynamics that he had taken during his conversations with Bill.

When they finally met for dinner, Larry handed Bill a typeset copy of the compiled notes, and proposed a toast. "To Bill, the man who stood behind me every step of the way, encouraging my confidence while discouraging my arrogance; applauding my ambition while making me cautious; forcing me to grow while protecting me from attempts others made to invade my turf; teaching me about power, and enabling me to feel empowered."

Deeply touched, Bill toasted Larry in return. "As Ralph Waldo Emerson said, 'A friend is a person with whom I may be sincere. Before him, I may think aloud.' I have thought aloud with you, Larry, and you with me. I look forward to enjoying our friendship for many more years."

"As do I, Bill. Rest assured, there will be times when I will need the benefit of your advice as I attempt to function as the chief marketing officer. I am sure that I am about to experience many more corporate power plays."

"And many more victories, Larry. You are a risk-taker with a vision. I applaud that. So would Theodore Roosevelt. I remind you of the Roosevelt philosophy that I shared with you on the eve of your graduation from Business School:

> Far better it is to dare mighty things, to win glorious triumphs, even though checkered by failure, than to take rank with those poor spirits who neither enjoy much nor suffer much, because they live in the gray twilight that knows not victory or defeat.

EPILOGUE: The Next Ten Years

Larry held the position of chief marketing officer for six years. During that time, the company maintained a steady and impressive growth rate of 30 to 50 percent per year. Much of their success was attributed to Larry, and to his ability to anticipate changes in the marketplace and then to use his astute political abilities to effect changes within the organization.

Larry's road during those six years was anything but smooth, however. Two years after Larry received the title of chief marketing officer, Topper left the company, impatient with corporate intrigue and anxious to return to the entrepreneurial world he found most exciting. Reginald Sterling was then named chief operating officer. The animosities that had once existed between Sterling and Larry resurfaced, rendering the executive suite more of a gladiator ring than a strategy center.

Larry once again found it necessary to call upon the services of his long-time mentor. As before, Bill helped Larry formulate a strategy that would permit him to achieve his objectives without exacerbating the adversarial relationship with Reginald. The Board was impressed. Larry's sphere of influence continued to widen.

Bill died suddenly at the age of seventy-three. Larry's grief was deeper than any he had ever known. For weeks, he lived in the past, reliving events he and Bill had shared. Thoughts of the man himself finally made Larry realize that Bill would not have approved of his prolonged grief. Larry began to work harder than ever.

His efforts were rewarded two years after Bill's death. Star retired. The Board chose to name Larry the chief executive officer. At thirty-nine years of age, Larry assumed the reins of a five billion dollar corporation.

Unable to tolerate what he regarded as the ultimate loss, Reginald Sterling resigned. Willing to let the past stay in the past, Larry named Joel Abramson chief operating officer. His decision was sound, for Joel was so impressed by Larry's ability to be "bigger than" historic allegiances and petty games that he worked extremely hard to impress his former adversary and current leader.

Meanwhile, Sandra Newman and George Foresight established a consulting firm that enjoyed a moderate degree of success. Foresight, however, was not happy in his new role. The incessant pressure to sell, to find additional clients, upset him. Respecting Foresight's expertise, and having tired of the incessant games that Buck played, Larry convinced the Board that Buck should be replaced. Foresight enthusiastically accepted the position of chief financial officer.

Hoping to minimize disruptive power plays within Textware Inc., and to ensure that talented employees got every opportunity to realize their potential, Larry introduced systems designed to identify talent early in the careers of newcomers to the corporation. He made it clear that he expected members of senior management to assume the role of mentor with such individuals. Executives were rewarded for nurturing the talent that lay within the corporation.

Attempts to shine at the expense of others diminished; innovation flourished. Management practices encouraged, rather than stifled, creativity. Regardless of divisional or functional membership, employees felt a strong allegiance to Textware as a corporation. Power plays that once robbed the organization of its energy were replaced by efforts to win in the marketplace. Textware's turf continued to expand until it had achieved a major share of the market with regard to books, software, and video products.

Thoughts triggered by the fifth year anniversary of Bill's death led Larry to envision a software package and book on corporate power dynamics. Working with Draft, he found a writer who was willing to take Larry's notes, and construct a full text illustrating the mentor's concepts. The product was introduced to the marketplace on the sixth anniversary of Bill's death.

Meanwhile, Larry maintained close contact with Bill's wife and family. He developed a particularly close relationship with Bill's grandson, Doug. Unlike his father, Doug had an avid interest in the world of business in general, and the field of marketing in particular.

It was with a great deal of pride that Larry witnessed Doug's graduation from the same business school he had attended. And it was with a great deal of excitement that Larry began to counsel Doug as he embarked on his career as a trainee with a large brokerage house. For many years, Larry derived a great deal of satisfaction from helping Doug to manage the power dynamics of business, and showing how to avoid the pitfalls as he maneuvered through the difficult and often confusing corporate maze.

APPENDIX:
Larry's Notes on Power

POWER CONCEPTS

People who view life in win-lose terms perceive of power as finite. Life for them is a perpetual contest; they are always trying to prove that they are better than others.

Flexibility is the key to the effective management of power.

**THREE KINDS OF FORMAL POWER
(CONFERRED BY THE ORGANIZATION)**

1. **REWARD: The ability to provide something of value to the other....** Do as I say if you want me to give you the things that you want or value.

   ADVANTAGES: rapid action

   DISADVANTAGES: desire on the part of the other to do the minimum required in order to get the reward; diminishing ability to influence as the reward is assumed to be a right; feelings of counterdependency get in the way of friendship

Be careful buying work with the promise of a carrot—you may run out of carrots or they may grow stale.

The candy store strategy for building reward power.... Corner the market on things that the other values.

2. **COERCIVE: The ability to punish, or to deprive the other of something of value....** Do as I say if you want to avoid injury.

ADVANTAGES: rapid action; absolute compliance

DISADVANTAGES: resentment, fear, desire to withdraw from the situation; need for constant surveillance

Avoid the consistent use of the stick unless you can be around all the time to make sure others are doing what you have directed them to do.

*The arsenal strategy for building coercive power.....*Gather weapons...find out what would hurt and get in a position to deliver that hurt....get in a position to deprive the other of something they value.

3. **POSITION: The power of role and the expectations associated with the roles we fill....** Do as I say because I have the right to tell you what to do.

ADVANTAGES: compliance without resentment.

        new relationships, triggered by role changes (e.g., promotions) enjoy a honeymoon period...can sometimes get things done in that period that you could not otherwise accomplish as easily.

DISADVANTAGES: lack of certainty that desired action will occur, as the other person questions "rights" and "privileges." Expectations regarding a new role are fuzzy; this can minimize position power.

The crown prince strategy for building position power.... Change either the role itself or the expectations.

- Change perception of key problems and opportunities
- Attract investment
- Find out; get in the information loop
- Try to get control of the resources you need to reach your objectives; minimize dependency

Ask these questions:

1. What work group or unit is perceived to be most vital to the ability of the organization to solve those problems it feels are critical?
2. What work group or unit is perceived to be most vital to the organization's ability to respond to key opportunities?
3. Which work group or unit is the least dependent on the resources of other groups in terms of its ability to reach its objectives?

4. On which work group or unit do many other work groups rely in order to reach their objectives?

5. Which unit or work group is thought to be most important in terms of grooming someone to assume a top leadership role?

6. In which work group or unit has the organization invested a significant amount of money?

7. Which work group or unit is perceived to be the most difficult to replace or replicate?

8. Which work group has the smallest margin for error; in which area are mistakes the most costly?

9. Which work group or unit has the greatest degree of control over information?

Formal power is efficient, but it does not build commitment.

Information can be an effective source of formal power.

Any of the three types of formal power can be exercised directly or indirectly. The indirect use of power occurs when one person relies on the power of a second person to influence a third person.... It is dangerous to get your boss to do the dirty work; reliance on your boss's formal power can antagonize peers.

THREE KINDS OF INFORMAL POWER (EARNED, NOT CONFERRED)

1. **EXPERT POWER: The power of respect gained as a result of what we know and what we can do.**

ADVANTAGES:	inspires commitment to your approach
DISADVANTAGES:	gap closes as other becomes equally expert
	need to work to maintain respect of other
	expert power does not generalize from one another; need to reprove expertise in the new area

    *The look-what-I've-done strategy to build expert power...*Keys are visibility, competent performance, and relevance to a pressing problem or opportunity.

2. **FRIENDSHIP: The power of trust, shared goals, sense of identification.**

ADVANTAGES:	inspires commitment to you as a person
DISADVANTAGES:	vulnerability
	need to work to maintain trust; trust is very difficult to build and very easy to destroy

The fraternity strategy for building friendship power.... Identify shared goals; talk the same language; listen actively; never win at the other's expense; make contracts and live up to them; show you care; band together to confront a common enemy.

It is possible to balance expert and friendship power, but it is difficult because expert power sets up a distance, while friendship power is based on a sense of similarities between people.

Balancing reliance on friendship and expert power leads to effectiveness regarding both people and task.

3. **PRESENCE: The power of image.**

ADVANTAGES:	gets attention
	people listen
	people assume you are worthwhile, with something to contribute
DISADVANTAGES:	establishes expectations which must be realized through words and actions

The public relations strategy for building presence power.... Put forth an image of competence and confidence.

- Stand erect
- Make good eye contact
- Dress the part
- Make your voice interesting in tone and choice of words
- Let people know you are in the room without being obnoxious

Informal power can also be exercised directly or indirectly.

Networking... Getting in a position to use indirect power, or the power of others to make things happen.

Never lose sight of the informal organization chart; the patterns of influence that are based on informal power and linkages between people.

OTHER CONCEPTS REGARDING
CHOICE OF POWER BASE

It is important to consider the personality type of the target of influence when selecting a power base.... Differences between people exist along the dimensions of reliance on facts vs. reliance on feelings and intuition; taking an active stance vs. taking a more passive stance; needing to be powerful vs. needing to be liked.

When we have formal power over someone, it gets more difficult to build informal sources of leverage, particularly the power of friendship.

It is always possible to stock the arsenal, to rearm; having done so, it may not be possible to build friendship or expert power.

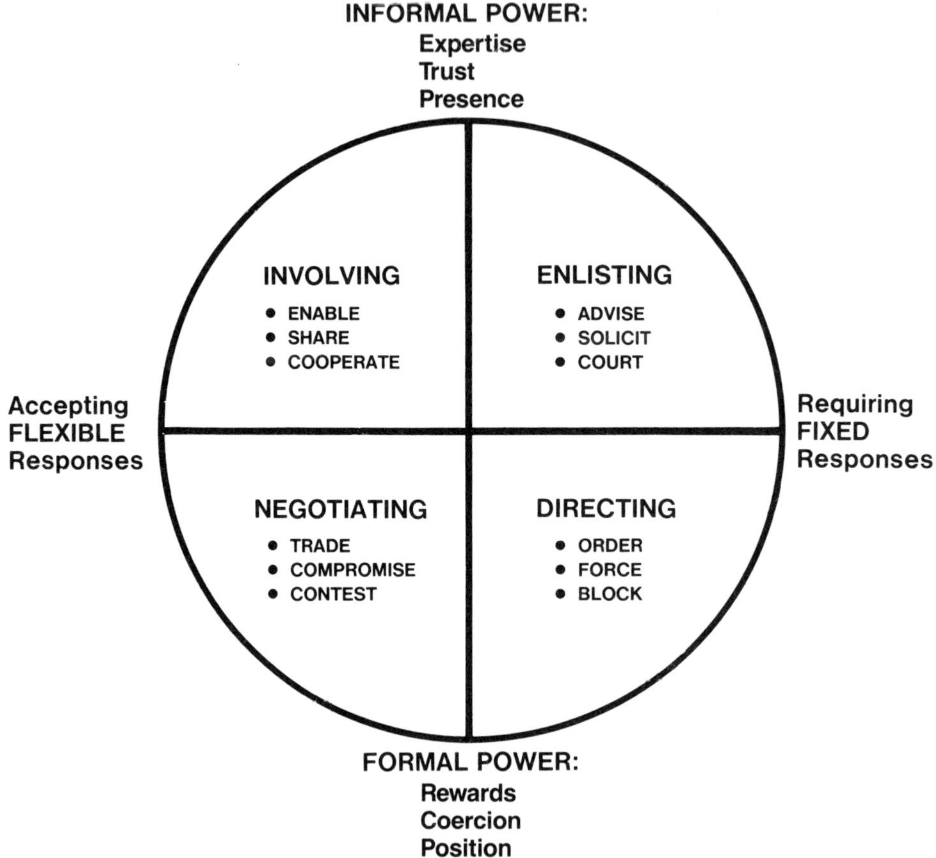

INFLUENCE STRATEGIES

INVOLVEMENT: Entails a flexible response and use of informal power.

Tactics:

> Sharing.... pooling resources; exchanging ideas
>
> Enabling.... offering resources (e.g., information, emotional support)
>
> Cooperating.... supporting or accepting suggestions of others

Involvement generates commitment (upside), but it takes time (downside).

Do not involve others whom you do not trust or whose expertise you do not value. To do so is to manipulate.

ENLISTMENT: Going after a fixed response while relying on informal power.

Tactics:

> Soliciting...pointing out need or worthwhile cause
>
> Courting.... relying on friendship and charm
>
> Advising.....using information to influence

To enlist is to make yourself vulnerable, to risk rejection.

When people are rejected, they tend to feel hostile.

NEGOTIATION: Accepting flexible outcomes, while relying on formal power.

Tactics:

> Trade...win-win; exchange of rewards, favors
>
> Compromise.....lose-lose; both give in; sometimes helps to achieve a longer-term gain
>
> Contest...If I win, we'll do it my way; win-lose; important to make sure the rules of the game are clear

DIRECTION: Pursuing a fixed response while relying on formal power.

Tactics:

> Force...with threat of coercion or promise of reward
>
> Order.... given the right to do so because of role
>
> Block...with threat of coercion or promise of reward, or through filibuster (using position power or the right to disagree)

Most productive influence strategies allow you to use power and enhance your power base simultaneously.

Criteria for choosing an influence strategy:

> Goals
> Controls
> Urgency
> Balance of power
> Commitment required

Selecting a Power Strategy

CONDITIONS	STRATEGIES			
	INVOLVING OTHERS	NEGOTIATING WITH OTHERS	DIRECTING OTHERS	ENLISTING OTHERS
GOALS	Your goals are interdependent; to reach yours is to contribute to the ability of others to reach theirs and vice versa.	Your goals are independent; not related.	Your goals are counter-dependent; if you succeed, chances are the other will fail.	You can't reach your goal without the others' help, but their goals are not dependent upon you.
CONTROLS	You rely on the on-going commitment and judgment of the other person.	"Rules" covering fair play and foul play exist and are understood by all parties to the contract.	You have ways to find out about "sabotage" before you're badly hurt; constant or frequent surveillance is possible.	The worst thing the other person can do is turn you down—they would not gain by hurting you in the other ways.
URGENCY (TIME)	Time is available for exploration and problem solving. Delay would not hurt either of you.	Delay would hurt the other more than you; you can tolerate a deadlock better than the other; or, delay would hurt both of you.	Delay would be detrimental to you.	Delay would hurt you more than the other person.
BALANCE OF POWER	Both parties have information or expertise the other party needs; or, both parties trust and respect each other.	Both parties can help (reward) or hurt (punish) each other.	You can reward or punish the other person more than (s)he can reward or punish you.	The other person likes you, respects you, and is not in a position to be hurt by you.
COMMITMENT REQUIRED	Long-term commitment of the others to your goals is sought.	Commitment to a contract or agreement is more important than commitment to goals.	Long-term commitment of the other person is not important; opposition or antagonism is acceptable (the other person can be "replaced").	Permission or acquiescence is more important than commitment; opposition or antagonism is not acceptable.

MANIPULATION

Manipulators attempt to conceal their objectives from their targets of influence; they pursue a hidden agenda.

SEDUCTION: The hidden agenda combined with the open use of informal power.

ENTRAPMENT: The hidden agenda combined with the open use of formal power.

DISCLAIMER: A double whammy...pursuing a hidden agenda while denying or falsifying the informal power base.

CAMOUFLAGE: Another double whammy...pursuing a hidden agenda while denying or falsifying the formal power base.

Manipulation is a dangerous tactic, and should be avoided if at all possible.... destroys trust.... makes it difficult or impossible to build and use expert power or the power of trust in the future.... creates suspicion and hostility.

Do not try to outmanipulate manipulators; both will end up losing.

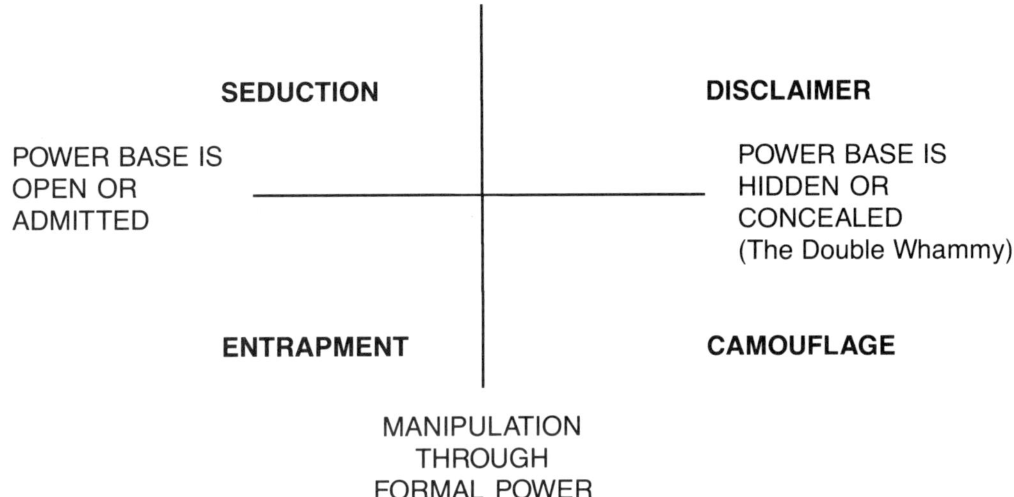

If something seems amiss, because of the history of the relationship, or due to a gut feeling, then stop and confront the other in a straightforward, direct fashion. Otherwise, you risk being manipulated.

Mergers Trigger

- Power plays
- Insecurity
- Attempts to protect turf
- Scramble for resources
- Ambiguity and confusion

To be part of the acquired company is to start one down; it is important to reestablish power bases, and to remain alert to power plays and manipulations.

The key to success is reliance on solid expertise and trust. Know what you're doing, and you won't have to rely on deceit. Inspire trust in others, and they will support you. There is then no need to manipulate or to engage in warfare.

Index